FAR FROM

THE ROOF

THE WORLD

FAR FROM

THE ROOFTOP OF

THE WORLD

Travels among Tibetan Refugees on Four Continents

. . .

AMY YEE

Foreword by His Holiness the Dalai Lama

THE UNIVERSITY PRESS OF NORTH CAROLINA

Chapel Hill

Cover art: Adobe Stock and Pixabay.

Library of Congress Cataloging-in-Publication Data
Names: Yee, Amy, author. | Bstan-'dzin-rgya-mtsho,
Dalai Lama XIV, 1935– writer of foreword.
Title: Far from the rooftop of the world : travels among Tibetan refugees on
four continents / Amy Yee ; foreword by His Holiness the Dalai Lama.
Description: Chapel Hill : University of North Carolina
Press, [2023] | Includes bibliographical references.
Identifiers: LCCN 2023014313 | ISBN 9781469675510
(paperback ; alk. paper) | ISBN 9781469675527 (ebook)
Subjects: LCSH: Bstan-'dzin-rgya-mtsho, Dalai Lama XIV, 1935– |
Refugees, Tibetan—Migrations. | Refugees, Tibetan—India. |
Refugees, Tibetan—Australia. | Refugees, Tibetan—Belgium. |
Refugees, Tibetan—United States. | Tibetans—Ethnic identity. |
Tibet Autonomous Region (China)—History—Uprising of
2008—Refugees. | LCGFT: Personal narratives.
Classification: LCC HV640.5.T5 Y44 2023 |
DDC 362.87089/9541—dc23/eng/20230503
LC record available at https://lccn.loc.gov/2023014313

[CONTENTS]

[AUTHOR'S NOTE]

Pseudonyms are used in some cases for Tibetans and others featured prominently in this book, or identifying details have been changed, to protect their privacy and the safety of their families in Tibet. I interviewed many people in an official capacity as a journalist and took notes as we spoke. Where I have made personal observations of people I met in an unofficial capacity, their names may have been changed or identities obscured to maintain their privacy.

I conducted most interviews and conversations myself in English or sometimes in Mandarin. Interviews and conversations in Tibetan were voluntarily interpreted by Tibetans present at the scene. I did not hire interpreters, fixers, or research assistants for this book or any of the two dozen or so journalistic articles I wrote about Tibetan issues.

I am very grateful to the many people who spent time and energy to interpret, answer questions, and provide valuable input.

A portion of any profits from this book will be donated to organizations working with refugees, Tibetans and Indians in need, and animals in need, especially in India.

[FOREWORD]

by His Holiness the Dalai Lama

In light of the Tibetan demonstrations in many parts of Tibet, including in the capital, Lhasa, in 2008, quite many journalists came to talk to me in Dharamsala about the developments. Among them was Ms. Amy Yee, the author of this book, *Far from the Rooftop of the World.*

Since then, Ms. Yee has traveled to meet with the Tibetan diaspora community around the world. In her book, she reveals how Tibetans in the diaspora have, even in the face of great adversity, managed to protect and preserve our distinct cultural heritage.

We Tibetans began arriving in India as refugees in 1959 after the failure of our sincere efforts for nine years at peaceful coexistence with the Communist Chinese authorities who took over our country.

In the period since then, Tibetans in Tibet have to endure unimaginable physical and mental challenges under the rigid Communist Chinese government. The Tibetan refugee community, although not having to go through the experience of their brethren inside Tibet, had to cope with difficult challenges, including having to adapt to a new environment. However, being a very resilient people, Tibetans' spirit and unswerving courage remained rock solid even in the face of great adversity. Today, the Tibetan people in exile have been particularly able to make a mark in the world.

It is my belief that the fundamental principles of nonviolence and compassion that lie at the heart of our culture have been a strong support to the Tibetans through the vicissitudes in their lives. I feel that these values also have the potential to make an important contribution to peace and harmony throughout the world.

I am confident that through this book readers will gain greater awareness of the Tibetan people's peaceful aspirations for freedom and dignity, and the values that have provided us succor.

Dalai Lama

October 7, 2022

A Hug from the Dalai Lama

We Are Not Writing a Novel.

We Are Facing Life and Death

DHARAMSALA, INDIA, MARCH 2008

. . .

When the Dalai Lama saw me, his wrinkled face lit up with interest. There were dozens of other reporters ready to surround him in a large room inside his residential complex, but he ambled over to where I stood and smiled kindly. The Tibetan spiritual leader had just finished a two-hour press conference at his exile home in the northern Indian town of Dharamsala. It was late March 2008. China had forcefully cracked down on the most violent unrest in Tibet in nearly two decades, and the Dalai Lama was pleading for calm.

On March 10, to mark the forty-ninth anniversary of a 1959 Tibetan uprising against China's rule, hundreds had demonstrated in Lhasa, Tibet's capital. As Chinese authorities tried to disperse Tibetan protesters, riots ensued. From March 14 onward, at least 100 Tibetans—men, women, and children—were killed in Lhasa and nearby areas in clashes with security forces or due to government repression. At least nineteen Chinese people, including civilians, were also killed in the riots. Many feared the violence could spiral out of control as China deployed police, soldiers, and tanks to stop Tibetans from protesting in the streets of Tibet and western China.

During the press conference, I sat on the floor near the front of the room. All the plastic chairs were filled with journalists like me because I had arrived breathlessly late after a flight from Delhi and five-hour car ride to reach the Himalayan hill town. Instead of showing despair after days of escalating tension or fatigue following a barrage of questions from reporters, the Dalai Lama exuded warmth. When the press conference finished, I stood up and he eagerly approached me.

"Chinese?" the Dalai Lama asked me brightly.

I hesitated. My parents are from Hong Kong and I am ethnically Chinese, as the Dalai Lama could see, but I was born and raised in the United States. That day, Tibet's spiritual leader had just spent two hours decrying China's aggressive crackdown. I told the Dalai Lama the truth—that I am American. The crowd of journalists I was usually a part of had surrounded us, yet for a moment, the Dalai Lama seemed to forget them and he gazed at me. Then he did something even more unexpected. The spiritual leader grabbed hold of my cheeks and squeezed them affectionately. When I was little, elderly neighbors in Boston had loved pinching my cheeks, and now here was a Nobel Peace Prize laureate doing the same thing.

The Dalai Lama grinned at me and his eyes shone behind his big rectangular glasses. Then he threw his arms around me and gathered me in a giant bear hug. He dropped his head against my neck. I felt the soft flesh of his bare shoulder protruding from the red robes he always wears. His loose skin felt surprisingly warm under my fingers as I hugged him back.

When the Dalai Lama released me, he gazed at me intensely and brushed my unkempt hair out of my eyes. I was the Delhi correspondent for the *Financial Times*, the British newspaper, and I'd slept only a couple hours the night before. The previous day I had been on a different reporting trip in Bangalore in southern India, so I took a rushed three-hour flight back home to Delhi, re-packed, then caught a 5 a.m. propeller plane to a city called Amritsar. From the small airport, I took a five-hour car ride up twisting mountain roads to Dharamsala, all while fielding phone calls from an editor breathing down my neck about an unrelated article I was also working on. I literally ran to the Dalai Lama's press conference, left my suitcase in the courtyard, and was still bleary-eyed as I found a place on the floor. Now he had hugged me and was making a request. Only talks between Tibet and China would resolve the current crisis engulfing his homeland, said the Dalai Lama. "You must tell them," he commanded.

I was speechless. I was just another reporter at a press conference on deadline. "I will do my best," I spluttered.

The Dalai Lama continued. "These others are just for show," he chortled, waving at the phalanx of reporters, photographers, and cameramen who had gathered behind him. I could see Somini Sengupta of the *New York Times* and Jonathan Allen of Reuters out of the corner of my eye. Cameras clicked as photographers focused on us. "Tibet and China must discuss," he repeated. "It is between us." I nodded.

Finally he turned away and began to leave the room. The crowd engulfed him once more, but the Dalai Lama didn't want the moment to end. "*Ni hao!*" he crowed gleefully in my direction, showing off a couple words in Mandarin.

When I later recounted to Tibetans and friends that the Dalai Lama hugged me, they were amazed. One friend told me devotees believe that just his gaze can change one's destiny. I didn't realize that my first visit to Dharamsala and my unexpected encounter with the Dalai Lama would spark a desire to know more about Tibetans in exile in India and beyond—people between worlds whose homeland is in crisis. Since China's 1950 invasion of Tibet and the Dalai Lama's subsequent exile in 1959, by some estimates 1.2 million Tibetans have died. Many other Tibetans—tens of thousands—have fled to and settled in India since 1959, and the Dalai Lama accuses China of waging "cultural genocide" on Tibet. At the same time, China has also oppressed its own: when it invaded Tibet, China was in turmoil when a civil war ended in 1949 after more than two decades of conflict. Over the next thirty years, as many as 47 million Chinese people died of starvation, political purges, and torture because of catastrophic government policies. Tibetans have suffered immensely and so have Chinese people, though the latter is less widely acknowledged and often taboo to discuss.

That week in late March 2008, frustration, anger, pride, longing, and solidarity were all on display in Dharamsala. Thousands marched daily for more than a week through the narrow streets of this small Himalayan hill town to protest the crackdown in Tibet—then also the worst violence in China since the 1989 Tiananmen Square demonstrations. I passed crowds chanting pro-Tibet slogans and waving hand-lettered signs. "World Stand Up: Don't Watch Another Genocide" and "China Stop the Lies" read two. Dozens of people sat cross-legged in a makeshift corral where they had launched a hunger strike. One sign summed it up well. A young man wore a hand-lettered poster over his chest. It read, "Thank you India for the support. But we want the freedom to go back to Tibet. I miss my family."

. . .

Before the Dalai Lama spotted me during his press conference, he urged all sides to "cool down" rising tensions in Tibet. He spoke to journalists with an intense firmness, sometimes shaking his finger accusingly and furrowing his brow. The crackdown in China reminded the Dalai Lama of the "terrible feeling" he experienced following the 1959 Tibetan uprising and his desperate flight to India. He described feeling like a deer caught by a tiger: the deer can fight and kick, but she cannot possibly win against the tiger.

"On one side, the Chinese were determined to crush. On one side, Tibetans were determined to resist," the Dalai Lama recalled. "I was between them. Neither side willingly listened. I felt too much anxiety and helplessness. This time it is the same."

Reporters pressed the Dalai Lama about how he reconciled his own measured approach toward China with the diverging views of some Tibetan activists who want full independence for Tibet; the Dalai Lama espouses autonomy while remaining under China. Some activist groups like the Tibetan Youth Congress wanted a full boycott of the 2008 Beijing Olympics, while the Dalai Lama said the games should go on.

"If we say complete independence, it is very difficult to get support," said the Dalai Lama. "Independence is out of the question. Just to express strong emotions is very easy. But we are not writing a novel. We are facing life and death."

There was a sense of gravity in the room, but the Dalai Lama punctuated it with jokes—often in the form of wry jabs at China—followed by chuckles. The cadence of his voice rose and fell, and he would often end sentences with a questioning harumph or sagacious "Hmmm." The Dalai Lama denied accusations from China's premier Wen Jiabao that he had masterminded the protests in Tibet. Government officials had called the Dalai Lama a liar, "a wolf wrapped in monk's robes," and "a devil with a human face and a beast's heart."

The Dalai Lama snorted. "You investigate who is a liar. I want to ask [Wen], please show proof," he demanded. He went on to invite the Chinese premier to come personally investigate his files, records, and speeches. The Dalai Lama added with a hoot, "They can examine my pulse, my urine, my stool!" The journalists laughed. Jonathan Allen from Reuters asked how the Dalai Lama could remain so composed and light-hearted during these tumultuous times. Was it because of his faith? The Dalai Lama laughed and said he never lost sleep and always slept a solid eight hours, then woke hours before dawn to meditate. Each evening when he settled down to sleep, his mind was completely clear.

I raised my hand to catch the Dalai Lama's attention and he turned my way. What did he think of allegations that Tibetans had initiated the violent riots happening that week in Lhasa? The Dalai Lama did not hesitate. If Tibetans had engaged in any violence, "it is wrong," he said simply. "It is wrong." The Dalai Lama shook his head sadly. He reminded everyone that he had voiced the same opinion in 1988 when pro-Tibet demonstrations erupted in violence in Lhasa: nonviolence was the only way. He had no tolerance for violence.

"If things become out of control I will resign," insisted the Dalai Lama. The statement set the room abuzz. Later, a reporter used that as the headline for their story, and soon other global news sites carried the same quote. What the Dalai Lama meant by that, a press release from his office later clarified, was that he could not represent the Tibetan people if violence continued, not that he would stop being the Dalai Lama. After all, he couldn't resign from being the fourteenth reincarnation of the Buddha of Compassion. The clarification went largely unheeded, though; the next day most newspapers and websites carried headlines provocatively blaring his threat of resignation.

Over the course of two hours, the Dalai Lama spoke unhurriedly and often went off on long tangents despite the urgent situation in Tibet. He touched on wide-ranging topics, including memories of meeting Chairman Mao Zedong in China in the 1950s, and "his friend" Jawaharlal Nehru, India's first prime minister, who gave the twenty-four-year-old Dalai Lama refuge in India in 1959. The press conference stretched on, and when it finally ended, the Dalai Lama wanted the conversation to continue. He wasn't shy. He got up from his chair to mingle with the journalists and chatted jovially with them. I stood up from my seat on the floor to stretch my legs, and that's when he saw me and gave me that hug.

. . .

The turmoil in Tibet did not end after March 2008. Over the next several months, security officials in China would go on to detain more than 4,400 people, nearly all Tibetan, in connection with the March protests. Government repression in Tibet would continue, as would tensions, anxiety, and uncertainty about what would happen next.

A few months after my first visit, I returned for a weekend trip to Dharamsala, home to the Tibetan exile administration, the Dalai Lama, and about 12,000 Tibetans. It was a grueling twelve-hour overnight bus ride from Delhi up and down the mountain sides. The afternoon of my arrival, I was so fatigued that I dozed off in the sun on a bench outside a restaurant. But I was intrigued by this place that had become a haven for Tibetans, where religion, culture, and politics could flourish freely, unlike in Tibet. Dharamsala is more than just an ethnic enclave; it is a unique microcosm of a culture fighting for survival. Tibetan residents have set up a democratic government-in-exile, complete with a parliament and prime minister; established a thriving spiritual center and nonsecular education system; and transplanted their culture to foreign soil while waging a struggle for autonomy and freedom. The plight of refugees and larger questions of how they adapt and assimilate to new cultures is also an important global issue. And as an Asian American, I have long been interested in multiple layers of identity and their accompanying insights and tensions. An Indian hill town that thousands of Tibetans call home seemed a place ripe to explore—and write a book about—cultural identity.

By fall 2008, I had left my nine-year tenure at the *Financial Times* to do freelance journalism. I moved to Dharamsala and lived there for nearly a year, then returned for years as I followed the lives of ordinary Tibetans: Topden, a monk and unlikely veterinary assistant; Norbu, a cook and political refugee; and Deckyi, a recent refugee, and her husband Dhondup. Their lives created a portrait of life in exile and beyond. A project I thought would take one year stretched to fourteen and extended to other parts of India and across oceans to Australia, Europe, and the United States—places where Tibetans have migrated while striving to keep their cultural and religious identities alive.

. . .

This book is not an academic history of Tibet; neither is it a memoir. It is a close-up look at the lives of ordinary Tibetans in exile who make their way in the world far from their homeland. It is also a window into what it was like to live in Dharamsala and India and to travel to other far-flung places that became their home. There are many narratives about the Dalai Lama and Tibet, but few about regular Tibetans who transplant their culture in other parts of the globe. Their stories, especially those of four Tibetan refugees I unexpectedly followed across four continents, are told against the backdrop of milestones and events in Tibet's recent history—some memorable, too many tragic—at home and in exile. I watched and listened and tried to tell the stories I heard and what I saw around me in India and beyond. I aimed to make the writing accessible; I wanted the people I wrote about—some of whom speak limited or no English—to easily connect with the book and any translations.

Writing this book was not a linear or clear-cut journey. I didn't know my destination, and much was beyond my control. The immersive travelog style of the book's first part transforms to reportage as the narrative progresses over time. This happened much the way the landscape and weather change during a long, transcontinental train trip, or the colors and textures of a patchwork quilt change when new fabric is serendipitously found.

The book's shift in tone in its second part also reflects changes in my own life. After seven years living in India, I began reporting mostly on human and economic development issues in Bangladesh, Australia, Africa, and later in the United States. Yet I followed the thread of Tibetan exiles that began in Dharamsala however I could, and naturally over time, its hues and textures shifted.

Through it all, I wanted to focus on the stories of Tibetan people and avoid focusing on myself. But the narrative lenses shift according to the situation. Sometimes the perspective is panoramic; other times it telescopes inward and even becomes microscopic. The balance between my role as reporter and observer and writer or protagonist also evolved with circumstances and time. I tried to strike a balance between journalistic objectivity and unexpected personal involvement; I mostly wanted to be a fly on the wall, but sometimes I became a fly in the soup. When that happened, my perspective became relevant and therefore took the fore.

．　．　．

During my first week in Dharamsala in March 2008 I fulfilled the Dalai Lama's advice to "tell them." I spent sleepless nights writing several articles for the *Financial Times*. I did my job and left when the other foreign correspondents departed. I didn't expect to return to Dharamsala, live there, and keep going back, let alone report more than twenty-five articles for US and UK media outlets. No one, not even the Dalai Lama, could have known that his advice to "tell them" would result in a book that spans fourteen years and four continents, but that is somehow what happened.

India
2008 to 2010
Dharamsala, Sarnath, Delhi, Bylakuppe

Monks and Basketball

It Is My Karma

DHARAMSALA, AUTUMN 2008

. . .

In Dharamsala I was told that there was an easy way to distinguish between monks from India and monks from Tibet. Those from India liked cricket, while the ones from Tibet preferred basketball. Topden was a monk who belonged to the latter group. He was crazy about basketball. When quizzed about his favorite player he answered without hesitation: Kobe Bryant. Basketball was popular in China, and the craze had spread to Tibet too.

One sunny autumn afternoon in 2008, Topden and I hurried up a hilly road that rose above Dharamsala to a "peace festival" featuring traditional Tibetan music and dance and children's games. But the highlight for Topden was a basketball game—the final contest in a tournament that had begun weeks earlier.

"These teams are very good," he said excitedly. Topden had a gentle smile and a low voice. When his voice broke out of its even cadence you knew he felt strongly about something. One team was made up of the Dalai Lama's bodyguards and the other was students from a school for newly arrived Tibetan refugees known for playing rough.

The basketball game had not yet started, but already the concrete steps that served as bleachers were full of people: monks in red robes, Tibetans in jeans and T-shirts, wrinkled elderly people in fedora hats, children, and foreigners with dreadlocks and baggy "MC Hammer" pants made of what looked like tie-dyed curtains. Topden and I found an empty spot in the sun. His head was shaved to a black stubble, and he wore a necklace of wooden prayer beads. His ears stuck out at an alert angle and he squinted to watch the game. Topden draped the shawl of his monk's robe over his head to shield his scalp from the strong sunlight.

During the day, the sun beat down on Dharamsala, perched at 5,500 feet in the Himalayan foothills. Blue skies looked over the bustling activity of a small, overcrowded mountain town, and dogs doubled as door mats as they napped serenely in patches of sun. But it was November, not long after I moved to Dharamsala from Delhi, and the warm days were deceptive. Once the sun started to sink below the distant, snow-streaked mountains, the air became chilly. Nighttime Dharamsala brought lonely winds blowing over the steep hillsides littered with garbage, fierce barking as dogs faced off in the streets, and flickering orange flames that dimly illuminated men burning cardboard scraps to fend off winter's approach. And then there was the Dharamsala you could not see: rumbling subterranean tremors that erupted without warning from previously tranquil earth.

Eventually the basketball players jogged one by one onto the court as a booming voice on a public address system introduced them in Tibetan. They waved to the cheering crowd and began to warm up by shooting baskets. The players wore T-shirts and long shorts made of shiny fabric, but you could recognize the Dalai Lama's security guards by their square crew cuts and burly physiques.

These security guards were ubiquitous wherever the Dalai Lama traveled in India. They wore dark blazers or zipped-up sports jackets as they scanned the crowd at a prayer, teaching, or press conference. One time I saw a beefy guard lean down and pick up a scrap of litter in the courtyard in Dharamsala's main temple where a large crowd of Tibetans eagerly awaited the Dalai Lama. Months later, at a Buddhist teaching in central India where thousands of Tibetans chanted prayers with the Dalai Lama, a guard mouthed along as he surveyed the crowd with a steely gaze. But that day, the security guards wore sneakers and sleeveless shirts and ran with puffed cheeks up and down the court.

Before the game, basketballs slapped against asphalt and players practiced jump shots, layups, and improbable three-pointers. Airballs sailed short of hoops. The first few minutes of the game were awkward as players missed their shots and stumbled over the court. Eventually, they loosened up and soon were scoring and blocking with skill. The crowd cheered wildly whenever the ball dropped through the hoop at either end of the court.

Topden was absorbed in the game, but I interrupted with an impulsive question. Over a cup of tea before the game he had told me about how he had come to India, how as a teenager he walked for twenty-three days from Tibet to Nepal. I was still thinking about our conversation.

"So you don't hate Chinese people? You're not scared of me?" I blurted.

He snorted at my question. "We don't hate Chinese people," said Topden with a short laugh, as though I had asked something absurd. "We hate the Chinese government."

I wasn't surprised at his answer, since Topden and every other Tibetan I had met in Dharamsala did not seem at all rattled by my Chinese face. In fact, some Tibetans wanted to speak in Mandarin with me or cheerfully called out "Ni hao!" as I roamed the few streets of this small town. They had no idea I was born and raised in America and happened to speak Mandarin because I learned it in college years before. They were friendly and warm to me, and that went against the grain of common perception—or misperception.

At first I was startled that these exiled Tibetans were eager to speak the language of the country that had repressed theirs for more than half a century. But many Tibetans, especially if they were from Lhasa or Tibetan regions of China, spoke some Mandarin or were fluent or were used to hearing it on television, radio, and in conversations. Most new arrivals to India did not speak English, and they didn't speak Hindi or other Indian languages. I wouldn't have blamed them if they had been angry at someone like me who wore the face of their "enemy." But in all the time I spent in Dharamsala, where I often approached strangers to talk to them, I never encountered any animosity for being ethnically Chinese. Usually it was quite the opposite: I was greeted with warmth and curiosity.

Most of the Tibetans I met also did not necessarily equate a Chinese face with political oppression. They could differentiate between the actions of China's government and those of an ordinary person who had no political influence. Some Tibetans I met had been imprisoned alongside Chinese people who had run afoul of the government. There were signs that there was more to the relationship between China and Tibet—or Chinese people and Tibetans—than the simple dichotomy of oppressor and oppressed, of enemies locked in a struggle with no way out.

Basketball games, however, produce diametric opposition and clear victors. In spite of their rough street basketball (mountain basketball?), the Recent Refugees lost to the Bodyguards on that sunny autumn day. The sweaty players shook hands then trotted off the court, which was just as well. With so many of the Dalai Lama's security guards at the game, I did wonder who was minding the shop?

• • •

I met Topden because of an injured street cat. One early morning after my arrival in Dharamsala on the nausea-inducing overnight bus from Delhi, I found a striped cat on the steps of my guesthouse. An elderly Indian woman and a little boy hovered over a brown and gray tabby cat protruding from beneath the staircase. The boy dropped a small white sweater on the cat who hissed and moaned. I couldn't communicate with the pair, but it was obvious the cat was injured; his nose was scraped and bloody and his eyes glowed with pain. The woman was trying to direct the boy to pick up the cat with the sweater, but the animal hissed and feebly tried to bite him. I asked some young Tibetan men sipping tea if there was a vet nearby. Miraculously there was a free vet clinic just a short walk down the hill.

Like many nonprofit organizations in town, the charity offered English and computer classes to Tibetans. It also had a health clinic and a small veterinary clinic. My visit coincided with Topden's second day there working as a vet assistant. When I barged in, a brown-haired woman was taking off her jacket and backpack. Beyond her a monk in red robes—Topden—was mopping the bathroom. "Are you a vet?" I asked the woman breathlessly.

"Vet student," she qualified. Her name was Martina, and she had just arrived from Germany to volunteer at the clinic. Together we walked back up the steep hill to my guesthouse. On the way there, Martina asked where I was from. I told her that I was born in the United States to parents from Hong Kong. "You must have a difficult time here, no?" she asked.

She assumed that Tibetans were hostile toward Chinese people, as non-Tibetans tended to. "No, not really. I feel very comfortable here," I told her.

When we reached my guesthouse, the Indian woman and boy were still hovering over the cat. Martina did not bother with a cloth to protect herself from the cat's bared teeth. She leaned over and quickly grabbed the scruff of his neck and plopped him into a lidded plastic basket. Back at the clinic Martina examined the cat, whose green eyes were now glazed with fear. She held him in the air by his scruff and the cat's back legs drooped lifelessly so he looked like a ragged accordion puppet. He couldn't move his back legs but Martina didn't think he was paralyzed. His bones and spine were intact. Probably a car had hit the cat, or worse, someone had kicked him.

Martina gave the cat an injection of painkillers and vitamin B for nerve damage. Topden meanwhile was cleaning the bathroom, and the pile of dust and muck included a large spider with ropey legs. Martina jumped and screamed at the sight of the mangled insect although she had intrepidly picked up a hissing, feral cat moments before. Topden looked up, also puzzled at the ruckus.

"Is it dead?" asked Martina apprehensively. "Or maybe you can't kill it because you're a monk?"

"Oh, it is dead. It was in water," said Topden slowly.

Martina watched in fear as Topden swept the already-drowned spider out the door with a straw broom. The cat crept warily to one side of the large plastic basin where Martina had put him. He laid his head down in misery, and his thin body trembled.

Topden told me the word for cat in Tibetan. It sounded like "shimmy," so that's what I called him. I came to the clinic almost every day to check on the cat, to whom I immediately felt attached. After several days Shimmy became more alert and during my visits stared at me warily but let me stroke his head. He could even relieve himself and twitch his feet, but his back legs remained completely limp, and he couldn't put weight on them. Martina thought Shimmy had a fractured pelvis, which might heal on its own with time. She wondered aloud whether it was acceptable to euthanize animals in India.

At the clinic one never knew what one would find. Street animals in India have a precarious existence; they are constantly hit by cars, or get into fights, or contract diseases or infections. One day a forlorn black puppy sat on a table with an IV drip in his leg as he battled a stomach virus. He died the next day. Then someone brought in a shaggy dog whose ear had been ripped by another canine down by the Tibetan library. At any given time, the vets might be neutering an anesthetized dog.

One time a young Russian girl of about ten dressed in the forest-green uniform of the Tibetan school in Dharamsala turned up with a tiny, days-old kitten that she carried in her hands. A few weeks later I saw the girl in the reading room of the Tibetan library. She tilted her freckled face and told me solemnly that the kitten had died days later.

. . .

Over the next couple of months I chatted often with Topden during my visits to Shimmy. After some initial shyness he spoke about any number of things in his slow, careful voice. Topden was from rural eastern Tibet where he loved playing basketball on his school's court. In 2008 he was "thirty or thirty-five. Sometimes thirty-six." (Many people in developing countries people do not have birth certificates; they were born at home or at informal clinics.) He became a monk as a boy, fled to southern India as a young man and joined a monastery there, so he had never worked a job before joining the charity.

Topden had come to Dharamsala when he took leave from his monastery to learn English—not an uncommon thing for a monk to do. "English is very powerful," Topden said. In September 2007 he started English classes at a nonprofit and studied diligently there for more than a year. Topden practiced English, memorized words, and did exercises in his textbooks. Of his own volition, he pulled all-nighters, studying until his head spun with English words. He went from speaking minimal English to being able to carry a fluid conversation a year later.

In late September 2007 a rabid dog bit an Englishman in town. The patient came to the vet clinic at the nonprofit where Topden happened to be studying English. "He asked me to help. I had not any idea. But I couldn't help. I get really guilty," he recalled.

Two days later—September 2—was World Rabies Day, an important event in a town home to street dogs, cats, and monkeys, the latter of which scamper precariously along electrical wires. The nonprofit director gave a speech to the students and kicked off a six-day rabies vaccination campaign. Volunteer veterinarians would vaccinate the dogs, but they needed extra help. Were there any students who would lend a hand? Topden didn't volunteer, but a week later the director asked if he would join the nonprofit's vet clinic, based on positive observations of him by staffers.

The offer came as a surprise. "I didn't think about it to get job because I'm monk," Topden explained. His answer to the director? "I said, 'No way. I have to go back to monastery.'" The director said Topden could think about the offer for a week, so he went to his cousin for advice. "I asked my cousin. He said, 'You like hospital to help human. You better help animals.'" Initially Topden didn't even like animals. "I thought dogs and cats were disgusting," he confessed, wrinkling his face. "I particularly didn't like cats."

In India, it's common for street dogs to roam streets, sleep in the middle of the road, and root through garbage. At night their guttural barks echoed through the streets of Dharamsala as they fought. Streets cats were not as common, but an observant eye could spot them slinking between buildings or prowling around mounds of trash.

Although not completely willing, Topden began to come around. He realized that helping animals was "a kind of practice. I think that. Don't know if it's true. Buddhism is to help sentient beings."

Topden began to change his mind about animals not long after working at the vet clinic. A few weeks after he started, he told me, "Now of course I like them. They are very poor. Of course I want to help them. The poor dogs, they can stay. Small puppies—I gave them fluid. And your cat always looks at my face." Before I could interject that he was not *my* cat—I didn't want that immense responsibility—Topden stuck out his tongue to mimic Shimmy's plaintive expression. "The cat looks like he's telling me something. Then my mind is changed. They are very pretty. They can't say, 'I'm hungry, thirsty, sick.' People can say, 'I'm very pain. Can you give me the painkiller?'" About his unexpected job helping animals, he said with a note of wonder in his voice, "It is my karma." There was the possibility that Topden would eventually enroll in a course to learn dog-catching and vet technician skills. He thought one day he might learn how to give injections, but now, "everything is difficult. Maybe I will get small experience," he sighed.

In those first few weeks, working in the vet clinic overwhelmed Topden. He was sickened when Martina spayed a female cat and he saw her shining innards. Another time she wanted him to cut a small infection from Shimmy's ear, but Topden refused. Once I came in as they were treating a dog whose injured leg had been splinted far too tightly by another vet. They unwound the bandage, and as blood returned to his bound leg the dog screamed in pain—a sound so keen and shrill that it was unlike anything I had ever heard before. Everyone in the room became very silent as though collectively holding their breaths.

In the commotion, Shimmy shimmied his way out of his basin and across the floor using his strong front legs. When he found he could not escape through the closed screen door, Shimmy slipped into a small space between the open inner door and the wall. The cat lay quietly in his shadowy hiding spot, probably thankful that he was not the poor animal in terrible pain that day. I crouched down to peer at Shimmy and then decided to leave him alone. From behind the operating table, Topden also looked at me with big, doleful eyes.

. . .

A circuitous road led Topden to Dharamsala. He was born in a small village in the Kham region of eastern Tibet. "When I was a child there were only farmers," he recalled. "There was no monastery, but we prayed. But the Chinese came to find out who prays and then punished them."

There was a village school that went up to sixth grade and about a mile away the ruins of a monastery that Chinese authorities destroyed after the 1950 invasion of Tibet. The place was deserted, and Topden's uncle took care of apple trees that grew among the ruins.

Locals began to repair the monastery, and by the time Topden was eleven a large prayer hall had been built. For reasons Topden couldn't fully explain, he desperately wanted to become a monk. His parents didn't want him to because they needed their sons to help with the fields and their yaks and sheep. "I wanted to become a monk. This is just my feeling," Topden recalled. When his parents forbade him, "I cried twice. My feeling was very, very sad."

His parents eventually relented, and Topden joyously became a monk when he was twelve. Another turning point came at fifteen, when he and three friends slipped away to Lhasa, Tibet's capital, to see the great Sakyamuni Buddha statue. They borrowed and scraped together enough money for the three-day journey to Lhasa via bus.

"I met lots of people on the way: poor people, rich people, farmers, city people, nomads." He began to hear more about Tibet's situation. "When I was home, I didn't know about Tibetan independence. We only know that His Holiness is in India," he said. "We didn't know why he couldn't come to Tibet."

Topden arrived in Lhasa two months after the 1989 protests, one of the largest demonstrations in Tibet's recent history, which were started by monks from major monasteries. He heard about what happened. "I said, 'What is Tibetan freedom?' People explained to me. At that time we were very poor in Tibet and we agreed China helped us. We didn't know China occupied Tibet." The way to Lhasa's holiest temple was still blocked by police, so Topden wasn't able to pray there during his monthlong visit. After the 1989 protests, China declared martial law in Lhasa for thirteen months.

He returned home and stayed in his village for two years until a restless older cousin convinced Topden to make the journey to India, where he could study as a monk far more freely. Flowers grew abundantly outside his family's house. On the day he left, Topden cut some blooms and put them in a bowl for his mother. She had no inkling of his plans. "I was really sad when I looked at my mom's face," he remembered. When she left to visit his uncle who lived nearby, Topden and his cousin slipped away. He left a note for his mother so she wouldn't worry, saying he would return in three days.

More than seventeen years later, Topden had not returned. Letters from his mother beg him to come back. "I want to go home but I have no passport," said Topden. "I miss my family, I miss everything in Tibet. I really, really miss home."

His escape to India was like that of thousands of other Tibetan refugees. He and his cousin went to Lhasa and found a guide to take them over the Nepal border. They begged for money in the city and then each paid the guide 450 yuan (about fifty dollars at the time; the price has gone up considerably since then). They took a bus to Shigatse, one of Tibet's largest cities, then another bus for two days to a large monastery. From there, a small truck took their group of six to the desolate landscape where they began their twenty-three-day trek.

"We walked at night. At that time moon was very good. It was like a dream. Lots of dreams come," Topden said. The journey became more difficult as they ascended steep mountains. Topden carried only his monk's robes in his small pack, while his cousin carried eating utensils and other supplies. Still, Topden recalled, "Small bag very heavy for me. I told my cousin, I want to throw them." The hiking shoes he bought for five yuan (about six dollars) in Lhasa "looks very good. But after ten days my shoes broken. Stones and water comes inside. Other person in group gave shoes." Nights were colder, and during the day the sun blazed. "My face is very easy to burn. My cousin said, 'You should cover your face.'" Topden wore sunglasses and a cap but couldn't breathe the thin air as they kept walking to "the top—not top." The mountain seemed to go on forever. "I said, 'I think it has no end.' I told my friends to go ahead. I couldn't go. They left and I tried to go home. I had no water. I tried to go back to Lhasa but I had no money."

Topden's gravelly voice rose a bit. "Then I thought I should go to India with them to see His Holiness. When I was a child I always pray: 'May I can see His Holiness as soon as possible.'" So he turned back up the mountain, prayed, and kept walking. "'Please, please help me.' Finally I was over the mountain. I could hear the sound of water." He caught up with the group and the next day they continued on together. "They made fun of me," Topden said, smiling a bit.

The journey wasn't over. China's border was easy to cross because the place was too cold and high for patrols. "It wasn't snowing but there was already snow on the ground." But the way into Nepal was quite risky, because it was close to a police outpost. The group waited until dark to sneak past. As they climbed over a gate, a dog started barking. Topden mimicked the "bad dog." "Ao, ao, ao," he called. Yet the group managed to sneak past into Nepal.

Getting to Kathmandu involved a grueling bus journey during which Topden rode on the rooftop luggage rack. When they finally arrived in the capital, they made their way to the Reception Center run by the Tibetan exile administration to receive new refugees. Frostbite and other health problems are common among new arrivals from Tibet, but Topden was in relatively good health. He remembered "five days of eating" after the Reception Center gave them rice, vegetables, and "lots of Tibetan cookies." Refugees then usually continue to Delhi by bus and then eventually to Dharamsala, where they register and stay at another Reception Center until they can have a group audience with the Dalai Lama. A big smile spread over Topden's face and his eyes shone as he recalled the audience. He cried during the meeting. Many others in the audience also wept at the sight of the Dalai Lama, who seemed like a dream come to life.

Shortly after, Topden went to join the Indian branch of his monastery in the southern state of Karnataka, home to the city of Bangalore, at the opposite end of India. The train journey took almost seventy-two hours, and for days after he reached his destination, he still felt like he was in motion. Topden finally reached a place where he could practice Buddhism freely with hundreds of other monks.

The next few years were very difficult. He desperately missed home and Tibetan food; even the meals in the monastery were "kind of Indian." For a time, his homesickness was so great that he considered returning to Tibet. But he knew that he would have a difficult time continuing his studies there. So he persevered, and gradually the homesickness subsided. He made friends in India and learned to speak Hindi. After completing his monastic studies, Topden went to Dharamsala to learn English. "I studied very hard." With a note of surprise, he said, "Now I have a job."

After the March 2008 protests in Tibet, Chinese authorities tightened security to the point that even phoning home to Tibet from India was risky. Topden learned that Tibetans were being shot and arrested. The time was "unforgettable. I feel very sad," he said, struggling for words. "If I had power I can help, I can discuss with the Chinese. I can tell them. The Chinese can change very easily. One minute, two minutes," Topden snapped his fingers.

It sounded strange and simplistic, but there was logic to his words. Chinese people adopted the mandates of their leaders quickly; they didn't have a choice. In 1978 after decades of bleak communism, Deng Xiao Ping became China's leader and paved the way for capitalism. Before, during the Cultural Revolution, grass was ripped out of soil for being too bourgeois. Topden mused that if he could get a "good passport" maybe he could go home. But would he really go?

"I can't come illegally to Tibet," he replied. His voice trailed off, and Topden shook his head in exasperation. "I don't want to think about the future. It makes me a little crazy."

[2]

Here to This Other Country

Since Then I Lost My Chance

WINTER 2008

. . .

The worst part was when the guard used an electric cattle prod on the prisoner. The guard had already beaten him to the ground. Then he stuck the prod into the man's mouth so he convulsed like a fish writhing on a hook. His arms and legs shuddered and his back arched. It wasn't real—this was a play—but just the sight was chilling. Then the group of Tibetans, including red-robed monks and nuns, started goose-stepping across the room with military precision. They marched in two straight lines, their sandaled and sneakered feet beating rhythmically on the floor. The prison guard barked numbers in Mandarin: *Yi, er, yi!* (One, two, one!).

The monks and nuns, all former political prisoners in Tibet, were eerily good at marching, and the lines remained two neat rows with all those feet stamping in unison.

These Tibetans were rehearsing an amateur play they would stage in Switzerland in a few months. Norbu, a Tibetan in his early thirties, had invited me to the rehearsal. The cattle prod used to shock and beat prisoners was actually a rolled-up newspaper covered with duct tape. It made a hollow whacking sound when it struck the guy on the ground.

Norbu was boyish and friendly with spiky, red-tinted hair. It was difficult to imagine he had been jailed in Tibet when barely a teenager. He sat in a plastic lawn chair and watched friends and coworkers reenact prison scenes. The actors wore olive Chinese police uniforms during dress rehearsals, which made Norbu confess, "I feel really afraid."

About twenty Tibetans took part in the play about the imprisonment of a man in Lhasa who had participated in a demonstration. A Swiss foundation would fund their travel to Europe to raise awareness about political prisoners in Tibet. I recognized several of the "actors" from around town. There were just three main streets in the main Tibetan neighborhood of Dharamsala, so it was common to see the same faces over and over, on the streets, in restaurants, and at talks and films. One was a scholarly looking monk with silver-rimmed glasses. Another was a long-haired Tibetan man in jeans with a lazy eye who often strummed a Tibetan lute outside the Internet café where he worked. One fellow wore a zipped-up sweatshirt with a fake Ferrari logo stitched on the chest. And there was Tsering, a cook in his early thirties at the same restaurant as Norbu. With an olive-drab cap over his shaggy hair and a brown T-shirt layered over a long-sleeved shirt, Tsering looked more like an urban hipster than a former monk.

The mood at the rehearsal was surprisingly jovial in spite of the grim events reenacted. The Tibetans laughed at the prison guard's overzealous assault or when someone bumbled a line or misstepped while marching in formation. The man acting as the cattle-prodded prisoner even chuckled self-consciously after convulsing on the floor. During the rehearsal the Tibetan man who played the guard fastidiously wrapped the baton in more tape when it began to sag. The tape made loud retching noises as he yanked it from the roll, but the dialogue between actors didn't stop.

After the monks and nuns marched in place for a moment, the prison guard's call in Mandarin reached a crescendo. *Yi, er, san, si!* (One, two, three, four!). The actor slurred four, so it became "su," as many Tibetans do. The Tibetans automatically marched in place, knees pumping, arms swinging, like mechanical soldiers. They came to an abrupt halt, stood at attention, then counted off, once again showing their Mandarin skills.

The "actors" were part of Gu Chu Sum, an association of Tibetan former political prisoners living in exile in India. They knew how to goose-step and march in formation because many of them had spent months or years imprisoned in Tibet. Some had participated in demonstrations or aided protestors in some way. One former prisoner was jailed for seven months for photocopying the banned Tibetan flag in a shop near Lhasa. He said he was routinely stripped naked and beaten outdoors in freezing temperatures; he still suffered health problems as a result. When asked if he regretted photocopying the flag, he wiped tears from his face and nodded.

A petite nun with a shaved head and apple-red cheeks marched in time with her much taller male counterparts during the prison scene. As we watched, Norbu said, "She was in prison." For years, he added.

Gu Chu Sum means "nine," "ten," and "three" in Tibetan. This signifies the months of major demonstrations in Lhasa: September 27, 1987, October

1, 1987, and March 5, 1988. On September 27, 1987, twenty-one monks from Drepung Monastery in Lhasa led a brief protest that was quickly quashed, though subsequent unrest flared up. Over the next few years, thousands of Tibetans who participated in demonstrations were arrested. Protests culminated in martial law in Lhasa.

. . .

On that cold afternoon in Dharamsala, the actors rehearsed in a clean, spacious room in Gu Chu Sum's red brick building. The room was also a mini-museum documenting imprisonment in Tibet and China. Framed photographs covering the walls showed handcuffs, a blood-splattered shirt smuggled out of prison by former Tibetan prisoners, torture devices such as cattle prods and batons, ruined monasteries, and other grim scenes. The actors rehearsed after lunch between English, Tibetan, and computer classes. An open window let in chilly air and limpid afternoon sunlight. Cars and motorbikes roared up the hilly road outside while drivers madly honked their horns, leaving behind noxious ribbons of noise.

The plot of the play was simple. A Tibetan man marches in a protest, is jailed and beaten. He falls ill and is released but can't find work; he is blacklisted and potential employers turn him away. Finally he gets a job moving boxes at a Tibetan shop, but Chinese police force the store owner to fire him. A friend visits the former prisoner and suggests they escape to India, but the man is too weak and sick. His sister arrives only to find he has died from a disease that left him hacking and coughing on his deathbed. The actors concluded the play by mournfully singing a song in Tibetan. The man with the lazy eye played a wooden flute and the lugubrious notes lingered in the air.

Norbu quietly explained what was happening in the play and peppered his comments with snippets of his own experience. He spoke English fluidly, but his grammar and pronunciation were sometimes rough, and he groped for words. I taught English in China for two years after college, so I understand how hard it is to learn. From my time there, navigating in Mandarin, I also know how exhausting and frustrating it is to fumble in a foreign language. I offered Norbu vocabulary and jotted words down in my notebook for his reference so he could see how to spell them. I printed them clearly in the margins in contrast to the scrawl of my notes. An odd vocabulary list resides in the margins of my notebook from my scribblings that day. "Regained consciousness," "solitary confinement," "pawn shop," "persist," "insist,"

"persuade." I explained to Norbu the difference between those last three
words in low tones as the rehearsal continued before us.

. . .

I met Norbu my second day in Dharamsala on a sunny autumn afternoon. I
was staying at a simple guesthouse run by friendly Kashmiris conveniently
located next to a Japanese restaurant that served delicious vegetarian fare. A
meal there quickly became part of my daily routine throughout the seasons
in Dharamsala. The cooks and staff were members of Gu Chu Sum and took
English classes or did vocational training there. A tailoring workshop in the
back was filled with women at sewing machines making clothes and crafts
sold in the restaurant's gift shop. Sometimes their children wandered out of
the sewing shop to play on the adjoining terrace. They played badminton or
chased each other, shrieking as I ate my lunch of miso soup, vegetarian sushi
rolls, and vegetable tempura. On sunny days, the terrace offered magnificent
views of lush green hills and snow-capped peaks in the distance. From there
I could also observe the balconies of nearby guesthouses. A Tibetan woman
washed her hair, coated in suds, over a basin. An older European man sat in
a chair absorbed in a novel. I was close enough to see he was reading *The
Devil Wears Prada*.

The friendly young chefs, including Norbu and Tsering, cooked in front
of windows in the kitchen. Above the din of oil crackling in woks, Norbu
and Tsering cheerfully called out, "Good afternoon!" They often joined me
on their lunch breaks. Both had come to India in their late teens, were now
in their early thirties, and tended to wear baggy jeans and T-shirts or, when
it got colder, hooded sweatshirts that seemed a bit youthful for their age.
Norbu had an especially round, boyish face though lines creased the corners
of his eyes. He also spiked his hair with gel, while Tsering's shaggy style hung
across his ears and forehead. Tsering had an earring made of what looked
like a scrap of black rubber pinching his earlobe, and he wore a black cord
wrapped around his bicep.

After lunch Tsering would puff on a cigarette and croon along with music
that blared from his cell phone with a tinny brittleness. He loved both Tibetan and Hindi songs. One Tibetan pop song was called "Pure Love."
Norbu and Tsering translated the lyrics into English for me:

I left my lovely country. I came here to this other country
I will be your good friend. If we have any problems, we will serve together.

In my heart we will together have happiness.

Long and winding life goes on. Please give your pure love to me.

Dearest parents are far away.

I don't know this other country but I feel like this is my country.

Tsering was also fond of beer. Kingfisher, the Indian brand, was his favorite, and he was no stranger to late nights of drinking and smoking. All this made it hard to imagine Tsering as a monk, as he had been for more than a dozen years both in Tibet and at a monastery in southern India. I couldn't quite picture his craggy, dark face with a shaved head rather than his trendy hairdo. Yet sometimes in an abrupt reminder of his former life, Tsering would burst out into guttural chanting—more deep vibration than song.

Did Norbu like beer too? He made a face. He didn't like beer, nor did he smoke. Besides, he woke up at 6 or 6:30 a.m. to walk the *kora*—the holy circular path around the Dalai Lama's residence—each morning. In his white zip-up jacket stitched with the words "50 Cent," he walked alongside the elderly Tibetans who circumambulated to receive religious merit.

He also went to a yoga class held each morning on the roof of Gu Chu Sum's building. Norbu, ever cheerful, invited me to join the yoga class. I attended a couple of sessions where mostly Japanese travelers and Tibetan ex–political prisoners contorted into awkward positions on the cold concrete rooftop.

Norbu was quick to smile, which crinkled his face. At lunch I showed him a slender orange book of prayers from a popular Buddhist philosophy class at the Tibetan Library. Norbu looked at it in recognition. He had taken a few classes at the Tibetan Library too but admitted he had trouble understanding the teacher because of his heavy accent from Amdo in northeast Tibet. Norbu's hipster appearance belied his interest in Buddhist philosophy classes, his habit of walking the *kora*, and doing morning yoga before he gelled his hair. On the streets of Dharamsala there were lots of young Tibetan men whiling away hours playing Indian checkers or hanging around trying to chat with foreign women.

One autumn morning I set out to walk the *kora* myself. It was about 6:30 a.m., and I had just arrived in Dharamsala after another overnight ride from Delhi on a bone-chillingly drafty and dilapidated old bus. I walked down the steep hill from my guesthouse and headed toward the small path that led to the *kora*. Before leaving the road I turned around to admire the dramatic view. Dawn was just breaking over the valley and mist swirled around the mountaintops. A vertical drop off the road made the sky all the more expansive as it brightened into the heavens.

A figure rounded the corner. It was Norbu, dressed in jeans and his white zip-up "50 Cent" jacket. We both started as recognition sank in, then happily greeted one another. He was incredulous that I had just gotten off the Delhi-to-Dharamsala bus. "On the bus, I want to vomit," he said grimacing. Norbu had a weak stomach: "I *see* the bus I want to vomit."

In the crook of his arm Norbu carried a tall plastic bag filled with white mush. Inside slopped noodles, rice, and bread he collected from the restaurant kitchen. "For the birds," he explained. A string of wooden prayer beads hung from his other hand, and he fingered it as we walked.

We left the paved road and stepped onto a smaller concrete path winding through thickets of trees. Norbu poured the bag's contents in a sweeping white arc onto the ground just off the path. Already large black birds—crows and kites—circled overhead as though they were used to this routine. Norbu folded the plastic bag and dropped it inside a green dustbin, one of the few in Dharamsala.

Kora is short for *lingkor*, the centuries-old circular path linking Lhasa's holy sites. In 1960, a year after arriving in exile in India, the Dalai Lama moved to Dharamsala. In the ensuing years, a new temple and *kora* were constructed so Tibetans could continue their rituals of prayer and circumambulation. In Dharamsala, the *kora* was the only well-trafficked route clean and free of the trash people discarded casually and liberally on main roads or in open gutters. Prayer flags stretched across the treetops like party streamers, and the bright red, blue, yellow, and green squares fluttered festively in the wind.

Cows managed to squeeze themselves onto the *kora* and Norbu and I were soon face-to-face with a large black bovine who stood squarely on the path and flared her glistening nostrils at us. We stepped around her and kept walking in a comfortable silence. Norbu pushed small barrel-shaped prayer wheels that line the *kora*; they are said to release prayers into the world with each turn. The wooden handles were smooth from the touch of countless hands. The path wound through the trees, past rocks painted and carved with the mantra "Om mani padme hum" in jagged Tibetan script. To one side of a courtyard, there was a small temple with rows of prayer wheels and stairs leading to a brightly painted shrine topped with a bulbous stupa. Some elderly people strained to push a gigantic prayer wheel. Each time it turned, a bell near the top clanged loudly. In the coming months, this tranquil courtyard would host many crowded candlelight vigils in response to China's continued and increasing repression in Tibet.

Norbu made his way to an open-air shrine that featured a large brass goblet filled with brown liquid. As he prayed, he closed his eyes, held his clasped hands to his face, and murmured. Afterward, he took out a small bottle of brown liquid and poured it over the goblet, making it overflow. Other bottles, including an empty whiskey flask, stood nearby.

"What was that?" I asked when we resumed walking.

"Tea," he said.

"Not whiskey?" I joked.

"Not whiskey."

The last stretch of the *kora* was a short, steep, uphill climb. I plodded and panted alongside wizened Tibetans who clutched walking sticks and muttered prayers as they walked.

"They do *kora* three times every morning. Some walk more," Norbu remarked. The *kora* ended in front of the gate that leads to the town's main Buddhist temple and the Dalai Lama's residence beyond that. By then it was past 7 a.m. and the town had woken up. The fruit and vegetable vendor laid out carrots and bunches of bananas; drivers stood next to their taxis hustling for customers; vendors squatted next to fresh bunches of spring onion and Chinese cabbage. Some older women sold *momo* dumplings and Tibetan bread from small stands right outside the temple gate. Norbu paused to buy two pieces of round bread that looked like oversized English muffins. The vendor wrapped the bread in newspaper and handed them to Norbu, who refused to let me pay.

We walked around the corner to a hole-in-the-wall café whose door was a Tibetan wall hanging with grease-blackened edges. Inside, other Tibetans sipped tiny glasses of steaming chai. Norbu paid for two despite my protests. A color TV rested on top of a refrigerator in a corner of the room.

In silence, we watched a morning program blare news of the recent terrorist attacks in Mumbai. Gunmen had laid siege to the city and its iconic luxury hotels on November 26 and held guests hostage for days. News channels had screened terrifying live footage of the attacks: gunfights and commandos stormed buildings. Nearly 200 people were killed as they worked in the hotels, ate dinner in the city's most expensive restaurants, or relaxed in posh hotel rooms. Inside those gleaming buildings, people had seemed protected, until terrorism's undiscriminating grip claimed them.

All this seemed far away from Dharamsala, but the attacks no doubt rocked India to its core. I had been on another harrowing overnight bus from Delhi to Dharamsala when I got a message on my Blackberry from my concerned mother asking where I was as the attacks in Mumbai unfolded. It reminded me of how people recall getting messages asking if they were okay on September 11, 2001, after the attacks on the World Trade Center in New York and the Pentagon.

As we watched the news from Mumbai, Norbu and I sipped the last drops of tea from our glasses, then headed out into the town's ruckus to start the day.

• • •

Back at Gu Chu Sum, the play rehearsal ended with a bustle akin to a class-room released for recess. Actors grabbed their belongings and chatted amia-bly. Norbu asked if I wanted tea, so we headed downstairs to where he lived. In addition to offices and classrooms, Gu Chu Sum had dorm rooms for members. Downstairs, the halls were dim, the walls and floor cheerless gray concrete. The building didn't catch the bright sunlight that warmed Dha-ramsala, so it was cold as a refrigerator inside. I zipped my green fleece up to my neck and stuffed my hands in my pockets.

Norbu shared a small and cluttered room with another young man from Gu Chu Sum. There were two single beds separated by a battered night-stand. The duvets and blankets were folded lengthwise like long sausages and stacked against the wall so the beds could be used like sofas during the day. One pillow was covered with a greasy yellow towel where a head rested each night.

Norbu had recently returned from a trip to Nepal to see his aunt, who traveled there from Tibet just to meet him. From Delhi, the bus ride to Nepal takes two days and is preceded by the stomach-clenching twelve-hour ride careening down the hills of Dharamsala. Yet there was no question that Norbu would go to Nepal to see his aunt. He would get news about his family in Tibet, so he weathered the journey to Kathmandu while clutching a plastic bag in one clammy hand in case he had to vomit. His aunt brought photos of his mother and their home in Tibet. The family house was bigger and stur-dier, but his mother looked so old, Norbu lamented. She was bent and her hair had turned gray. He worried he would never see her again.

Norbu paused to offer something to eat and eagerly pulled out a plastic sack from the nightstand's shelf. Via his aunt, his mother had passed along treats to her son. He held up a large plastic bag filled with walnuts. I declined, knowing nuts are expensive, and said he should enjoy them himself. Next Norbu pulled out a big bag of dried yak cheese. Cubes of the whitish-gray substance were strung together like Christmas tree garlands.

Dried yak cheese is pungent and so hard that it can be chewed for hours. He offered some, but I insisted he keep it too. Finally Norbu offered a bag of roasted soybeans. I finally agreed to eat some, and we munched on those crunchy yellow beans and chatted. I asked him when he left Tibet.

"I left my lovely country in 1994," he answered and waved to a large poster of Lhasa taped above his bed. In the photo, the city is stunningly beautiful: all sky, mountains, and water.

• • •

Norbu was from a village east of Lhasa. In March 1988, when he was twelve or thirteen years old, he was in Lhasa during his school holidays when a big demonstration swept through the capital. He was a bystander, a child who didn't fully understand the banners that read, "China Quit Tibet." But Norbu did understand the ones that said, "Long Live the Dalai Lama."

"I always go to the temple to pray," Norbu remembered. That habit brought him to Lhasa's main temple. When protestors surged through the streets, the crowd carried him along. He started shouting and chanting slogans too. Before long, Chinese security forces descended on the temple and dispersed the unarmed crowd with gunfire. "I felt bullets fly over my head," he remembered.

Protestors ran for cover. Norbu cowered in a public bathroom with other Tibetans who sought refuge there. "The police said, 'Come out or we'll shoot you.'" Norbu stayed inside until the police burst in and began dragging people out by force. One Tibetan woman begged them to let her go: she wasn't involved with the protest, she had just been using the bathroom, she had children. They dragged her out with the others.

What followed was a blur for Norbu. Sitting on the edge of his bed, he told his story quickly, as if he couldn't get the words out fast enough. The security forces beat him, twisted his arm, and tied his hands behind his back with his belt. They threw him into a truck "like luggage" and he blacked out. When he regained consciousness, his eye had already become very swollen and green and his arm was badly hurt. Police dragged him into a detention center where they beat him some more.

"I feel like I died," said Norbu simply. The detainees were forced to stand in line, but most people could barely move. "Every day they interviewed us.

I don't admit I join the demonstration. If I admit, they sentence me five to seven years. I said, 'I'm a student. When I was coming back from school there were demonstrations.'"

After three months of interrogations, Norbu was finally released from the detention center and he returned to his village. But his life was irreparably changed. "I couldn't go back to school. Police came to check on me. The headmaster said, 'You can't go to school.'" The same thing happened when Norbu tried to enroll in school in a nearby village. He stated simply, "Since then I lost my chance."

What did he do after being barred from school? "I just help my mom," he replied. "My mom—she was always crying." The blacklist extended beyond school. "If I tried to sell something, the Chinese police came and said, 'Not allowed.'"

This limbo continued through Norbu's teenage years. Finally his older brother said, "If you stay here you can't do anything." His brother scraped together 1,000 yuan, about $125, and hired a guide to take Norbu to Nepal with a group of 18 other Tibetans. Five were children younger than ten years old. The guide said the trek would take seven days, but it lasted seventeen. Norbu ran out of food and supplies.

"The weather was so cold. Sometimes we had no food for two days." They walked at night on ground covered with "ice and dirt mixed." Sometimes they fell through quicksand-like mud. "I felt so sad and nervous," said Norbu.

When he finally arrived in Dharamsala, Norbu enrolled in a school for older Tibetan refugees who didn't have much formal education. The Transit School, as it is called, is today a neat cluster of buildings on a spacious campus complete with a well-used basketball court. But when Norbu was there, the school was still under construction. Classes were held on the muddy ground in shacks made of corrugated metal sheets that were stiflingly hot in the summer and bitterly cold in the winter.

"I couldn't study very well in school. I was very sick. I had diarrhea. I had no relatives." He loathed lentil dal and other Indian food served at the school. "If I see dal I want to vomit. I want to eat *thukpa*." Norbu was so weak and miserable that the school bus driver took pity on him and gave him 100 rupees, about $2. The gesture made Norbu brim with gratitude even years later. He immediately went to a food stand to buy *thukpa*, yellow stew with thick noodles that he missed so much from home.

The first couple of years in India were miserable for Norbu, but he still sent cheerful letters to his mother. "I'm very happy. I'm working. His Holiness is here. Everything is good," he wrote. After two years of school, he joined Gu Chu Sum, where he trained for three months to cook Japanese food. Seven years later he was still working at the Japanese restaurant, which was co-owned by a Japanese man who supported Gu Chu Sum. Norbu mastered making homemade miso paste and hand-rolled sushi, but he still much preferred a simple bowl of *thukpa*.

Now Norbu spoke English fluidly, but he often groped for words. While we were talking, I helped Norbu with his pronunciation, especially the sounds of *p* and *f* and *b*. He often confused the latter two. When he said the word "café" it sounded like "cabin." He patiently repeated the words, rolling them over his lips, or pursing his lips. He didn't get frustrated or angry; he just said the words over and over again and remained patient and composed. Norbu took a thick, worn book from a cluttered shelf: *The Name of the Rose* by Umberto Eco. A foreign tourist had given it to him so he could practice English. Norbu admitted he couldn't understand most of it. I told him that many native English speakers would have a hard time with it too.

A few days earlier, I had heard of some dramatic developments for Norbu. On a cold night, I ate at the Japanese restaurant with Tsering and another staffer from Gu Chu Sum. The ceiling was strung with colorful paper cutouts. Badminton rackets and, inexplicably, some pink hot-water bottles hung in a window like the Himalayan version of the lobster pot buoys that decorate New England clam shacks. Most of the glass-topped wicker tables were empty. Business was slower in the winter months, as tourists fled the cold northern mountains for the tropics of Goa.

With fewer customers to cook for, Tsering wandered out of the kitchen. The smiling young Tibetan woman who minded the restaurant's gift shop sat at my table too. For some reason, Norbu wasn't there that night. Then Tsering revealed the dramatic news. Norbu was one of fifteen Tibetans chosen in an annual immigration "lottery" sponsored by the Australian government. According to the Australian government, it wasn't a lottery; political asylum was granted to some Tibetans after an application process and interview. Those who were chosen got visas and could eventually apply for Australian citizenship after resettling there.

Tsering made no pains to hide his envy. He had applied too but wasn't selected. "Lucky number seven," Tsering muttered. Norbu's number included a bunch of sevens. "If I go, I make money to open a hospital in my village in Tibet," he pouted. The Tibetan woman from the gift shop chortled loudly. Tsering shot her a stern look. "It's true," he said, almost bashfully. "My village has nothing."

. . .

As Norbu told his story, I waited to see if he would announce his news, but he didn't mention anything. So while munching soybeans, I asked casually, "What about Australia? Are you really going?"

He seemed unsurprised that I knew. "I'm waiting for visa," he explained. From a jumble of books and papers on a shelf he extracted a long envelope and unfolded the letter within. The creamy stationery was still crisp and bore Australia's kangaroo and emu crest in gold. The letter was written in formal, British-tinged English, and Norbu asked about the meaning of a few big words. It cautioned Norbu not to give up his accommodations or job or to buy airplane tickets in anticipation of getting a visa. The letter told him to wait until the Australian embassy asked him to go to Delhi for an interview.

Norbu remained matter-of-fact when I asked what he would do in Australia. He didn't really know. There would be government-sponsored English classes, a stipend, job training, he said. Above Norbu's bed the poster of Lhasa was taped to a smudged wall. The panoramic view showed dramatic white snow peaks cradling the city against a brilliant azure sky. The enormous Potala Palace was reduced to miniature, like a child's toy instead of a 1,000-room ziggurat atop a hill. In the maze of buildings, one couldn't make out the sacred main temple in Barkhor Square in the heart of Lhasa, where Norbu had been swept up in a protest as a boy. It was a mesmerizing photo that captured the city's landscape, its hyperbolic colors and beauty. A river wrapped around one side of Lhasa and formed lacy waterways on its edge. It was surprising to see that the city was surrounded by water, seemingly incongruous because it was so close to the sky.

"Where in Australia will you go?"

"Sydney." Norbu pointed over my head. There on another smudged wall behind me was a poster of Sydney with a glorious vista of Sydney Harbor. White sailboats dotted the harbor, and the spectacular Sydney Harbor Bridge stretched to the opposite shore. The eggshell shards of the opera house formed a giant white flower. A former roommate had taped the poster to the wall a few years back.

"Have you been to Australia?" Norbu asked me suddenly.

I hesitated, then admitted I was there for two months more than a decade ago, just after backpacking in Tibet in 1998.

"Why you go?"

Sheepishly, I said was traveling. I didn't tell him that I had finished two years teaching English at a university in Nanjing, China, and took the long route home. After several weeks in Tibet and Nepal, I flew to Australia and went to museums, beaches, and rainforests across the country. I hugged a koala, snorkeled in the Great Barrier Reef, and slept in the red desert in a swag roll beneath a sky bright with stars. I took the Manley Ferry across Sydney Harbor one afternoon and admired the sublime view of a beautiful city that, like Lhasa, is surrounded by water and sky. I didn't tell Norbu these details of what seemed like an utterly indulgent trip. Instead, I simply remarked, "It is a beautiful place."

"You are lucky. You can go anywhere," Norbu said, looking at me. An unfamiliar edge of frustration crept into his voice. "In Australia maybe I can get passport. My wish is to go to Tibet to see my mother. I wish we could meet again before she dies. Every day I go to temple to pray."

That helped explain why Norbu woke up early to walk the *kora* each morning. During his recent trip to see his aunt in Nepal, he had lost weight and his thinned body slumped on the bed as we talked. Spidery wrinkles radiated from the corners of Norbu's eyes and hinted at what his open, youthful face and cheerful demeanor did not.

[3]

Dharamsala Means Shelter

Everything Has Changed in the World
Except This Place

FALL/WINTER 2008

· · ·

Dharamsala is an apt name for a town that is home to thousands of Tibetan exiles: in Hindi the word means "shelter" or "rest house" for spiritual pilgrims. The town was so named long before the Dalai Lama appeared on its hillsides in 1960 and serves as a reminder that Dharamsala has its own distinct history. The curious names of parts of town hint at this too: McLeod Ganj, named for an administrator of the British Raj, is the bustling Tibetan hub most familiar to tourists, while further along, Forsyth Ganj is the military camp named for another bygone British administrator. Dharamsala's fascinating history rests under the surface, beneath the pollution, grime, and blaring car horns.

One shop in McLeod Ganj's busy main square embodied the crossroads of Dharamsala's past and present. Through autumn and early winter I walked past many times every week and noticed that it was the only one-story wooden building amid narrow concrete storefronts stacked atop each other. Signs above those shops announced in gaudy letters, "Hooka Bar, Discotheque Lounge Bar," "Xcite!," and "Hot Spot, a Family Restaurant." "The Pastry Den," with its glass cases full of gooey cakes, stood steps directly across from "The Pastry Shop." The small square thronged with honking cars, pedestrians, cows, roaring motorbikes, autorickshaws, street dogs, buses belching black exhaust, jeeps crammed with passengers, and lumbering trucks taking improbable U-turns.

The modest shop was the only one without a garish sign or colored lights in its windows. Instead, a plain blue board with white lettering reticently stated,

Estd. 1860 Nowrojee & Son General Merchants
House & Estate Agents, Auctioneers Manufacturers
High Class Mineral Waters

In front of the words "General Merchants," the words "Wine &" had been half-heartedly rubbed out but were still visible beneath the whitish blur.

As I stepped inside, wooden floorboards sighed wearily underfoot. Antique glass display cases stood in aisles that seemed luxuriously long in this cramped town where nothing was spacious except the sky and mountains. An ancient Petromax kerosene lamp hung from the ceiling, but it hadn't been lit for ages, much less lowered by the intricate web of thin ropes and pulleys strung down the walls.

One autumn afternoon, I encountered Kurush Nowrojee in the store. A descendant of the store's founder, Nauzer Nowrojee, Kurush grew up in Dharamsala but moved to Calcutta as a young man. From there he attended to his family's tea business in northeast India until his father, Jimmy Nowrojee, died in early November 2008 in his eighties. Black-and-white photos of Jimmy Nowrojee hang in the Kangra Art Museum in lower Dharamsala. One old photo shows the storefront. Its blue sign looks almost exactly the same, but the area in front of the shop is a bare, earthen lot that gives no hint of the haphazard urban development to come.

Jimmy had looked after the store in McLeod Ganj after his brother Nauzer's death in 2002. The eldest of five brothers, Nauzer Nowrojee was born in 1915 in Karachi, decades before the city became part of Pakistan when independence cleaved India into two countries. He was a merchant of Parsi origin with roots in Iran whose family had lived in India for generations. Nauzer was known for more than owning Dharamsala's oldest store: he had helped bring the Dalai Lama to town. In 1959, Nauzer was one of a handful of residents still living in the ghost town that Dharamsala became after a catastrophic earthquake in 1905. Legend has it that Nauzer sent word to Prime Minister Jawaharlal Nehru that the abandoned town would be a convenient haven for the recently exiled Dalai Lama. While some dispute Nauzer's starring role and say he did not have a direct line to Nehru, he is nevertheless remembered for playing a role in the Dalai Lama's move to Dharamsala. Nauzer died in Dharamsala after sixty years of tending the store. Then after his father Jimmy's passing, Kurush returned to Dharamsala to put things in order and that is when I met him.

It wasn't clear what would happen to the archaic store now that the elder generation of Nowrojees had passed on. Its role as a commercial hub in the late 1800s selling tobacco, soap, and sundries to British settlers and officers at nearby military camps had long faded away. Middle-aged Kurush was still deciding what to do with the shop. That afternoon, he emerged from an office in the store dressed in a green button-down shirt, maroon sweater vest, black loafers, and square bifocals. Kurush had a quiet, avuncular air and was not puzzled or bothered when a random visitor showed up and started asking questions about the place's history. In fact, he accompanied me and seemed pleased and proud as I walked up and down the aisles and peered into dusty display cases.

Kurush reminisced that his grandfather was the first person in Dharamsala to have a car: a Chevrolet Hudson. Back then Dharamsala was pristine, he recalled. Its thick forest sheltered barking deer, wild leopards, and bears. Well before the British arrived, the nomadic Gaddi people lived in the area and herded goats and sheep over the verdant hills surrounding Dharamsala. A photo of a Gaddi dance festival showed men wearing big white turbans, knee-length tunics tied with layers of rope-like belts, and leggings. Their feet were bare, and they stared into the camera with serious faces. The Gaddi women covered their heads with white shawls and wore heavy necklaces.

The area eventually changed from the hilly abode of nomads to a colonial outpost. In March 1849, as the British East India Company expanded, the British annexed the area after the Second Anglo-Sikh War, when they wrested control of Punjab State from the Sikh kingdom. The British then established a military camp in the scenic foothills of the Dhauladhar mountains above Dharamsala. This would become the village of McLeod Ganj, named after Sir Donald Friell McLeod, a lieutenant governor of Punjab who was born in Calcutta. Hill stations of northern India, including Dharamsala, became summer retreats for British administrators and their families seeking refuge from the stultifying heat of Calcutta and Delhi, along with an influx of military personnel.

Ghosts of the British Raj still lingered in a pocket of greenery a short walk from McLeod Ganj along one of the five roads radiating from the main square. I often ran along a wider, flat road that lead toward Forsyth Ganj, which today houses an Indian army base. There, the town's noisy traffic eventually faded away. The quiet stillness, though periodically disrupted by shrieking, speeding vehicles, was as much a relief as the serene thickets of trees flanking the road. After half a mile, the forested hillside on one side of the road became a clearing. A stately neo-Gothic church of gray stone sat in a meadow surrounded by deodars, the Himalayan cedars that carpet the area's rolling hills. I explored its history-rich grounds several times. St. John in the Wilderness was built in 1852 for the British who settled or summered in McLeod Ganj. The church, with its long nave, survived the 1905 earthquake, though its tall bell tower was destroyed. A new bell was made in 1915 by Mears & Stainbank, which became Whitechapel Bell Foundry—Britain's oldest manufacturing company until it shut down in 2017. Shipped from England, the one-ton bell remains at St. John in the Wilderness today.

Adjacent to the church stood a graveyard with dozens of well-kept headstones nestled in trimmed grass. The clear inscriptions told of an era when McLeod Ganj really was wilderness, with all its risks and dangers. One tombstone embedded in the grass read,

> In loving memory of Thomas William Knowles,
> who met with his death at Dharamsala by an attack from a bear
> on the 25th October 1883, aged 50 years.

Twin headstones told of hardships that claimed lives early:

> In the memory of Ethel Emily,
> the dearly loved child of Walter and Lucy LeMarchand, born 9th
> December 1880, died 10th June 1881, aged 6 months.

> In loving memory of Edith Mary Dixie
> The Beloved Infant Daughter of Col. and Mrs. C. A. R. Sage
> 2nd Battn 1st Gorkha Rifles
> Whom Jesus called to himself on June 17th, 1898, age 10 weeks
> Jesus called a little child unto him

Others agreed this was a comfortable place to rest. An empty Kingfisher beer bottle, whiskey bottles, and a crumpled package of Goldflake cigarettes lay on the grass. Cows found their way into the tranquil graveyard and lounged on grassy mounds while gently swishing their tails.

Next to the church, in the shade of tall deodars, lay St. John's most famous denizen. A tombstone with a towering stone crucifix read,

> In memory of James Bruce,
> earl of Elgin and Kincardine, viceroy and governor general of India
> who having previously served his country as Governor of Jamaica,

> Governor General of Canada, High commission and
> ambassador to China

And in other high offices
Died at Dharamsala

In the discharge of his duties On the 20th of November 1863 Aged 52 years
and 4 months "He being dead yet speaketh!"

In 1852, Dharamsala became the administrative capital of Kangra district. Lord Elgin, viceroy of India from 1862 until his death the following year, liked the area so much that he suggested it become the summer capital of India. The British Raj's highest administrator in India, Elgin lived in Shimla, the northern hill town today an eight-hour drive from Dharamsala, and he made it the viceroy's official residence. But before he could shift the government there, Elgin died of a heart attack.

Dharamsala's reputation as a desirable retreat for the British Raj evaporated in 1905 when a 7.8-magnitude earthquake destroyed the area and killed an estimated 20,000 people. The 1924–25 *Kangra Gazetteer*, a local almanac, noted,

> At six o'clock in the morning of April 4, 1905 Kangra District witnessed an earthquake which by the ruin it caused and the consequent loss of life can scarcely be equaled by any other calamities recorded in the history of this part of the Province. . . . The morning was calm and beautiful and then in a moment with two fearful lurches every house in the affected area collapsed amid the thunder of falling rocks, the roar of the falling rafters and walls and the thousand shrieks for mercy, confusion and terror and death. Every second or third hour there was a shock although not very severe and a roar like the boom of a cannon.

Kurush Nowrojee told me his grandfather helped unearth people trapped in the rubble and was later awarded for his service during the earthquake.

After the disaster, survivors fled the town, and it fell into disrepair. After Partition in 1947, everyone left, said Kurush—"the Britishers," Hindus, Muslims. In 1959 few people lived in McLeod Ganj, including Nauzer Nowrojee. Dharamsala seemed to be gasping its last breaths. According to lore, when Nauzer wrote to Nehru he imagined that bringing the Dalai Lama to Dharamsala would make the "place jump back to some sort of prosperity," said Kurush.

Nauzer Nowrojee could not have envisioned how the town would change. Even the McLeod Ganj of Kurush's boyhood had been idyllic wilderness. I followed him to the rear of the store and a wooden porch elevated above a hillside. "The whole place was forested, and the sky was crystal clear day and night," Kurush remembered as we gazed toward the horizon. "You could see all the way to Pathankot," he said of the nearest railhead, more than two hours away by car. As he spoke, a dusty haze obscured the skyline and its view of distant treetops and buildings. "Look, garbage is dumped here," he said pointing below us. Sure enough, some bloated cows rooted through piles of rubbish heaped on the hill. "Believe you me," Kurush said. "There were no mosquitoes or flies or dust." He gazed nostalgically at the scenery. "This was a beautiful place before the Dalai Lama got the Nobel Prize. Then it became a concrete jungle." He waved in the direction of the main square and its vertical patchwork of buildings. "Subsequently these monstrosities have come up," he said.

Traffic and crowds weren't the only changes after the Dalai Lama's 1990 Nobel Peace Prize propelled him onto the global stage. In the winter, snow used to fall so heavily that the store would be buried nearly to its eaves. An old photo showed the store wrapped snuggly in a ten-foot high duvet of fluffy snow. By 2008, snow rarely appeared in McLeod Ganj. And a 1965 photo of Dal Lake, near the Tibetan Children's Village—the big Tibetan school a couple of miles away—showed a picturesque pond surrounded by trees. By 2008, Dal Lake had become a muddy depression that filled with stagnant water during dry winter months. A couple of years later, Dal Lake was no more than a swampy field.

Over the decades, as Tibetan refugees followed the Dalai Lama into exile, forests of Dharamsala were cut down to make way for roads, buildings, and eventually restaurants and shops. A grove of enormous deodars near Nowrojee's store was cut down to make way for a Tibetan temple ringed with prayer wheels. In the 1980s, more cars, trucks, and buses wound their way up to McLeod Ganj from the commercial hub of lower Dharamsala. Before long, the small clearing amid tranquil woods were but a memory. Dharamsala's population swelled to 19,000 according to a 2001 census, and to over 31,000 by 2011. It was a number unimaginable in 1925 when the *Kangra Gazetteer* said about the area, "There does not appear to be much scope for an increase in population. . . . There seems to be no prospect of any industry developing sufficiently to attract many artisans or laborers."

All the while, the little store run by the Nowrojees stood as witness to the transformation. Kurush looked wistful as he said, "People would tell my father, everything has changed in the world except this place." Indeed, little had changed at the store in the last fifty years, and the place was more of a down-at-the-heels museum. Painted wooden signs on the wall declared,

"Take Andrews Liver Salt and Keep Fit" and "Palmolive Keeps Skin Clear."
There were ads for White Horse Scotch, Bluebird Toffee, Cavanders Navy
Cut Cigarettes, and Spring's Chocolates. One advertised leather shoelaces.
That autumn day when I chatted with Kurush, no other customers came
inside to peruse long aisles of glass-topped wooden display cases or examine
the candy jars arranged on a tall three-tiered table. A look at the goods told
you why. Nothing seemed to have been disturbed for decades; perhaps not
even the last big earthquake in 1986 had wrinkled the thick blankets of dust.
A wooden box with a glass cover displayed different types of cookies cloistered in small, labeled compartments. The gingerbread and Boston cream
were so ancient they had disintegrated into heaps of powder against the glass,
like corpses in a cell. These cookies were once precious goods, carried by
ship across oceans from England to India, hauled from a port, and put on a
train that chugged to the northern hills. The words painted on the box spoke
of a congenial, bygone era: "When the samples in this case become faded,
kindly return them to Reading. We shall be pleased to replace them with a
fresh set upon request." In another case, boxes of metal pen nibs rested next
to dusty bottles of ink. Stacks of "mourning stationery" bundled in black
satin ribbon sat nearby. In another era, someone dipped pen nibs in ink to
write a condolence letter on creamy stationery edged with black piping.

Yet there were some signs of contemporary life. The candy jars were filled
with new penny candies in plastic wrappers, and a hand-lettered sign read,
"Please do not touch these jars! Thank you!" The vessels were seventy or
eighty years old, Kurush explained. Near the front of the store, display cases
offered an odd medley of modern Indian sundries: Harpic toilet bowl cleaner
in dark blue bottles, packets of Nestlé dairy creamer, and orange plastic pack-
ages of sanitary napkins.

Kurush and I looked out at McLeod Ganj's main square. Autorickshaws
honked madly and swerved in front of pedestrians. Customers lined up in
front of a nearby shop that sold cigarettes and *paan* chewing betel. Idle Indian and Tibetan men sat on metal benches along a road that reeked of urine
and led to a rutted, muddy taxi depot. Inexplicably, an Indian man on stilts
walked past.

"The party is over. This is today's McLeod Ganj," said Kurush, gazing
at the chaotic scene. "There is a lot of history here but most of it is gone."

• • •

Shards of another history predating the British Raj emerged in Kangra, the
district that is home to Dharamsala. Buddhist influences in the area date

from the first century CE. In 1997, stone sculpture, pottery shards, bricks, and inscriptions were excavated at Chaitru, a town almost twelve miles from Dharamsala. Some of the materials were likely used for raising a stupa, while bricks in another trench could have been the outer wall of a "huge" Buddhist complex, said Ramesh Chander, curator of the Kangra Art Museum since 1992. Even the name "Chaitru" is probably a distorted form of the word *chaitya*, or stupa. The seventh-century Chinese Buddhist monk Xuanzang, famed for his seventeen-year journey to India that inspired the classical novel *Journey to the West*, wrote that fifty monasteries housed more than 2,500 monks in the Kangra region. Other Buddhist relics also were found in Kangra: two Buddha statues were discovered in Chaitru during road construction in the early 1900s. One was sent to Lahore Museum in Pakistan, while the other remains near Chaitru.

India is today a Hindu-majority country where Buddhists number fewer than Christians. In 2011, Buddhists comprised 0.7 percent of India's 1.2 billion population. And yet the Buddha lived in India, home to the major Buddhist pilgrimage sites, and was born just over the border in Lumbini, Nepal, in 623 BCE. Buddhist followers traveled and settled across northern India and what is today Pakistan more than 1,500 years ago. The religion spread to the north and west, to modern-day Pakistan and Afghanistan in a region known as Gandhara, which was part of the Silk Road between China and the Mediterranean. From the first century CE, Buddhism spread to Southeast Asia, then Central Asia, China, Korea, Japan, and finally Tibet in the seventh century. Meanwhile, Buddhism shrank in India by the twelfth century due to factors including Islamic conquests and the rise of other religions.

In spite of the discovery of ancient Buddhist statues in the area, few Buddhist objects are held in the Kangra Museum, a large two-story villa in lower Dharamsala, the town's larger, more urban, and less Tibetan area. Notable items in its airy galleries included an embroidered elephant saddle used by the Lamba Gaon Royal Family, and a ninth-century statue of Lakshmi, goddess of wealth, whose stone breasts were worn smooth by fortune-seekers who rubbed them for good luck. When I visited one cold afternoon, the place was virtually empty; just one or two other visitors' footsteps echoed in the marble-floored halls. No other traveler I met in Dharamsala had ever visited the museum.

I arrived at the museum unannounced, but its curator, Ramesh Chander, spoke candidly to me in his office. He was scathing about Indian youth's lack of interest in their country's history. "Ancient people have a lot of knowledge. Young people are doing nothing. They have no interest in preserving," he said. "They don't have patience, and the present generation is not capable of creating that type of heritage."

Chander continued to talk even though dusk had fallen. His small office descended into black, and soon the curator was just a shadow outlined against the window. "India is a very great civilization. The museum's role is just to preserve it." From the deepening shadows, he repeated, "We are trying our best to preserve it."

. . .

Overshadowing any reverence for the past in Dharamsala was a fervent race to accommodate the new. The number of Buddhist students, Tibetan refugees, and foreign and Indian tourists swelled, and construction boomed in McLeod Ganj. Machines pounded, pummeled, and gouged the earth in a quest to erect new hotels, guesthouses, restaurants, and stores. On the steep hillside of Temple Road, the main street that led to the Tibetan temple and the Dalai Lama's residence, a three-story building was razed to the ground in weeks. A bulldozer crushed the narrow concrete structure and workmen yanked out the remains like dentists conducting an architectural root canal. When they finished, only a yawning slot remained next to a neighboring three-story building that clung perilously to a steep dirt hill. Next, a gigantic machine drilled at the earth until a geyser of muddy water spewed out. The operator held an umbrella while brown sludge showered down on him. Dumbstruck bystanders stood on the roadside to watch as the machine continued to wrench itself into the ground. It was creating a bore well—yet another to drain Dharamsala's already receding water table.

All these buildings were being erected on fragile, volatile ground. Dharamsala is, in geologist-speak, a "disturbed area" that is never stable. It sits in a "zone five" area for seismic activity, with five as the highest rank. In 2005, a 7.6-magnitude earthquake in nearby Pakistan killed at least 86,000 people along the same fault line that runs through Kangra District. Tremors in Dharamsala were frequent though usually undetectable to the average person. A journalist friend from Japan—a country plagued by earthquakes—remarked that he felt the earth sway one night during his visit to Dharamsala, though I had felt nothing. Every so often a sizeable quake occurred. One measuring 6.8 shook the region in 1975. Another measuring 5.5 struck in 1986. Yet the threat of earthquakes was not top of mind in Dharamsala. I didn't come across any hotels, restaurants, or government buildings posting notices to remind people of emergency procedures. The average person did not talk about earthquake precautions or safety measures. Beginning in 2009, a nongovernmental organization called GeoHazards International and various Tibetan groups organized emergency exercises at Tibetan schools on the April anniversary of the 1905 earthquake. GeoHazards matter-of-factly acknowledged that a "major earthquake during school hours centered anywhere along the Himalayas would kill thousands of children and wipe out years of development gains in education." A 2006 GeoHazards report noted that most of the town's buildings have unreinforced brick walls and rooftop water tanks: "Were these objects to fall during a daytime earthquake when the narrow streets are crowded with people, they would kill many. Many buildings, especially the newer ones, are constructed on slopes prone to landslides. As McLeod Ganj continues to be built out, this situation will only worsen."

Two geologists noted in a 2006 paper in *South Asian Journal* that earthquakes on the Indian subcontinent had left "a trail of ruin on its west, northwest and eastern boundaries." They sounded a clear warning of the looming threat: "Like an alarm clock that won't be silenced, this activity represents a wake-up call to the governments and citizens of South Asia. If steps are not taken now to reinforce cities, future earthquakes will cause future disasters on an unprecedented scale."

. . .

One place in Dharamsala took careful notice of earthquakes. The tree-lined road running past St. John in the Wilderness church led to the Tibetan Children's Village. At a bend in the road a nondescript concrete government building housed the Naadi Geological Survey, also known as Central Recording Status of Seismological Network. They let me in to have a look. Offices and large rooms were empty except for odd, lonesome objects. A big barrel-shaped contraption was connected to a seismograph brought to India from California in 1990. The box-like machine silently and continuously excreted a length of paper along which a stylus skittered, leaving a slightly spiky black line. On days when the earth murmured or shrugged or convulsed, the stylus frantically jumped up and down so the seismogram looked like the wild electrocardiogram of a patient having a heart attack. Twenty such government earthquake-monitoring stations were scattered across the geologically unstable state of Himachal Pradesh, home to Dharamsala.

Landslides, their cause undetermined, were also growing increasingly common around Dharamsala. All the construction on Dharamsala's temperamental land surely didn't help. In a case of subduction—giant slabs of earth sinking and sliding beneath an adjacent plate—the road from McLeod Ganj to lower Dharamsala sunk a few inches every year, an Indian official at the geological survey office explained. Because he wasn't authorized to speak on the record to media, I have omitted his name. Wasn't it dangerous to build on such unstable land? "Yes!" cried the Indian official. Will there be another earthquake? "There will be! Certainly!" The 1905 earthquake killed nearly 20,000 in Kangra when the population was far smaller than today. "You can magnify the picture if there will be a big earthquake what will be the result," the official told me.

In addition to population growth, other factors added to the danger. Buildings in the area shouldn't be more than three stories tall. Yet four- and five-story brick and concrete buildings—very unyielding materials for buildings that sway and buckle in an earthquake—were being built on precariously steep hillsides. Light materials like wood better withstand earthquakes, but in India, concrete was cheaper. Even if earthquake-proof building codes were enforced, it would be easy to circumvent them with a bribe.

What about preparation for earthquakes? At this, the official became animated and reached for a thick folder on his desk. "I have given a lot of lectures on this everywhere," he said. He ticked off a list. One should have a battery-powered radio and supplies of water. In the event of an earthquake, turn off electricity and gas switches. Don't keep heavy objects on high shelves. Heavy furniture should be kept in "certain places where you think it will never hurt you."

Next was the list of things to do during and after an earthquake. First, be calm. Then he advised standing against a wall near the center of a building or in a doorway. Wood has maximum elasticity while concrete may crumble. Stay away from windows, electricity poles, and big trees. Don't use candles or open flames. If driving, stop the vehicle. If at work, get under a desk or sturdy furniture. Use stairs, not the elevator. The list did not include what to do if the metal gate of your hillside guesthouse was padlocked shut at night, as was later the case for me in Dharamsala.

Geologists at University of Colorado, Boulder, and the US Geological Survey in Pasadena, California, pointed out that mandatory rules to make new buildings earthquake-proof could increase safety with "minimal effort." In their paper they wrote, "We envisage a time when, looking back at the 19th to 21st centuries, people will marvel at the waste and short-sightedness of governments that allowed their people to construct, and then live in, buildings that fall down in earthquakes."

The geological evidence for earthquake risks was clear, but there was no slowing the frantic construction on the tremulous ground of Dharamsala, a town creaking with history and bursting at its seams with uncertainty and change.

[4]

Winter Audience with the Dalai Lama
We Have Truth on Our Side

DECEMBER 2008

. . .

As autumn slipped quickly toward winter, the sun warmed Dharamsala during the day, but temperatures plunged as soon as the last rays withdrew for the night behind snow-capped mountains. I walked around town bundled up in layers of coats and a wool hat with ear flaps made by a Tibetan artisan. One afternoon when warmth still lingered in the air, Topden and Sarah, a new volunteer veterinarian from Scotland, walked up the steep hill of Jogiwara Road to collect an injured dog. I was walking down when I saw them, and we paused on the roadside to greet each other. Topden normally wore his monk's robes at the clinic but that day he wore a dark T-shirt with a hip design, jeans, and shiny leather shoes. In his layperson's clothes, Topden became a good-looking young man—a startling fact that one defused or ignored when he wore his monk's robes. He looked tan and robust next to Sarah's pale complexion and long blond hair.

Topden had talked about the inconvenience of wearing his robes in the clinic, where he cleaned "cat shit and dog shit" from the cages on the roof. He had mentioned the robes a couple of days before when he rushed after work to visit a friend's relative in lower Dharamsala's hospital. He described the misery there where people moaned in pain complained about the cold, or needing to urinate, and any number of other discomforts. The old man he planned to visit was so ill that if he drank a spoonful of water he would throw up "more than a spoonful" seconds later. The vet clinic's atmosphere was far better, said Topden. He added that he didn't want to visit the hospital in his robes so had to hurry home to change. He said goodbye, then thumped off down a shortcut home.

From then on at the clinic, Topden dressed in surprisingly fashionable layperson's clothes: slightly baggy jeans, T-shirts with funky logos, two pairs

of shiny leather shoes (one black, one brown), an off-white twill jacket and a
blue wool one for cool weather. Sometimes he topped off his ensemble with
a Nike baseball cap at a jaunty angle. Topden confessed that his roommate
and cousin, also a monk, disapproved of his layperson's clothes and thought
them disrespectful to monastic life. Topden had, after all, reached a level of
distinction at his monastery, as indicated by the yolk-colored vest he wore
beneath his robes.

After that, I saw him wear his robes only once, several months later when
Tibetans flocked to the main temple to pray for the Dalai Lama's long life.
Topden was part of a stream of crimson-robed monks walking uphill after
the ceremony. By then I was so used to seeing him in jeans and T-shirts that
it took me a moment to recognize him in his robes at all.

. . .

Through the autumn, I lived at a simple but clean budget guesthouse run
by hospitable Kashmiris. There was Amin, the friendly manager who spent
a good deal of time drinking tea with guests—especially female ones—on
the rooftop terrace; Samir, an elfin older man whose quick grin cracked his
weathered face; and a few other young men whose names echoed in the halls
when Amin called them to clean rooms. On Ramadan, Amin offered me
milky white sweets from a gift-wrapped box. A small mosque with green
metal gates was wedged onto a crowded street in lower Dharamsala, but
Amin went there only on special occasions, he told me.

On top of the guesthouse sat a rooftop living room with a wall of windows
like a solarium. The flimsy glass panes revealed a magnificent view of hulking
green mountains on the other side of a dagger-shaped valley. At night, distant twinkles inched across the inky black mountainside as cars chased their
headlights up the winding road.

In the evenings I often sat with the staff on the Kashmiri rugs and rested
against the fat bolster pillows lining the walls. Temperatures dipped to the
forties and thirties once the sun set, but the Kashmiris kept the windows
open to let in fresh air. Sometimes they treated me to tea or to "hot ginger
lemon"—a brew of hot water, lemon juice, and shards of ginger that turned
the liquid rosy inside a steaming glass. Best of all, there was an electric
heater—the only source of heat in the uninsulated guesthouse—that swiveled
with a robotic stutter and glowed cherry red. With the day's work done, the
Kashmiris watched Bollywood movies that blasted on the television in one

corner. To stay warm, I hovered near the heater while clutching my glass of hot ginger lemon until the men started unrolling their sleeping pallets on the rug, signaling bedtime.

In my room downstairs, the cold made it painful to change before going to sleep. The moments when skin was exposed to the frosty air even for just a few seconds were dreadful. I went to bed dressed in thick layers: wool socks, fleece pants, sweatshirt, and fleece hat. Under a thick quilt and heavy blanket, I turned my face beneath the covers to thaw my numb nose. Bathing was an ordeal best done after lunch when the day was its warmest: the guesthouse was fortunate to have hot water, but, as is the norm in India, the bathroom had a hole in the wall for ventilation that created a funnel of bone-chilling air. Still, I was far luckier than most in Dharamsala who bathed outside at taps, shared primitive bathrooms, or lived in far flimsier buildings than the sturdy Kashmiri guesthouse.

In the winter, when the tourists and backpackers migrated south to Goa, the normally congested streets of McLeod Ganj seemed roomier, cafés and restaurants emptier, and the town had a more intimate feel. Although fewer tourists visited Dharamsala, winter months were busier for Tibetan refugees because more of them crossed the border into Nepal and onward to India. Fewer Chinese guards patrolled the border in winter, and frozen streams and rivers along the escape route were easier to cross.

On a sunny December morning, Chhime Chhoekyapa, joint-secretary in the Dalai Lama's office, called me. Chhime was one of the Dalai Lama's right-hand men, and he told me the spiritual leader was about to greet newly arrived Tibetans. Virtually all new arrivals have an audience with the Dalai Lama, which creates a bond they all share. Because the Dalai Lama traveled so much, new arrivals might stay for weeks in the open dormitory of Dharamsala's Reception Center until he returned home to meet them.

At this last-minute invitation, I rushed to the main temple and the Dalai Lama's residence and offices. I passed through the security check—a metal detector, pat-down, and cell phone confiscation—and hurried across the compound, along spacious pathways and past manicured shrubs. Chhime and Tenzin Taklha, another joint-secretary, stood outside a long hall. The open-air room looked small, but inside about 100 Tibetans sat cross-legged in silence as they waited for the Dalai Lama. They settled so close to one another that knees and folded legs brushed against the backs and limbs of neighbors.

Some of the Tibetans were dressed in their best finery: silk brocade, stately dark *chupa* dresses and chunky turquoise or coral necklaces, pendants, and hair ornaments. Tenzin Taklha, who also happened to be the Dalai Lama's nephew, quietly told me that thirty-seven Tibetans had arrived in Dharamsala just that morning. He looked down at a sheaf of notes in his hand. Of that group, nineteen were school age, thirteen were monastics (monks and nuns), and the rest were on pilgrimage. Of the entire group, seventy-one did not have official travel documents while thirty-five did; twenty-three were ages six to thirteen years old; sixteen were fourteen to seventeen; and twenty-three were eighteen to thirty.

For months after the March 2008 protests, China severely tightened security and arrests and detentions surged in Tibet. Some 6,500 Tibetans were arrested by the end of 2008, according to the Tibetan Centre for Human Rights and Democracy in Dharamsala. The flow of refugees from Tibet ebbed to a trickle. It was an especially dangerous year to flee, but in early winter, refugees began to edge into India again, though numbers were still low. The Tibetan Children's Village normally receives about 850 new students each year from Tibet. In 2008, only 20 enrolled.

Finally, the Dalai Lama entered the hall, one shoulder bared beneath his red robe. With little fanfare, he took his spot behind a table and stood to address his audience. The Dalai Lama had a different air as he spoke in Tibetan. When he spoke in English to foreigners, he was often playful, laughed a lot, and seemed to enjoy hamming it up. In front of the Tibetans, he was no-nonsense, serious, and focused. In a whisper, Tenzin Taklha translated the Dalai Lama's words into English, and I wrote everything down.

· · ·

The Dalai Lama scanned the room where all eyes were fixed on him. "Any problems? Was anyone caught? Was anyone seen by the border police?" he asked.

His head swiveled as he surveyed the room, and he read through a list of monks in the audience as though taking roll call. "Anyone going to Sarnath?" he asked, referring to an upcoming weeklong teaching he would give at the Buddhist holy city in northern India. After these routine questions, the Dalai Lama spoke calmly yet hurriedly, as though he were a father with just a short time to impart advice to his children. All was quiet except for the sound of his voice.

"Many of you have come under difficult circumstances. This is a happy occasion for you," he said of their meeting.

I am also happy. But these days, Tibetans are immersed in a complicated problem. For me, for the last fifty years in exile I have been separated from my country. Generation after generation is facing great difficulty in their mental state.

The situation in Tibet sparked the nonviolent demonstrations across Tibet. The generation from 1949 when the Chinese came, those people [Tibetans] are already gone. The next generation is slowly disappearing. In all regions in Tibet, most demonstrators are very young, but the difficulties in our mind continue to remain. I frequently meet with Tibetans who care for Tibet. One Tibetan said he can earn a good living there. His children get education. But he said, "I am a Tibetan. In my mind I always feel like I'm being suppressed. In my mind, I feel anguish." Then he started crying. It is not just a problem of earning bread. Inside our mind we are not satisfied and not happy.

Though the generations change, this problem remains. For the Chinese government, this is embarrassing and it forces them to lie. Sometimes they make unbelievable lies. But we want to solve this problem. It will be helpful to China and then they won't have to lie. If they respect Tibetan culture, give us meaningful autonomy, really look after minorities, then China can be proud. Everything should be transparent.

If truly China is united, they won't have to rule with suppression. Other minorities are facing problems. In order to deal with these problems, Chinese are using terror as a tool. When we give our presentations, they just dismiss our requests.

The Dalai Lama let out a short burst of wry laughter. "We can't do anything. Even if we swear to the Communist Party, it doesn't help. They don't trust us. They don't believe us. Some Chinese people believe we are sincere but they can't do anything. The People's Republic of China was founded more than sixty years ago. There are many changes taking place in China. Many of you have seen it with your own eyes." The Dalai Lama surveyed the room. "One very big change: even though it is the Communist Party, Communist ideology is almost gone. Communist Party without ideology—very strange. One Westerner familiar with international affairs said it's not communism. It's capitalism. Totalitarian capitalism.

"However, the power kept by the CCP [Chinese Communist Party] remains the same. The government is ruling by power. Under the government, loyalty to our country remains the same. Besides the older generation, the younger generation feels even stronger nationalism." The Dalai Lama spoke fluidly and did not pause as he switched to another topic.

"The most important thing is higher standard of education. Then we can fight for our rights. In villages there are no educational facilities. Monasteries are no longer there. Rural people have great difficulty. For Tibetan people it is important to have a high level of education. It is not enough to make money, gamble. I heard a report that many Tibetans are drinking inside Tibet. That's not good. I'm not asking the monks. You're not supposed to be drinking!"

The Dalai Lama laughed. "I went to Spiti monastery," he said, referring to Spiti, a remote region in northern India with strong Tibetan influences. "I asked the monks, 'Is the *chhaang* better in Spiti or Shigatse?'" Was the Tibetan barley beer better in Spiti or in one of Tibet's largest cities? "One monk answered, 'Spiti.'" The Dalai Lama chuckled when recounting the monk's inadvertent admission to drinking alcohol.

Then the Dalai Lama grew serious once more.

If we have money and spend it on drinking, it is not good for your health or good for anything. It is better to spend on food or education or learning how to read and write Tibetan. The reason Tibetans face so many difficulties is because we lacked education. In religion, too. People have great faith, but they don't understand the philosophy of our religion. Even if you ask someone, they don't know the dharma, sangha, and Buddha. It is not enough to have faith in the religion. You have to study. If you think this is the job of a monk not a layperson, that's wrong, backward. Buddhist religion is something very wide and deep. With pride, you can have dialogue with scientists. You can have dialogue with modern science. Many scientists are taking notice of Tibetan Buddhism. It shows Tibetan Buddhism is very deep and profound. You can be very proud of this. Many scientists say, "I don't have a religion but if I did, it would be Buddhism." Without knowledge of this religion, there's not much we can do. At initiations, many people come. But fewer people come to teachings, even in Singapore. This shows that people are not interested in studying. People think faith is enough. This is not the case! Wisdom has to be attained through study. We need to investigate reality and look at modern study. We lack this. This is the big drawback of the Tibetan nation.

The most important thing is to study and learn. With that we can
compete in a modern world. If we have to talk with the Chinese,
we have truth on our side. When we have truth on our side, we can
explain and reason with them. But to reason, we need knowledge.
There are two types. One is traditional Buddhist tradition. There are
many texts and great scholars. Second is a modern education to know
what's happening in the world today. Please do your best to study
hard. We Tibetan exiles represent the Tibetan people. We are trying
our best. Carrying on the struggle are you people inside Tibet.

China is changing. There is growing interest in Tibet even among
many Chinese intellectuals.

A number of you are here to study. So don't waste your time.
To the monks: study hard and follow the rules. Some of you are
returning to Tibet. Talk about the situation. Look at the situation.
You know what you've seen. You can explain what you've seen.

With that, the Dalai Lama finished his monologue. The room stirred as everyone stood and calmly lined up to receive a blessing. From behind the desk
he handed each person an envelope that contained blessed "pills"—small
sugar tablets—and a colorful picture of the Buddha of compassion. In the
past, the Dalai Lama gave a photo of himself as a keepsake, but this endan-
gered those returning to Tibet with what the Chinese government considered contraband material.

As the Dalai Lama spoke, the hall remained remarkably still. It was understandable that many Tibetans said they could not remember what he said
during their welcome audience: they were too dazed. Later, when I asked
Topden and Norbu about finally meeting the Dalai Lama in Dharamsala,
they both remembered little except being happy beyond words and overwhelmed with emotion.

But the silent rapture in the hall soon broke. After the Tibetans received
their envelopes, some milled around in the courtyard outside. Men and
women, young and old, sobbed or wiped tears from their faces. I imagine
they felt a range of emotions: joy and relief at finally meeting their exiled spiritual leader, or perhaps his words articulated their frustrations and grief. One
teenage girl wailed as her father, dressed in a formal gray *chupa*, led her away.
Tenzin Taklha murmured, "It seems like she has to leave school here. Her
father is taking her back to Tibet." The girl bent her head toward her father
and covered her face as she wept. Many parents in Tibet sent their children
to India so they could attend the Tibetan schools in exile.

A wide cross-section of Tibetans were included in the audience. Their origins were distinguishable to a Tibetan from their clothes, the way they tied their *chupas*, their jewelry and hairstyles. Older women from western Tibet displayed distinct long, thin braids that reached down their backs like black whips. Tall, rugged men from Amdo wore white shirts, and long ponytails braided with red tassels swept up the sides of their heads. A woman dressed in a green brocade *chupa* and black pumps wept. An elderly woman in a long brown *chupa* with big turquoise earrings shuffled past. A gaggle of students dressed in uniforms of blue gingham shirts and navy trousers wandered by.

An old man with white hair and a walnut-brown face spoke intently to the Dalai Lama as the spiritual leader nodded sympathetically. "Take medicine," he advised the man. Some Tibetans expected the Dalai Lama to cure them of ailments. But the Dalai Lama regularly described himself as a simple monk, and sometimes he expressed impatience or exasperation when people expected him to cure them. A documentary called *The Unwinking Gaze* shows the Dalai Lama giving an audience to a group of ordinary Tibetans in Dharamsala, similar to the scene that had just transpired. In the film a man carries his toddler daughter in his arms and holds her up to the Dalai Lama. The girl is quiet but the camera focuses on a greenish, open wound in her arm.

"Is that her bone?" the Dalai Lama asks incredulously, clearly horrified as he peers down. "Take her to a hospital immediately!" he commands. "The cost doesn't matter!"

In addition to being a spiritual leader, the Dalai Lama is a strong champion of modern science who has said he might have been an engineer had he not been a reincarnation of the Buddha of compassion. He regularly reminds people that he cannot call up miracles or cures. But he does create change in more mortal ways. This is the case with education. When the Dalai Lama arrived in India in 1959, just twenty-four years old, he was ill with dysentery and surely frightened and miserable after his harrowing escape from Tibet. Nevertheless, just weeks later, he began trying to set up a Tibetan school for refugee children, even before establishing a monastery or religious institution. He valued and longed for modern education even before leaving Tibet.

"In Tibet I had a great desire to establish a modern school," he told John Avedon, author of *In Exile from the Land of Snows*. "From the early fifties on, I felt the need very strongly. Without knowledge of how such a school functions, I just thought over and over, 'We must have a modern school. We must have a school.' But I didn't even know how many classes to have."

Nearly fifty years later in 2008, the Tibetan school system counted about eighty schools across India, Nepal, and Bhutan. The exile education system, which includes Tibetan schools run by the Indian government under the Central Tibetan Schools Administration, enrolled some 28,000 students in 2008 and included day schools, nurseries, vocational institutes, and training centers. India was home to some seventeen branches of Tibetan Children's Villages (TCVs), schools funded by many international philanthropies, with at least 12,000 students across India, from the tropics of Orissa in the east to the hinterland of Madhya Pradesh in the country's middle.

The first exile school in India opened in 1960, less than three weeks after the Dalai Lama's arrival in Dharamsala, as a ramshackle nursery for Tibetan orphans. New Tibetan refugees—former farmers and nomads—found back-breaking work building roads in Jammu, Kangra, Kullu, and Manali. Children were born on Himalayan roadsides, lived in rough conditions in tents near construction sites, and died of illnesses. Some were crushed by falling rocks. Hearing of these harsh conditions, the Dalai Lama persuaded families to send their children to homes in the hill towns, and those eventually turned into nurseries and schools.

In Dharamsala, the Indian government provided a large bungalow to house children. That quickly filled up and more bungalows were allocated, included one that is today the site of the Upper Tibetan Children's Village in Dharamsala. The Dalai Lama put Tsering Dolma, his elder sister, in charge of the nursery. Children over eight years old were sent to boarding schools established in the hill towns of Mussoorie, Darjeeling, Shimla, Kalimpong, and Dalhousie, while the youngest stayed in Dharamsala. Still, the facilities were not enough for the constant influx of refugees. "No sooner had one hundred children been sent to the schools than twice as many more arrived. Dharamsala had certainly ceased to be a ghost village, but chaos was increasing," recalled Jetsun Pema, the Dalai Lama's younger sister, in her memoir *Tibet: My Story*. A 1961 photo at the Kangra Art Museum showed a Tibetan boy and girl dressed in rags standing next to a crude water spigot against a backdrop of dirt and rubble. A shack stands behind them, its cloth roof held up by sticks. Jetsun Pema wrote, "Many children died the first winter in Dharamsala, with only the toughest surviving. . . . There were not enough blankets and food was terribly scarce. When at last we were able to give a blanket to each child, 200 more arrived all at once after having been cut off several days by the snow."

In spite of the initial hardship, over the years the nursery grew into a building, matured into an actual school, expanded onto a campus, and then became a network of campuses across the country. In 1964, when Tsering

Dolma died of cancer at age forty-four, Jetsun Pema took over and remained at the helm of the Tibetan Children's Village until retiring in 2006.

The promise of the exile schools in India was appealing enough that Tibetan parents risked sending young children, even toddlers, over the mountains for a chance to attend. In exile, they could learn Tibetan language, culture, and religion free from repression. It was telling that the Dalai Lama devoted much of his audience with the new arrivals to education; he spoke on the theme again and again, though education did not make headlines the way tension with China did. The Tibetan exile education system had its flaws, but it was critical to keeping Tibetan culture and identity alive. The Dalai Lama often visited the children at school. He "was like a father to all the children," Jetsun Pema remembered. "He spoke to them, saw how they were getting on with their Tibetan writing and always told them that they were the 'hope of Tibet' and the 'seed for the future of Tibet.'"

．　．　．

The flagship Tibetan Children's Village in Dharamsala, or "Upper TCV," is a common stop for diplomats, donors, dignitaries, and other guests visiting town. A couple of miles north of McLeod Ganj, past St. John in the Wilderness Church, up curving roads, and nestled among evergreens rests a spacious campus for some 2,000 students. It has basketball courts, a sunny library lined with books, classrooms decorated with posters and student artwork, and a Tibetan Buddhist temple crowning a hilltop. In the Montessori nursery school, children played with blocks and flashcards on the wooden floor. During recess the sound of games and laughter filled the air.

A look inside a dorm revealed neatly made bunk beds and clean-swept wood floors in a room shared by at least a dozen children. A resident house mother or father looked after the children, made meals, and oversaw study time in a common room lined with little desks. The same space served as living room, dining room, and study for dozens of children. Recycling bins for plastic and paper sat outside dorms.

To a visitor from a rich country, TCV's classrooms and buildings might seem threadbare and worn. Although the facilities are modest, they are adequate, especially for India, where many communities and schools have sparse resources. Dormitories—small brick houses with corrugated metal roofs—dot the hillsides. Small brass plaques on buildings announce benefactors: the Norwegian government, the Himalayan Society of San Francisco.

One morning, a house father energetically punched a large mound of dough to make dumplings. In another dorm, a house mother opened a cupboard to show tidy shelves filled with small piles of clothes children had meticulously folded. For some students, TCV serves as a boarding school, so they return home during holidays, often taking long train rides alone across India by themselves. But for the majority of students, TCV is home. In 2008, about 70 percent of the 2,000 students at Upper TCV came from Tibet. Sometimes Tibetan parents accompanied the children or carried the youngest ones during the arduous journey over the Himalayas, enrolled them in school, then made the dangerous trek back to Tibet. Other times parents hired guides to shepherd children over the border and deliver them to the school. Parents might not see their children again for years or decades.

A photo exhibition in Dharamsala in March 2009 featured images that documented the journey's risks. Photos showed Tibetans with blackened feet gnawed by frostbite, and mangled stumps that used to be fingers and toes. One refugee's experience was described in an exhibition wall note: "After three days we reached an encampment of Tibetan nomads in Sikkim. We were totally exhausted and suffered extreme pain from our frostbite. The nomads took us to an Indian army post for medical treatment. I was more worried about being reported back to the Chinese than about my health. We were hospitalized in Gangtok but my condition did not improve. After six months my legs and some of my fingers were amputated."

Other images showed a queue of Tibetans walking across an icy landscape as inhospitable as the moon. In 1995 a Swiss photographer, Manuel Bauer, famously captured the journey of a Tibetan father and his six-year-old daughter, Yangdol, by walking, climbing, and driving with them for twenty-two days from Tibet to Nepal to Delhi then Dharamsala. One photo early in the journey was taken during a truck ride to Tingri, a town in southern Tibet near the Nepal border. Yangdol is bundled in warm clothes on her father's lap. Outside the window a desolate landscape flashes past. The camera focuses on the girl's face: a pale scrap sharply creased with fear and apprehension.

Dramatic photos from later in the journey show the pair, unrecognizable in their coats and hoods, climbing chalk-white crags of a 5,700-meter (18,700-foot) mountain pass as wind whips snow into gauzy streamers. As they descend, both sprawl face down in the snow, exhausted from the trek and the dizzying effects of high altitude.

Why did some parents return to Tibet after taking their children to the schools in India? Sometimes it was because of work. Finding steady jobs in India, especially as refugees with limited status and language skills, was difficult. Parents also had other obligations: relatives to care for or land that needed tending.

Given the risks and sacrifices, weren't the schools in Tibet enough? For a better-off Tibetan living in or near a major city, the answer might have been yes. Some Chinese schools offered Tibetan language as an elective course, though it was likely taught in a perfunctory way. But the Chinese government controlled any education about Tibetan culture and language, starting with a ban on mentioning the Dalai Lama. For poor Tibetans in rural areas, schools were few and far between. About a third of Tibet's 6 million inhabitants live as nomads in desolate areas with no schools at all. The prospect of free, quality education for Tibetans in India in "the Dalai Lama's schools," as Tibetans called them, was enough to make them endure the risks and sacrifices of fleeing their homeland.

Even some Indian parents enrolled their children in TCV in Dharamsala because they thought it offered a better education than local Indian schools. Of the 2,000 students at Upper TCV in 2008, 150 were non-Tibetan. They were Indian or children of foreigners who had settled in the area, sometimes to be part of a Buddhist community: Russians, Japanese, and Koreans. I sometimes saw Caucasian or Indian children speaking fluent Tibetan in Dharamsala or wearing TCV's school uniform, like the Russian girl with her kitten.

One of the best-known Indian alumni of TCV was Vinayak Sharma, a serious lawyer in his thirties who ran a legal aid service for Tibetans in McLeod Ganj. His parents enrolled him in a Tibetan school, and he attended from the age of three to sixteen. Vinayak switched easily between fluent Tibetan, English, and Hindi to speak to Tibetans who crowded his small office and waited for him to advise on their legal problems. Many exiles said Vinayak's Tibetan was better than theirs since they had not formally learned it in Tibet. He also spoke Pahari, a local dialect, and counted Hindi as his weakest language. Months later, I unexpectedly needed Vinayak's help and saw his vital legal and Tibetan-language skills in action.

The Tibetan school system had its share of shortcomings. Common complaints, especially from Western guardians of TCV students, focused on lack of creativity and emphasis on rote memorization; lack of rigor; and teachers with insufficient training. Much the same could be said of Indian schools in general, apart from expensive private ones. Yet results showed that TCV students did not perform as well as students at good Indian schools. They did worse on the country's stringent university entrance exams and often failed to gain admission. The education ministry in the Tibetan exile government acknowledged the flaws and tried overhauling its system. In 2005 it launched a new policy that attempted to modernize curricula, raise academic standards, and give better training and salaries to teachers. TCV also opened its own university, a college focusing on teacher training in south India near Bangalore, to give Tibetan students better access to higher education.

The schools faced the perennial challenge of straddling several worlds: preserving Tibetan language and culture while providing competency in English so students could compete for jobs and college admissions in India. Curricula had to adhere to Indian standards, but it was also "Tibetanized" as much as possible with Tibetan culture, history, geography, and religion. A new rule in 2006 mandated that Tibetan schools must use the Tibetan language, not English, as the mode of instruction before fifth grade.

Even champions of TCV sourly noted that many high-level officials in the Tibetan exile government sent their children to English-language private schools in India rather than TCV. But ultimately, the free schools were a sound and appealing option for many Tibetans. One measure of their success was simply the fact that in spite of great risks, parents in Tibet continued to send their children to India. Thupten Dorjee, secretary-general of TCV, put it more bluntly. "We give an education that allows our children to grow up as Tibetans," he told me during a visit to his office at Upper TCV. "The Chinese are destroying Tibetan identity. If Tibet is to survive as a race and a nation, our hope is our children."

[5]

The Longest Night
One World, Many Dreams
DECEMBER 2008

. . .

To stave off the day's chill, Ngawang Choedon sat in the small front yard of Upper TCV's nursery with her back warming in the sun. She was head of the nursery at Upper TCV, more commonly known as the "Baby Room." NC, as her friends called her, cradled a plump toddler while another child in a striped fleece hat crawled on the cement floor. When she picked up the baby with the hat, the other one wailed.

"He's jealous," NC explained about the child's screaming. The one in the striped hat was her own baby, Pasang, who would soon celebrate his first birthday. He was a good-natured boy with lusciously fat cheeks. The other fussily tried to push his way back into NC's lap. His mother had died of AIDS and his father had HIV. The baby would grow up in the Baby Room and then at TCV.

Months before, a mutual Tibetan friend invited me to a party at NC's house to celebrate the success of her eldest son on recent exams. The party (minus the honored son, who was at a Tibetan boarding school in Karnataka) was held in the front yard around a makeshift table. The six male guests celebrated by drinking glass after glass of whiskey far into the night. By the end of the evening our mutual friend—previously a monk for twenty years—staggered to his friend's car to return to McLeod Ganj beneath a dark sky smeared with stars.

After that introduction, I sometimes visited TCV to chat with NC and glimpse the Baby Room. By the end of 2008 about thirty Tibetan toddlers ranging from three to five years old or younger lived in the Baby Room. At bedtime, toddlers trooped to the bathroom or plastic potties, then climbed into cribs with wooden slats painted turquoise. Tibetan pop music blared from loudspeakers, and the sound of children singing in unison from their beds filled the house.

The Baby Room had a cheerful atmosphere. During the day toddlers played in the yard or with toys inside a sunny room with wooden floors. At lunchtime the children sat at miniature tables and chairs in a small dining room. One little girl walked methodically back and forth, serving each child a bowl of food that a Tibetan woman doled out from large pots.

After eating, the children unrolled quilts on the playroom's wooden floor for naptime. They lay down, nose to the back of their neighbor's neck, pressed together like little sardines. The house mother stood over them, speaking in a firm tone, and they stilled as they snuggled under blankets. When the house mother slipped into another room, the children stirred, picked up their heads to look around, whispered, and giggled. They quieted when the house mother reappeared in the doorway.

In her *chupa*, striped *pangden* apron, and leather dress shoes, NC seemed older than her thirty-six years. She had three children of her own, ages one to sixteen, all born in Dharamsala. Her own early years were spent in Nepal after her parents fled Tibet; she had no memory of her homeland. NC's parents died when she was young, so she grew up at TCV in Dharamsala like the toddlers she cared for. She and her husband, Dawa, a former teacher-turned-administrator at TCV, both graduated from the school. They lived in a small house located just below the Baby Room down a flight of concrete stairs.

One Sunday morning in December, I jogged up the winding road to the school and arrived unannounced at NC's home. We had met only a few times, but her hospitality gave me a glimpse into the life of a Tibetan family in India. She graciously chatted as we shared glasses of steaming, milky chai. NC wore a long fuchsia house coat. Her husband sat on a low stool in the front yard and soaked up the sun with his back as he and a boy pored over a math book. Pasang was slung into a circular toddler walker tied to a post with rope. He grinned and drooled as he tried to walk, but the rope went taut and he could only shuffle his feet in place.

The TCV campus seemed well run and lively, yet NC had her criticisms. She thought the school was too lax compared to the strictness she experienced as a student. Back then pupils couldn't show up to class with shirts untucked; they were more respectful of teachers, she recalled. Now the attitude was too casual. Tibetans were losing their culture, NC said. Some young men even dressed "like hip hop" in baggy, ragged jeans, she sniffed.

NC shook her head. Women should wear traditional Tibetan clothes like she did and retain their culture. Even her own sister, adopted by a Swiss family as a child, could barely speak Tibetan, she said.

In the early 1960s, during the chaotic influx of tens of thousands of Tibetan refugees into India, resources were scarce; so about 200 Tibetan children were adopted by Swiss families. The practice lasted ten years. By 1970, when the tumultuous first stage of exile had eased, the Tibetan exile administration decided not to give children up for adoption except for extraordinary reasons. Today, foreigners are not allowed to adopt Tibetan children except in extremely rare instances. Switzerland remained a special case because it was home to a Tibetan community of roughly 2,000. "The children are therefore not cut off from their roots," wrote Jetsun Pema, the Dalai Lama's sister, in her memoir. But when she visited the Tibetan children in Switzerland in 1975, she wondered, "Why had we given them up for adoption? I then had a strong feeling of sadness."

Family separation, especially for the sake of education, was still common among exiles in India. NC's older sons both lived away from home in Tibetan boarding schools in India. They had been admitted to the elite test-based Tibetan schools in the states of Karnataka in the south and Uttarakhand in the north. She wasn't worried they were forgetting their culture. In fact, NC and Dawa were interested in their son applying to college in the United States. They wanted him to go overseas, and perhaps they would eventually follow. This would "be better for him and for us," explained Dawa.

• • •

On another wintry Sunday afternoon, silver clouds swirled around Triund, the gleaming white peak that overlooks Dharamsala from some 9,300 feet. An icy drizzle fell from the misty sky. At one edge of the Tibetan Children's Village, a coffee-colored goat stood on a stairwell bleating next to clusters of small houses. Some Tibetan men played cards near a wall painted with the interlocked Olympic rings. The slogan for the recent 2008 Beijing Summer Olympics had been, "One world, one dream," but the version at TCV read, "One world, many dreams." Across a dirt sports field a troop of Indian ladies carried on their heads bundles of leafy branches so voluminous that they obscured the women's bodies from view; they resembled trembling green bushes with legs.

That day NC's cottage stood empty and gray; no sun warmed the yard. There was a spark of life when she opened the door wearing her long fuchsia housecoat, gray woolen leggings and socks, and fake Croc clogs. Her long black hair was pulled back from her oval face. "Hello!" NC greeted amiably. "We are watching *Rambo!*"

They were indeed watching *Rambo*. Her husband sat cross-legged on floor rugs, playing with baby Pasang as Sylvester Stallone's muscled chest and sad dog eyes flashed across the television screen.

"Come sit by the fire," Dawa called, referring to the shiny electric heater. Pasang was not wearing a cap, so wisps of curly black hair spilled over his head. The baby wobbled on his socked feet, pursed his red lips, and happily blew spit bubbles. I sat cross-legged on the rugs and held my arms open to him. Unlike most days he spent in the Baby Room with NC and other children, that day Pasang was the sole focus of his parents' attention. Both father and mother played with Pasang and cooed over him as he toddled about and observed them with keen curiosity. Pasang was just a nickname; it means "Friday" in Tibetan and marked the day of his birth. The gleaming three-foot-tall Black & Decker electric heater, imported and especially expensive, glowed a fiery red and warmed the room generously.

"We bought it in Chandigarh," Dawa noted. "It was more than 2,000 rupees." Salaries were modest in Dharamsala and the heater (about forty-five dollars then) could have easily been a third of a monthly wage. They bought it the previous winter when Pasang developed breathing problems soon after his birth at the hospital in Dharamsala.

"The hospital here is not very good," said NC. Dawa nodded in agreement. After the breathing problems emerged, the family rushed down to the larger, more modern hospital in Chandigarh, six hours away, where Pasang was admitted for several days. I knew from my bus rides between Dharamsala and Delhi that Chandigarh was the halfway point. Before reaching the city down mountain roads, it wasn't uncommon for Tibetan passengers to vomit out the window. Yet Dawa and NC were matter-of-fact about the trip to Chandigarh and didn't mention anything more about their emergency journey.

NC bustled about in the kitchen and then brought tin plates of food into the living room, which doubled as a bedroom with two beds against the walls. We ate chapatis—round flat bread—and fresh peas and carrots in a spicy tomato sauce. At the end of the meal she brought a porcelain bowl filled with Tibetan rice wine soup. Whitish and thick, the liquid tasted like alcoholic egg drop soup.

We basked in the warmth of the Black & Decker heater, which was far more powerful than my very basic 250-rupee (eight-dollar) heater I had splurged on to heat my room. My flimsy metal contraption was less than a foot long and only large enough to warm my feet. It had two "bars" that resembled a toaster's heating elements; within a week one of them burned out. I once reheated leftover pizza with it by propping slices on a fork outside the protective metal cage surrounding its red-hot bars.

As we ate, NC and Dawa gently asked for advice about sending their eldest son to university in the United States. He was sixteen and attended school "in the south" in Karnataka, more than forty-eight hours away by train. He had attended a Tibetan gifted-and-talented middle school in Dehra Dun in the northern state of Uttarakhand where his twelve-year-old brother was still enrolled. After graduating, he started high school in Karnataka and came home only during winter and summer holidays. It was the best Tibetan high school in India, so NC felt that the sacrifice of separation was worth it.

"He wants to study business," NC said in a slightly bashful tone.

I briefed them about college applications, deadlines, and costs. It would help to ask any Tibetan friends with children at US universities since their experience would be recent, I suggested.

NC and Dawa looked at me blankly. Some Tibetans in Dharamsala send their children to the United States but they don't share information, Dawa replied. "Tibetans should help each other but they don't," he said. That was just one opinion, but it hinted that Tibetans were of course fallible like any other humans, and not paper cutouts of virtuous, enlightened beings.

After a while their eldest son and their twelve-year-old burst through the door. They were home on their winter holiday and had been out with friends on the school grounds. The eldest, tall and thin, gelding-like, had wavy hair like little Pasang. He smiled shyly. The two boys picked up Pasang like a doll and hugged and kissed him affectionately. The two draped themselves over their father, hugging and clinging to him as Dawa smiled and laughed.

The television was still on and the screen showed Rambo leaping out of a muddy river bank in Vietnam to cut a Russian soldier's throat. Then Rambo tenderly cradled a raven-haired female companion as she gasped her last breath in his arms. Her makeup was immaculate. The Tibetan family paid Rambo no mind and continued to hug and play with baby Pasang.

. . .

The Kashmiri guesthouse where I stayed my first months in Dharamsala was comfortable, but in December I moved to a room in a Tibetan Buddhist nunnery a short walk away. My new abode cost $100 dollars each month, half the price of my room in the Kashmiri guesthouse. For a freelance journalist on a shoestring budget, the savings were significant. Plus, living in a Tibetan

Buddhist nunnery promised to be a unique experience. The place didn't look like a nunnery. It was a plain four-story concrete building sandwiched between other concrete buildings. The nunnery perched on a lane up a steep hill a few minutes from the main Buddhist temple. The road wasn't much wider than a footpath, too narrow for cars, though motorbikes did roar obnoxiously up the hill. Weary donkeys clopped along the pavement carrying heavy loads to a construction site. The incline was so steep that I usually arrived at the nunnery doorstep panting.

The nunnery annex where I lived housed some fifteen senior nuns who took classes at the nearby Institute of Buddhist Dialectics, located a short walk down the hill. Its main nunnery was about a thirty-minute drive away. Two nuns shared a room simply furnished with bookshelves and a pair of twin beds they sat cross-legged on by day. Small tables in front of the beds served as both desks and dining tables. Each floor had a common bathroom shared by a dozen people. Senior nuns had lived there for more than a decade and remembered when trees covered the hillside. Most of them were born in India and had grown up in Kinnaur, in Himachal Pradesh near Tibet's western border. Like monks, the nuns wore crimson robes and shaved their heads. To earn income, the nunnery rented out eight rooms to paying guests like me and to nuns from Germany, Japan, or other countries who were studying in India.

My third-floor room faced squarely east, so it brightened and warmed as soon as the sun rose, then blazed with light as morning progressed. The space felt large compared to the nuns' rooms, and though my attached bathroom often lacked water, it felt relatively luxurious for Dharamsala. There was a desk, plus a wobbly round table in the middle of the room, ample cabinets, and shelves with statues of the Buddha and Buddhist books left over from previous tenants. A single bed with a thin foam mattress stretched out next to a row of windows. Dawn often broke to the sound of hooves clopping on cement and bells clanging from necks. A troop of donkeys hauled heavy sacks of sand, gravel, and bricks to a construction site up the lane. An overseer's voice urged the donkeys on as the animals bowed their heads and forged uphill. I recalled that near the vet clinic, a lonesome donkey stood idly on the roadside every day. He had a marvelous view of the valley, but his foreleg jutted out at a grotesque angle. I suspected he had been a work donkey and got terribly injured carrying heavy loads.

The balcony outside my room commanded an expansive view that unfolded in layers toward the horizon like a long tapestry. Down the hill through groves of deodars and firs, the white rooftop of the Dalai Lama's residence emerged. In the distance lay the sprawl of the Kangra valley. From afar, clusters of buildings resembled Legos. On clear days unobscured by haze or mist a vivid red circle shone; it looked like a giant had dropped a bright bracelet. My neighbor in the nunnery, a gray-haired fifty-something American from Berkeley, California, and the nunnery's only male guest at the time, told me that the crimson structure was not a temple but a cricket stadium. When a new cricket league launched a couple years later, more tourists than ever overran Dharamsala, particularly those from neighboring Punjab State. Traffic jams choked McLeod Ganj.

Winter in Dharamsala meant cold rain, which erupted from the sky in great gusty storms. I huddled in my bed at night with a rubber hot water bottle beneath a duvet and two wool blankets. Sometimes the nunnery cat, a hyperintelligent gray striped tabby named Wangmo, would insist on getting under the covers even though I resisted at first. Eventually I relented and found myself quite cozy with a hot water bottle under one arm and a warm cat under the other.

Howling winds sent the nunnery's loose windows banging in the night. More than once, glass shattered as panes broke in the dark. I worried about Shimmy, the injured cat I rescued, in his metal cage on the vet clinic's roof. Every morning I still rushed down the hill to him with a plastic basket of food, medicine, and supplies to clean him. Sometimes I feared the worst, but Shimmy was always there, his thin face looking expectantly through the cage grate, bent legs nestled on a feces-stained wool blanket. I had started hand-feeding Shimmy white rice and boiled chicken from a Korean restaurant that served delicious meals. He became practically possessed, yowling and clambering wildly, when I took out the plastic box of food.

Because I visited Shimmy every day at the vet clinic, I saw Topden almost daily as he and an Indian vet technician tried their best to minister to the sick and injured animals that kept arriving. I was giving Shimmy vigorous physical therapy: rotating and bending his back legs. It seemed to be working. I watched, elated, as Shimmy put his back legs underneath him and struggled to stand up. He still couldn't do it, but that he could put his haunches under him was an encouraging sign.

In December, Shimmy took a turn for the worse and I spent more time at the clinic. The cat could move around using his front legs but couldn't support weight on his back legs. Just when he started getting stronger, he was stricken with diarrhea. Shimmy ate like a horse, but partially digested food poured out of him soon after. His cage was perpetually smeared with feces and his fur would get soiled and matted. I visited Shimmy morning and night to feed him, administer him a range of human antidiarrhea medicines that didn't seem to work, and clean him with baby wash and water so he wouldn't develop sores and infections. These were extraordinary lengths to go through for a street cat. Shimmy was eating better food than many people in Dharamsala. But I couldn't stand the thought of leaving him to fend for himself; I knew he would die if the diarrhea didn't subside. The situation grew worse because new volunteer vets wouldn't arrive for several months.

One cold, gray afternoon, after feeding Shimmy, I stopped by the clinic downstairs. The room, with its one operating table and cabinets of medicine and equipment, was empty and quiet—a contrast to recent months when it was full of Dharamsala's sick animals. Topden sat at a table, nattily dressed in wool jacket and baseball cap, fingering his wooden prayer beads and murmuring a mantra. He nodded and smiled but continued his prayers. After a few minutes, he finished and put the beads down. "I woke up too late this morning to do my prayers," he confessed sheepishly.

We chatted for a few minutes until a Tibetan man swung open the screen door with a brown mutt in tow. A rope tied around the dog's neck served as a leash. Topden and the man spoke in Tibetan and then hoisted the compliant dog onto the operating table. The monk bent over the dog and confidently poked and prodded his belly, then reached for some instruments. It wasn't so long ago that Topden had started working at the clinic, looking overwhelmed as he wielded a mop. Now he was single-handedly diagnosing and attending to the dog. I quietly slipped out the door to let him focus on his work.

As I walked toward Jogiwara Road the sky darkened and sleet streamed down from the sky. The road jutted around a precipice with an expansive view of the valley. A glimmer appeared and an enormous rainbow poured from one corner of the sky and swept over the valley in a long, shimmering arc. A European man also stopped and busied himself capturing the magnificent sight with his camera. Sleet soon turned to hail and chunks of ice pattered loudly as they struck the ground. A dog barked behind me and I saw the Tibetan man from the clinic and his canine companion running through the wet haze. He bent down to untie the rope from the dog's neck and the mutt bounded happily up the road. I could see rust-colored streaks of iodine on the dog's belly from Topden's ministrations.

"He's okay?" I called to the Tibetan man.

He waved and hurried up the hill behind his joyous dog as they disappeared through the white veil of hail.

. . .

Across from the nunnery, a stone's throw across a narrow lane, sat the largest monastery in McLeod Ganj. Home to hundreds of monks, Kirti Monastery was small in comparison to the sprawling ones in southern India that housed thousands. This was a branch of the main Kirti Monastery in Amdo Ngaba, a Tibetan region of China's Sichuan Province. The Dharamsala branch sat on the hilly slope below the nunnery where I lived, so my room had a prime view of its flat roof and offered glimpses of monastic life. The large building housed offices and classrooms at the front and monk's rooms at the back. At the rear a big terrace-like yard served as a recreation area. On weekend afternoons monks sat at square tables and played Indian checkers, and milled around chatting with each other.

Both Kirti monasteries in Amdo Ngaba and Dharamsala played influential roles in the March 2008 protests. A pro-Tibet march in Amdo Ngaba turned deadly when Chinese forces opened fire on the crowd of unarmed civilians. Men, boys, and a young woman were shot dead on streets close to Kirti. Monks rushed to safeguard the bodies and helped move victims inside their monastery. Someone photographed corpses with chests and limbs riddled with bullet holes, dead eyes in faces that dripped blood. The grisly images circulated by email and mobile phones and found their way to monks at Kirti in Dharamsala, many of whom had relatives and friends in Amdo. Later, one Kirti monk told me that when Chinese authorities realized the images had been disseminated far and wide, soldiers came to Kirti in Amdo to take the bodies away in an effort to erase the evidence.

The Dharamsala monks sprang into action. They emailed the images to Indian and foreign media and copied the images onto CDs to distribute to journalists who flocked to Dharamsala after March 10. Within days the bloody images were splashed on television screens and newspapers. I walked past many plastered on posters and banners in the streets of Dharamsala during my first visit in March 2008. More than a dozen images formed a grid on the posters' black background. Each square showed a picture of a nearly naked male corpse stripped to reveal black, deceptively small bullet holes puncturing chests, legs, and heads. Blood streamed across skin in crimson rivulets. Some bodies lay in dark pools of liquid. The worst images showed peoples' faces, their dazed eyes and shocked expressions. One haunting image depicted a black-haired teenage boy whose eyes were half-open as though he had just woken up. A stream of blood seeping from a corner of his slack mouth signaled the opposite.

On the first day of my visit to Dharamsala back in March 2008, a middle-aged monk from Kirti Monastery pressed a CD and press release in rough English into my hands outside a press conference in an exile administration building. He couldn't speak English but was excited that we could speak in Mandarin. He told me that the monks had no experience with journalists, but they were well versed with publishing Buddhist texts in the form of books and pamphlets and making CD and videos of teachings. The computers and equipment in Kirti were all unexpectedly handy when this urgent mission arose at its sister monastery in Amdo Ngaba.

. . .

Most days, all seemed calm at Kirti in Dharamsala. Monks walked to and from their bedrooms, the prayer hall, classrooms, or canteen, sometimes chummily slapping each other on the back as they moved along outdoor corridors. From the nunnery's higher vantage point, I could usually see only the tops of the monks' shaved heads and their robes. They favored knockoff Crocs—those slip-on rubber sandals—that peeped from beneath the hems of their robes. Monks were constantly removing their shoes to go into prayer halls and their rooms, so slip-on rubber clogs were convenient, and the muck of the streets could be easily washed off. Somehow a spa shoe for yuppies had become standard footwear for monks in Dharamsala.

These Crocs cost just a couple of dollars from the street vendors in McLeod Ganj who piled their tables with sundries from China: polyester socks, jars of chili paste, and packs of plastic chopsticks. On weekend mornings I could see monks tidying their rooms and flapping dust from pillows outside their windows. Other days the sound of prayers droned from the monastery, particularly on special holidays. The cacophony of voices and hands slapping together when monks debated often drifted into my room at the nunnery.

Gigantic plastic vats containing the monastery's water supply sat on the flat roof. Sometimes mischievous monkeys tried to pry off their covers until monks chased them away. Street cats strolled and sunbathed on the roof that commanded a marvelous view of the valley. Monks took morning or evening walks around its perimeter, talking on their cell phones or just admiring the vista.

During a gray drizzle, a solitary monkey sat quietly on the roof's edge so only the humped mound of his hirsute back was visible. The scene looked like the simian version of a German Romanticist painting where a man stands on a precipice, back to the viewer, while gazing over misty mountains contemplating existence. From the roof of Kirti Monastery, the spectacular view could even stop a monkey in its tracks.

. . .

One December morning, Kirti Monastery bustled with even more activity than usual. It was a bright, crisp Sunday, and from the earliest hour the sonorous drone of chanting prayers rippled the air. Monks bent over as they systematically placed small circular objects along the edge of the roof, and soon they lined the entire perimeter. This was no ordinary day.

At the main temple, crowds streamed through the gate. Tibetans filled the large courtyard: toddlers and wrinkled grandparents, parents with kids and young people too. People sat or stood, chatting and cavorting as if attending a big picnic. Monks walked by with buckets overflowing with snacks—packs of cookies or spicy potato chips—and handed them out like Halloween treats. Devotees had brought these items as temple offerings, and the monks were redistributing them.

Up a flight of stairs, colorful *thangkas*—Tibetan tapestries—decorated a prayer hall packed full of cross-legged and chanting monks. Here, the atmosphere was more solemn than the casual air of the courtyard downstairs where families frolicked and relaxed. The crowd spilled from the prayer hall to the concrete floors outside crammed with Tibetans and foreigners sitting cheek to jowl. Some listened attentively while others chanted along, textbooks in hand. Many had brought their own cushions and mats to sit on; they had been there for hours already since the prayers had started early that morning. Somewhere inside the hall, at the nexus of all those people, was the Dalai Lama.

It was Gaden Nga-Choe, also known as Tsongkhapa Day, a holiday commemorating the death day of the founder of the Gelugpa school of Tibetan Buddhism, to which the Dalai Lama belongs. A lama named Tsongkhapa founded this Tibetan Buddhist sect in 1409 when he established Gaden Monastery in Tibet.

The chanting and prayers continued into the afternoon. Finally, the droning and cymbal clashing ceased and the Dalai Lama's security guards cleared the stairs that led from the prayer hall to the courtyard. When a beige Toyota sedan rolled into position near the stairs, the picnic-like atmosphere in the courtyard immediately dissolved. The crowd quieted and stood up expectantly. People rustled and leaned forward as the Dalai Lama descended the stairs surrounded by an entourage of senior monks and security guards. He smiled and clasped his hands together as he scanned the crowd of Tibetans, who clasped their hands and bowed their heads in return. As his security guards surrounded him, the Dalai Lama slipped into the sedan, which slowly rolled 200 feet across the courtyard to his residential compound, cleaving the dense crowd, then disappeared through the gate. The crowd seemed to collectively exhale, then the Tibetans streamed out of the courtyard to resume their day.

Tsongkhapa Day wasn't over. After dusk fell, the streets of McLeod Ganj remained magically illuminated. Shops and restaurants hung long strands of fairy lights from rooftops, so storefronts radiated vertical stripes. Candles flickered in windows and on their ledges. All was unusually quiet and the ear-splitting noises that normally permeated the air—honking, roaring cars and motorbikes—seemed subdued. As I walked up steep Jogiwara Road, light transformed the town so that its grime and garbage faded away. At Gaden Monastery's annex near the post office, light burned from molten wax stumps on windowsills. In the middle of the street Indian boys gleefully played pickup cricket and used plastic stools as wickets. The other main street, Temple Road, was a lonelier stretch at night. One side overlooked a sharp drop-off, and shops usually stood ominously dark and empty. But that evening, twinkling lights draped over the buildings created bold strands of brightness. Even the eerie wind that normally whistled across this road was hushed.

On one side of the narrow lane leading home to the nunnery, a stone wall pocked with crevices had been turned into tiny shrines with flickering candles. On the hill above me, Kirti Monastery was transformed into a beacon. Its rooftop was ringed with intense flames of hundreds, perhaps thousands, of tiny brass oil lamps. That's what the monks had been doing that morning: lining the balconies and roof with oil lamps. Strands of fairy lights cascaded down walls so the monastery was ablaze with light against the velvet darkness of night. It was an awesome sight.

That year, the holiday happened to fall on the winter solstice. The longest night of the year in this mountain town started with raucous noise, then settled into peaceful stillness; light silently illuminated the dark. I slipped through the door of the nunnery and climbed upstairs to my room that overlooked Kirti's radiance piercing the darkness.

[6]

A Chance to Enhance

I'm Always Praying Inside

SARNATH, INDIA, JANUARY 2009

. . .

It was early morning but already the shrieks of playing children filled the train. Indian kids raced up and down the aisle as we lurched and trundled along. They wielded miniature cricket bats and turned the aisle into a make-shift pitch. One boy, about six years old with a mischievous grin, wore a red sweater embroidered with large letters across the chest that read, "Tex-Ass."

In my compartment sat three Indian electricians on a bottom bunk that served as a sofa during the day. On the top bunk, I rubbed my bleary eyes. The day before, I had boarded the train at Chakki Bank, a station a few hours' drive from Dharamsala, and was headed to Varanasi, the city on the Ganges known for riverside funeral cremations and ashes scattered into the holy river. My neighbors wore button-down shirts, slacks, and thick mustaches. They were headed home to Varanasi after their pilgrimage to Jammu, the mountainous state bordering Pakistan, for a festival called Vishnu Devi.

My ultimate destination was Sarnath, about six miles from Varanasi. The Buddha gave his first sermon there more than 2,500 years ago, making it a Buddhist holy site and part of a pilgrimage route in northern India. Sarnath is normally a quiet town but would be transformed into a Buddhist jamboree with the Dalai Lama's ten-day teaching that January. In Dharamsala, many people—Tibetan and foreigners—talked about going to Sarnath for the event. At the December audience I attended, the Dalai Lama had asked who was going to Sarnath. Ultimately about 25,000 people registered for the teaching—in addition to 1,300 foreigners—and came from all over India, Nepal, and even Tibet to hear the Dalai Lama. I decided to attend to see how Tibetan Buddhists outside the haven of Dharamsala and in the heart of India communed.

The Indian electricians in my compartment were curious, frank, and opinionated. The day before, on the first leg of our eighteen-hour journey, they launched a barrage of questions as we sat across each other on bunks. Their English was good and we talked about a range of topics: the "26/11" terrorist attacks on Mumbai in November, less than two months before; Pakistan; Tibet; the recent Satyam scandal, in which one of India's largest IT companies spun a $1 billion fraud. The man in the middle wore a blue shirt; he was the most assertive of the three. He steered the conversation again to the terrorist attacks in Mumbai.

"You are a journalist. What should we do?" he demanded. He quickly offered his opinion: "India should attack Pakistan." There had been too many terrorist attacks in India and "attack is the best form of prevention," he intoned knowingly. The other two electricians nodded in agreement.

When I turned away and started writing in my journal, the electricians stared.

"What are you writing?" one of them asked. "Are you writing about us?"

The scenery outside flew by in a blur as hours of the day slid into one another. There was no dining car on the train, not even hot water to make instant noodles. When we stopped at a station somewhere in northern India, I ran outside like a ravenous dog to the food stands and bought potato chips and "glucose biscuits" for dinner. One of the electricians had said the train would stop for twenty minutes. Instead, it restarted after barely five, while I was still on the platform. It rolled away, and after a moment of panic, I sprinted and hoisted myself through the door. Once safely back onboard, my stomach growled persistently. The only food came from a porter who carried a stack of small rectangular dishes covered with tin foil. They contained semi-warm dal, rice, and curried potatoes that even the blue-shirted electrician complained were too spicy.

Night fell and the blackness outside the window obscured the landscape except for lonely glimmers of light from distant houses. Every so often the train rolled into a station. Then India burst into life in a glare of naked light bulbs illuminating shops that sold fried snacks stacked in pyramids, bottles of water, potato chips in miniature bags hanging in vertical strips. As it approached 10 p.m. the hum of conversation and tinny Hindi music played on phones eventually faded. Almost on cue, the passengers unlatched bunks from the wall. They spread starchy train-issued white sheets and brown wool blankets on the vinyl cushions and kicked off their shoes. Someone flicked off the overhead light in our compartment. I lay down and waited for the train to rock me to sleep.

Hours later I groggily rubbed sleep from my eyes and sat up cross-legged, scooching my head down so it wouldn't hit the ceiling. The electricians were already awake, their linens heaped messily on a bunk. They laughed as they pored over an IQ test in an Indian magazine that showed the palm of a hand. The kids continued their cricket match in the aisle. My watch showed we had less than four hours before reaching Varanasi. Through the window the scenery flew by in scattered fragments of color. By late morning the train began to slow, then it spluttered as it rumbled down the tracks, gradually losing steam. After pausing at stations on the city outskirts, we lumbered into Varanasi station.

Impatient passengers erupted from the train, flowed through the station, and spilled onto the street like human lava. Central Varanasi was expectedly chaotic, and traffic was loud and piercing. Dilapidated buses, cars, and scooters tangled in a messy knot outside the station, which made crossing the street a death-defying ordeal. I clutched my two backpacks—laptop bag on my back, the other slung over my chest—and dodged careening scooters and cars that kicked up thick swirls of dust. All the guesthouses were fully booked in Sarnath, so I had reserved a room in Varanasi at a budget place called Hotel Shivam. I would commute about thirty minutes to the teachings each day by autorickshaw. Days before, the receptionist had told me over the phone that I could walk from the train station to Hotel Shivam. I naively believed I could find it myself. But I couldn't locate the side street where I was supposed to turn. Overwhelmed after just a few minutes by the noise, traffic, crowds, and pollution, I paused at a hole-in-the-wall pharmacy and leaned limply against the counter. "Where is the UP Tourist Bungalow?" I asked, practically shouting over the noisy traffic. If I could find this landmark, Hotel Shivam was supposedly next door. A customer, a pudgy middle-aged man with his young son, pointed in the direction I came from and gave some instructions in English. It was hard to process anything in my disoriented state. "Is it close?" I asked. "Can I walk there?"

"Walking, yes," he replied.

He pointed down the daunting, horribly congested road. I sighed loudly. "Are you sure it's nearby?"

"Yes." Then he said decisively, "Come." He and the boy, about nine years old, started walking. "Come," he told me again.

"You don't have to—" I started to say but the man and his son were already walking, so I trotted to catch up with them. They forged ahead briskly, unbothered by the broken pavement, shrieking horns, and buses roaring dangerously close since the sidewalk was crumbled into coarse chunks and pedestrians were forced to walk in the road. We turned onto a narrower, less frenetic side street lined with shops and guesthouses. The boy skipped alongside his father, and they walked with me until reaching a large yellow building with a sign: UP Tourist Bungalow. Hotel Shivam was around the corner. I thanked the man profusely for guiding me. He nodded and smiled, then headed back toward the main road with his son still skipping carefree beside him.

. . .

Early the next morning I hailed an autorickshaw outside my hotel and bargained the price down to 100 rupees, about $2. It wasn't the real rate (60 rupees, or $1.25, is what a local would have paid), but it was cheap enough, so I climbed in. The driver asked where I was from. I didn't feel like dealing with prying questions or surprised, incredulous exclamations if I explained I was American, so I replied, "China."

"China!" The driver cried. "China very good! Football! Table tennis! Basketball!" Apparently, the fervor of the previous summer's Beijing Olympics still lingered. As we cut across the city, the streets were a wild, rolling cinema playing the spectacle of daily life in Varanasi. In front of us a man briskly pedaled a bicycle cart piled high with boxes, while another man in a blue sweater sat precariously on the cart's edge and chatted on his cell phone. On the pavement, reed-thin Indian men with sparse towels around their waists bathed by sudsing themselves then pouring water over their heads from small plastic jugs. A man opening his shop yawned and stretched, revealing a roll of fat hanging over his waistband. Cows and dogs standing shoulder to shoulder nosed through colorful mounds of rancid garbage. A mangy dog ate from dry rice fanned out onto the dirty street. Fat hogs trotted along, hairy snouts caressing the pavement like porcine vacuum cleaners.

After half an hour, we arrived in Sarnath and the autorickshaw slowed. Vehicles were not allowed on the road leading to the teaching, so I got out near a metal barricade. Crowds of Tibetans streamed down this road, past the large, tranquil campus of the Central Institute of Higher Tibetan Studies, a college founded in 1967 after conversations between Prime Minister Nehru and the Dalai Lama. The entire road was flanked by vendors manning cluttered stalls and tables. They sold religious books, Tibetan trinkets like prayer wheels, beads and amulets, white *khata* scarves made of polyester, bottled water, oranges and bananas, squishy squares of gray Styrofoam to sit on during teachings, plastic tarps, sun hats, cloth shoulder bags for carrying all that stuff, and anything else one might need during ten days sitting under a big tent in a field.

The bustle of commerce also included plenty of beggars and wild-haired children in rags. Like seasonal workers, they migrated to holy sites during various religious pilgrimages when thousands gathered. The beggars looked especially destitute and amputees bared the stumps of their limbs. Some wrapped bandages around their limbs and daubed red paint on them for dramatic effect. The road continued past the gauntlet of vendors and beggars. Megaphones jutted from tall utility poles, and near a T-junction I suddenly heard the Dalai Lama's familiar voice speaking Tibetan. I couldn't understand what he was saying, yet his calm, disembodied voice was soothing, almost palpably so, like ocean waves or leaves murmuring in a breeze. His voice, amplified by more megaphones, grew louder as I approached the source. A gate led to the teaching venue through metal detectors monitored by security guards. A sign by the entrance read,

The following items are not permitted in the teaching premises:
Handy cam recorder, cameras, mobile, cell phone, lighter (2 horse), match box, cigarette, pen knife, revolver / gun / chemicals.
Thank you for your cooperation.

At a large tented area, an orange and maroon canopy covered thousands of people—old, young, families, children, couples, monks, and nuns. Some spilled out from under the tent and sat on the pavement. The crowd displayed many distinct styles of *chupa* shirts and dresses. A group of middle-aged men wore tartan *chupas* and striped knee socks, like a highland tribe, though they perhaps were from Bhutan. Twin girls with pigtails in identical *chupas* of magenta silk brocade sat near their mother. An old woman wore a dark *chupa* cinched with a belt of bleached, round shells. There were plenty of non-Tibetans too, including familiar faces from Dharamsala: the Australian woman from philosophy class; the silver-haired woman from New York; the German guy who volunteered in town. At the front of the tent onstage sat a familiar and welcome figure: the Dalai Lama perched cross-legged on a raised platform decorated with flowers. Colorful *thangka* tapestries illuminated by drooping chandeliers hung behind him.

That morning, the Dalai Lama spoke on Buddhist texts called Kamalashila's "The Middling Stages of Meditation" (*Gomrim barpa*) and Shantideva's "A Guide to the Bodhisattva's Way of Life" (*Chodjug*). Non-Tibetan speakers followed along by listening to English interpretations broadcast via an AM channel on handheld transistor radios. For ten days from 9 a.m. to 3 p.m. the Dalai Lama talked almost nonstop, except an hour for lunch and some tea breaks. This exhausting teaching schedule was scaled back from even longer days when the Dalai Lama was younger.

Before long, there was a tea break and I entered the tent after burly Tibetan security guards inspected my pass. Suddenly, a stampede of young red-robed monks pounded down the aisle like linebackers. The tea truck had arrived and monks raced to fill their kettles. They clutched large metal tea pots by handles made of twisted cloth, then ran back up the aisle to pour tea into bowls held out by monks in the first few rows. Some guards held people back so they wouldn't get knocked over by the monks barreling past.

Finally, I reached the nearly empty press area in the first aisle in front of the Dalai Lama and sat down cross-legged. He sipped from a white mug, yawned like a lion, then leaned forward and spoke in a concerned tone into the microphone. He cautioned the monks not to run or else someone might get hurt. "Tea servers, you should be careful you don't fall," he warned gently, according to an interpreter whose voice piped through my headphones. "You could tumble off, spill tea on your face. Do you feel happy dashing?" Nevertheless, the monks kept sprinting with their teapots. After pouring tea, they lugged large plastic crates filled with round bread up the aisle. They handed large doughy discs to the audience, monastics and laypeople alike. A monk handed one to me and I hungrily bit into the bread.

The Dalai Lama drank some water before resuming his talk. His complex lecture was based on slim Buddhist texts held by many audience members. But he often veered off onto tangents and spoke spontaneously, hopping from one topic to another and interspersing anecdotes. One moment he was talking about transforming miseries: "Instead of adversity as cause of losing our patience, it becomes a chance to enhance." A few minutes later his thoughts about greed led him to warn about encroaching on the habitat of wild animals and the abhorrent practice of smuggling animal hides: "Human beings sometimes even worse than animals." Later he spoke extensively about anger:

> If you have anger for a long time and fear, they eat up your immune system. Jealousy gives you energy to catch up to others but in reality leads you to exaggerated qualities of object and self-destruction. . . . There was a conference in the USA a few years ago. There was a scientist who said a person who uses words "I" and "me" is more prone to heart attacks. The more you think about yourself, gross self-centeredness, then more you tend to narrow the scope of your

thinking. The more you are thinking about others, the broader your thinking.

After the audience cleared out of the hall, I talked to a young Tibetan man in his early twenties who had recorded the teaching and was packing up his video camera. He looked hip in jeans and a T-shirt that read "Property of Team Tibet / Olympics Exiles Beijing 2008." It was designed to look like a team athletic T-shirt, complete with a snow lion mascot. The young man told me he was studying in the United States at Hampshire, a very liberal liberal arts college in western Massachusetts. His name was Khemrab and he was born in Bir, a town a couple of hours' drive from Dharamsala known as one of the world's best spots for paragliding. Khemrab had been a student at the Central Institute of Higher Tibetan Studies in Sarnath when he met some Hampshire students studying abroad there. He later transferred to Hampshire. Then twenty-six and a senior, he was loving his college experience. He was back in India for a school project to make a documentary about Tibetans newly arrived in India from Tibet.

Khemrab peppered his speech with Americanisms. "Sweet!" he exclaimed when I said I was from Boston. "Seriously!?" he cried when I told him I was working in India.

Did this Americanized, liberal arts college Tibetan guy identify himself as Tibetan? He replied decisively: "I am 40 percent Tibetan, 60 percent Indian." He used surfer dude expressions but also mused eloquently about the plight of Tibetans. "Any people who are devoid of land create their own small community wherever they go. That's the positive side of being a refugee. It's also beautiful. From one side, it's a terrible thing Tibet fell. But every day more and more people are getting into Tibetan Buddhism and everything Tibet."

Khemrab was overwhelmed just by the Dalai Lama's presence at the teaching. "When you have so much reverence for someone you will get goose bumps, your hair will stand up," he gushed. "I'm always praying inside when I'm in his proximity." Then he confessed with a sheepish laugh, "This is the hundredth time I've promised myself I'm going to quit smoking and drinking."

That afternoon after the teaching I took an autorickshaw to Deer Park to see Dhamek Stupa, Sarnath's famous temple. All was serene, with just a few people inside the expansive grounds dotted with ancient Buddhist stupas, ruins in various conditions, and pits in the midst of excavation. To one side,

separated by a chain link fence, herds of deer with fuzzy antlers huddled
and vied for treats from tourists. The name Sarnath seems to derive from
"Saranganath," meaning "Lord of deer." According to one Buddhist tale,
the Buddha in deer form offered his life to a king in lieu of a doe he planned
to kill. The king was so moved that he created the park as a deer sanctuary.

The Dhamek Stupa itself was an enormous mound of brick and stone,
140 feet tall and 91 feet in diameter. It marked the spot where, according to
lore, the Buddha gave his first sermon to five disciples weeks after attaining
enlightenment. That afternoon, two Tibetan women prostrated on the paved
path around the stupa, lying full-length on the ground with arms extended,
then standing up, over and over again. Nearby, on the other side of a fence,
beggar children quietly watched.

Sarnath fell into ruins in the thirteenth century and lay forgotten and in
disrepair for centuries. Excavations began in 1798 when workmen disman-
tling a stupa to use its bricks for a local Indian ruler's construction project
uncovered relics. British archaeologist Alexander Cunningham later excavated the site in the 1830s. The first director of the Archaeological Society of
India in 1861, Cunningham was involved with excavation of Buddhist stupas
across India, including at Sarnath. The Dhamek Stupa bore an inscription
from 1026, "perhaps commemorating the spot of Buddha's first sermon,"
read a more recent plaque. It added, "Alexander Cunningham, in search of
the relic casket, bored nine vertical shafts through the center."

From Sarnath, the Buddha's influence spread far and wide—and returned
in the form of temples built with donations from Buddhist communities all
over Asia: Japan, Thailand, Sri Lanka, Myanmar, China. The temples scattered across Sarnath created a microcosm of the different forms of Buddhism
around the world: tall, stacked cupolas of the Thai temple; understated,
tranquil grounds and spare calligraphy on a stele at the Japanese temple;
prayer wheels and hundreds of blazing candles at the Sri Lankan temple.

As I exited Deer Park, I passed an Indian family. The father, an older
man, marched up to me and his familial entourage surrounded him. "Are
you Buddhist?" he queried, friendly and frank, and full of cheerful curiosity.

"Are you?" I asked.

He paused and crowed, "I am a human being first!" Then he said he was
Hindu but liked Buddhists too. He announced he was a management professor and planned to buy land nearby.

The Sarnath Archaeological Museum across from Deer Park showcased artifacts excavated from the site. Visitors—mostly Tibetan and some
Indians—milled inside the bright, airy galleries. Glass cases did not protect

sculptures, so people were free to rub their hands and press foreheads against objects that were 1,800 years old. Several of the stone Buddhas were alarmingly smooth and glossy from countless oily hands.

After the teaching, I headed back to Deer Park. It was around 5 p.m. and the empty, tranquil place of the afternoon was completely transformed into a kaleidoscope of humanity. Now the grounds pulsed with people. As dusk fell, the Dhamek Stupa was the center of a buzzing human vortex as hundreds of people swirled and walked around it. A few monks in crimson robes wore white face masks as they walked the paved path. An old woman in a turquoise cardigan and striped *pangden* apron over her *chupa* led her small granddaughter, who wore a sweater with a backpack slung over her chest. A young man with a black T-shirt that read, "Justice has been raped in Tibet" walked alongside a woman in a *chupa*. A little girl dressed in a pink dress munched from a bag of Lay's spicy tomato-flavored potato chips as she walked. A gigantic, burly monk did full body prostrations on the concrete path. To protect himself, he wore mittens made of metallic material and around his waist an apron of burlap sacking. The monk was so tall that he had to wait for the woman in front of him to finish her prostrations lest he overlap and crush her. A barefooted young man in T-shirt and jeans also prostrated around the stupa, his skin rubbing on the abrasive pavement.

People threw white *kathas* onto the stupa, trying to lodge them into window-like crevices high up in the stone. Scarves flew into the air, streaming cloth behind them like reversing meteors. On the grass, a worn cream-colored dog sat on his haunches and calmly observed the activity around him. In the plum sky, a single star emerged to the left of the stupa and winked down on the commotion below. A monk held a bundle of burning incense that glowed in the dark as he circumambulated. One section of steps was covered with candles and entirely aflame with burning, melted wax.

Around the stupa, people sat on the sloping lawn, their shapes fading into twilight shadows. Some chanted prayers, others sat lounging with companions. Dozens of red-robed nuns sat on the grass, chatting leisurely. Children's laughter wafted through the air. To one side, three old men wearing dress slacks and neat wool sweaters sat together. Their felt caps with an upturned forest-green flap were typical of northern Himachal Pradesh. At some point they stopped talking and began to prostrate in place, touching their foreheads to the grass toward the stupa.

Suddenly I spotted a familiar face in the crowd. It was Zhu Rui, a woman in her mid-forties from northern China who was visiting Dharamsala for several months to write articles. She had lived and worked in Tibet for several years in the 1990s as a journalist for a Chinese newspaper and had emigrated to Canada. Before moving to Tibet from her hometown of Harbin, Zhu Rui admitted she knew as much about Tibet as the average Chinese person, which was not much. She had believed the stories that Tibetans were "savages" and that the Dalai Lama was the devil. But after living in Tibet for several years and seeing things with her own eyes, Zhu Rui was convinced of the oppression there, grew enamored of Tibetan culture, and became an ardent supporter of Tibet. In Dharamsala, Zhu Rui had many friends, particularly Mandarin-speaking Tibetans. Simply put, she was popular. I sometimes saw her walking arm in arm with a female Tibetan refugee journalist who seemed thrilled to speak Mandarin; she had grown up in Lhasa. Zhu Rui's access to the exile government was excellent; they warmly greeted any Chinese-speaking visitors and prioritized their welcome. She loved Dharamsala and often sighed about how much she liked India.

Zhu Rui walked around the stupa with a group of monks. She wore her usual outfit of a black Tibetan high-necked shirt and long skirt. Her round face and nose and chin-length bob made her look distinctively Chinese. Zhu Rui's cheeks were rosy and she smiled easily. She went to Sarnath with a group from Gu Chu Sum, the nonprofit that supports Tibetan former political prisoners like my friend Norbu, the chef. She couldn't communicate with the group's president, a middle-aged Tibetan monk, who spoke neither English nor Chinese. Yet Zhu Rui was staying in a one-room brick shack in Sarnath and sleeping on the floor with eight men from Gu Chu Sum. When she first saw the basic accommodations she immediately volunteered to find another place to stay. The monks innocently insisted that Zhu Rui stay so they could make sure she was safe during her visit. They seemed oblivious to the idea that a woman might need privacy. Zhu Rui admitted to me that she didn't want to insult or embarrass them by excusing herself, so she hadn't changed her clothes yet. There was no bathroom or plumbing in the shack; the communal toilets were a short walk down a dirt path. Beyond washing her face, Zhu Rui also hadn't bathed in days.

When I told her I was staying in a guesthouse with a good bathroom and hot shower for 400 rupees (about $8), her face lit up. She could come and shower at my hotel, I offered, and Zhu Rui eagerly agreed. The next day we met for an early dinner in Sarnath at a big temporary roadside restaurant comprised of plastic chairs and tables within tarp walls. It had the feel of a tent at a county fair. The food was unappetizing: greasy fried noodles, fried rice, and gloopy noodle soup. After dinner, we hailed an autorickshaw and

Zhu Rui haggled with the driver. He tried to extract more than 100 rupees, but she barked at him ferociously. Zhu Rui was from China; she knew how to bargain. The driver sensed this and shrank back, visibly cowed. We set off for Varanasi after Zhu Rui haggled him down to sixty rupees, the local price. In the middle of Varanasi, near the train station, our autorickshaw got stuck in an ugly snarl of traffic. Huge, ancient-looking buses jammed into a cruel jigsaw puzzle of metal and noise surrounded us. The autorickshaw driver tried to move his tin can of a vehicle between two behemoths, but we were wedged in. We could only wait for the buses to inch forward, giving a vehicle locked diagonally behind it a chance to pass. "Oh," gasped Zhu Rui. "Maybe this is the real India."

In my hotel room, Zhu Rui made a beeline for the bathroom, like someone offered water after a long journey in the desert. After her shower she emerged looking a little dazed, her face scrubbed and shiny. She had brought socks and underwear to wash and she clutched the clean items in a wet ball before dropping them into a plastic bag. It was after 8:30 p.m. so I told her she could stay with me for the night rather than travel all the way back to Sarnath by autorickshaw. Zhu Rui shook her head; her "eight Tibetan fathers" would be worried, she joked. I accompanied her to the street to hail an autorickshaw. Zhu Rui climbed in and waved goodbye with one hand while her other hand clutched her bag of wet clothes.

· · ·

The next morning at the teaching, the formerly empty press area was jam-packed. Someone realized that the most precious real estate in the audience had been unused except by me and quickly made sure it was well occupied. I squeezed in among a group of middle-aged Tibetan-looking men who wore heavy black wool tunics with upturned turquoise-colored cuffs. More security guards scanned the crowd from the foot of the stage where the Dalai Lama sat. The men next to me were from Arunachal Pradesh, a state in India's far northeast near Tibet. They were relatives and colleagues of Dorjee Khandu, Arunachal Pradesh's chief minister who was onstage with the Dalai Lama in a special ceremony. Some monks passed out red satin ribbons to the audience. As the Dalai Lama chanted, the men around me put the ribbon over their eyes like a blindfold.

Arunachal Pradesh, India's easternmost state, is particularly remote. For years, tourists needed special permits to go to most of the seven northeast states in India's "chicken neck," which stretches out and over Bangladesh.

Though far-flung, the states are geographically strategic because of their shared borders with Bangladesh, Bhutan, Myanmar, and Tibet. Some also had natural resources, most notably oil in Assam.

Arunachal Pradesh was politically sensitive because of its geography. The 1914 Simla Accord drew a border between British India and Tibet. Britain and Tibet signed the pact, but China refused. Today China still refers to the area as "South Tibet," and Chinese officials have declared this rugged strip of mountainous land part of China. Only about 13 percent of Arunachal Pradesh is Buddhist, according to a 2001 Indian census, but the state is heavily influenced by Buddhism because it borders Tibet.

The following year, in the fall of 2010, the Dalai Lama's plan to give a teaching in Arunachal Pradesh created a political firestorm. China took it as an affront and warned India not to let him travel there. Tensions escalated and a media circus ensued. Indian and foreign journalists booked flights, but at the last minute, India's government barred them from traveling to Arunachal Pradesh at all. Nevertheless, the Dalai Lama went. He visited a historic monastery built in 1861 in Tawang district where about 30,000 people ardently greeted him during his weeklong visit.

Later that afternoon in Sarnath there was a long-life ceremony for the Dalai Lama and an offering to White Tara, a female Buddha. The ceremony was held on the grounds of the Dhamek Stupa, and its grassy field turned into a sea of Tibetans. The Dalai Lama sat on a stage far in the distance. People sat in clusters as though picnicking. Some chanted along from thin prayer books. A young woman shyly told me she was from Madhya Pradesh in central India. Someone next to me peeled an orange so its citrus spritz perfumed the air, then offered me a slice. A middle-aged man sat with his wife, children, and a flock of relatives, fourteen of whom had come from all over India and Nepal. The man was a teacher from the TCV in Dharamsala and taught English and social sciences. He wore a T-shirt with the homemade Tibetan Olympics logo.

Near the end of the week, the Dalai Lama held smaller morning audiences specifically for "foreign friends." He held separate audiences for overseas Chinese, people from Taiwan and Japan, and other groups. At the one I attended, the miscellaneous group of several hundred foreigners gathered before 7 a.m. on a lawn on the serene campus of the Central Institute of Higher of Tibetan Studies. They waited quietly in the cool sunshine until 8:30, when the Dalai Lama finally appeared. He smiled broadly as he made his way to the front of the audience and, much to their delight, laughed in greeting.

The Dalai Lama took a short poll of where the visitors came from by calling out a country and asking for a show of hands. There were people from Australia, Canada, Italy, France, Germany, Poland, Bulgaria, and the United States, among others. He thanked them for coming to learn about Tibetan Buddhism and for supporting Tibet. Then, just as warmly, he said in English, "People from non-Buddhist countries are showing genuine interest in Buddhism. At the same time, it is important to keep one's traditions rather than change religions." Most religious leaders want to grow their membership, not dissuade people from conversion, but the Dalai Lama had always been adamant about this. Non-Buddhists could learn and borrow from Buddhism, he said, but converting could lead to confusion if one expects it to solve all their problems.

· · ·

The trains back to Delhi were nearly fully booked, so I left Sarnath before the teachings ended. On the dirty platform in Varanasi railway station, a gaggle of people waited. They wore white surgical masks over their faces, presumably to block out germs and pollution. They were East Asian, their clothes subtly designer and high-end. Once onboard the train, I went for a walk and wandered into the next car. A young man with a face mask looked up from where he lounged on his bunk. On a whim I asked in Mandarin where he was from. "Taiwan," he answered. His group was coming from a visit to Bodh Gaya, a city east of Varanasi, and the Buddhist holy site where the Buddha became enlightened. The Karmapa, the twenty-something head of the Karma Kagyu school of Tibetan Buddhism, had given a teaching there that week. Through his face mask, the man estimated at least 1,000 Taiwanese attended the teaching and plenty of Chinese from mainland China too. He heard there was no problem for them to get visas from India. In China, interest in Buddhism was growing, the Taiwanese man told me. This contrasted with the lack of interest in religion I had observed in China when I lived there in the 1990s. Under decades of communism, religion was expunged as "opium for the masses," according Marxist ideology. One theory for the recent revival in religion was that as living conditions improved and prosperity grew more widespread, people had time and leisure to think beyond day-to-day survival. For some, rampant materialism and consumerism in China also created a void that caused them to ponder spirituality and explore religions.

Back at my bunk, I settled down for the overnight journey back to Delhi. Across from me sat a young man from Bhutan who worked for a UN agency there. He was Buddhist, as are about 75 percent of Bhutanese, so I asked what he thought about the teachings in Sarnath. He sheepishly admitted he didn't know much about it. Most Buddhists just have "blind faith" and don't know the details of Buddhism, he opined. In the Dalai Lama's audience to Tibetans, the spiritual leader also mentioned the importance of studying Buddhism and trying to understand it, not just memorizing prayers and going through the motions of religious ritual. The man from Bhutan and thousands of others had come to Sarnath for the Dalai Lama's detailed teachings about Buddhism. Perhaps they came away with a deeper understanding from their journeys, spanning thousands of miles for some.

Around us, fellow passengers began the nightly railway ritual of unlatching bunks, arranging bedding, rustling plastic bags, and kicking off shoes. Someone flicked off the overhead light. Soon the only sounds were of the train lurching, carrying travelers back from pilgrimage, rushing through the night back to Delhi.

No Losar and Murder in the Snow

If You Have Something Inside,
Just Let It Out!

DHARAMSALA, FEBRUARY 2009

· · ·

The Dalai Lama bent his head and gazed through the airplane's oval window at the landscape below. The view of craggy brown mountains and snow peaks reflected in his square glasses, visible even from where he sat a few seats behind me on the small propeller plane heading to Dharamsala. It was February 2009, after my trip to Sarnath and a whirlwind stay in Delhi, where I wrote a travel article for the *New York Times*.

Earlier at the airport while the plane waited to take off, I was surprised when a commotion ensued. Several red-robed monks got onboard, which was unusual since the relatively expensive flight meant most Tibetans took the bus or train. At the time there was only one flight between Delhi and Dharamsala. Then activity buzzed near the rear door and Indian passengers turned to stare. One headed down the aisle with his camera; the Dalai Lama had mounted the plane's folding staircase.

Dressed as usual in his robes and heavy brown shoes, the Dalai Lama was accompanied by a group of bodyguards, monks, and aides, including joint-secretary and nephew Tenzin Taklha dressed in a dark suit. The Dalai Lama smiled graciously, clasped his hands, and nodded at the passengers who ogled and snapped photos of him. Then he slid into a window seat near the back. Another red robed monk sat next to him for the forty-minute flight. When the plane was aloft, I stared at the undulating switchbacks carved into the mountains below, incredulous that I was normally inside a bus careening over those harrowing roads for twelve hours instead of gliding far above them with the Dalai Lama a few seats away.

Surely his surprising presence was a good omen for Shimmy. While I was in Sarnath the cat had taken another turn for the worse, and I splurged on the flight to Dharamsala so I could hurry and tend to him. The Dalai Lama wrote in his autobiography *Freedom in Exile* about his own experience in Dharamsala caring for three cats. I was surprised that all of them had crippled legs like Shimmy. The Dalai Lama's first cat, called Tsering, fell from the top of a curtain rod and eventually died of her injuries. Not long after, the Dalai Lama discovered an abandoned kitten in his garden whose "hind legs were crippled in just the same way as Tsering's were when she died." This cat eventually regained her health, was able to walk, and became good friends with the Dalai Lama's two dogs, particularly one called Sangye, "against whose furry chest she liked to lie." Eventually she passed away along with the dogs, and the spiritual leader decided against having any more pets. His senior tutor observed, "Pets are in the end only an extra source of anxiety to their owners." I well understood that anxiety as I tried to help Shimmy. But in the winter of 1988 the Dalai Lama discovered another sick kitten near his home. "To my surprise, I found that she too was crippled just as her two predecessors had been." He fed her and gave her medicine until she recovered and joined his household, proving herself to be "a very lively individual and very curious."

Before leaving Dharamsala for Sarnath a couple of weeks before, I was hopeful that Shimmy would recover. I'd been giving him physical therapy at least twice a day—rotating and flexing his back legs—and it seemed to help; he could actually move them. After weeks of struggle, just before I left for Sarnath, even Shimmy's diarrhea abated. I had searched desperately for someone to care for him in my absence. Topden first declined, saying he would be too busy with his driving lessons; the vet clinic was paying for them so he could transport sick animals to and from the clinic. Finally, perhaps sensing my desperation, Topden agreed to care for Shimmy. While in Sarnath I called Topden, who reported that Shimmy's diarrhea had stopped. "I give him physical therapy every day," Topden announced proudly. "He is improvement!"

"Does he try to bite you?" I asked.

"No, he knows me. He knows I help him. He is very quiet."

"How are his legs?"

"They are stronger. Yesterday I helped his two legs and Shimmy is almost standing. It was beautiful. I love him!"

Overjoyed at Shimmy's progress, I hoped even more for his recovery. But after I arrived in Delhi from Sarnath, I called Topden again. Things had changed with shocking swiftness.

"Shimmy is not eating his food," Topden said in a low voice.

"What? How long?" My heart sank. Shimmy was always ravenous.

"Since yesterday. He is very weak now. Just sleeping. Oh, I think he will die!" he moaned.

Shimmy had suddenly become very lethargic and barely responded when Topden opened his cage. He could hardly lift his head. He didn't touch his food or drink water. Something was terribly wrong.

On the little plane with the Dalai Lama behind me, I fidgeted in my seat, anxious to get to Shimmy. When we landed at the airport near Dharamsala, the Dalai Lama and his entourage sprang into action and quickly disembarked in a flurry of robes. Through the window I could see the group moving with a practiced swiftness across the tarmac, forming a crimson cloud with the Dalai Lama at the center. In the small airport, I waited impatiently for my luggage then jumped in a taxi to Dharamsala. After dropping my things at the nunnery, I grabbed my kit of cat food and medicine and ran down the hill. I could envision Shimmy looking up at me with wide, expectant green eyes and meowing loudly as he did each time I visited. When I reached the clinic I went straight to Shimmy's cage on the roof but found it bare, bereft even of the wool blanket he usually sat on. All the rooftop cages were empty.

It was late afternoon and the sky was overcast, the color of dull steel. There was hardly any wind and the clouds squatted stagnantly in the sky. I took out my phone and called Topden.

"Topden, where is Shimmy?" I asked breathlessly when he answered.

"Oh," he replied. "Where are you?" I could hear noise in the background; he was at a basketball court.

"I'm at the clinic."

"I just left the clinic."

"The cages are empty."

Then he said, "Shimmy died this morning. I felt so sad the whole day."

Shimmy had deteriorated quickly. The day before, Topden placed a bowl of chicken porridge next to him, but the cat only picked up his head then put it back down. This was a very bad sign; Shimmy never refused food. That morning just after dawn, the clinic's caretaker heard the resident street dogs barking loudly. He checked on Shimmy, who barely opened his eyes. When the caretaker checked again an hour later, the cat was dead. Topden wanted to keep Shimmy until I could see his body, but the caretaker advised otherwise. That afternoon, Topden put the cat "in the earth" near the clinic and placed a large rock over Shimmy's grave.

I hung up and gazed at the empty cages on the rooftop I had visited so many times in a hurry as Shimmy cried for food. The air was unusually still and nothing moved in the queer air. Even the street dogs stopped barking. The thick clouds portended rain, but that day, none came.

· · ·

Losar, the Tibetan New Year, ushers in weeks of festivities in Tibet. The biggest holiday of the Tibetan calendar, it falls in January or February, sometimes around the Lunar New Year. For Tibetans in India, Losar is a weeklong celebration when shops close, people break from work, and routine life gives way to feasting, singing, dancing, visiting family and friends, playing cards, and, last but not least, drinking *chhaang*, Tibet's barley beer.

But in 2009, when I was in Dharamsala, no Losar celebration happened in Tibet or India. That year, the first day of Losar fell on February 25, two weeks before the fiftieth anniversary of Tibet's failed uprising against China in 1959. The mood in Tibet, and subsequently Dharamsala, had become even more sober in recent months. That January, in anticipation of the fiftieth anniversary and potential unrest, China launched its "Strike Hard" campaign in Tibet. The crackdown brought a sharp rise in arrests, raids, and interrogations as authorities tightened control, according to the Tibetan Centre for Human Rights and Democracy in Dharamsala. Chinese authorities forced Tibetans, especially monks, to take part in "patriotic reeducation" campaigns.

For months, Tibetans in Dharamsala debated what to do instead of Losar celebrations. One evening, about two dozen people led by local activists braved the cold for a public discussion in an empty classroom at a Tibetan school. While sitting on plastic sacking printed with the USAID logo, as well as wooden planks on the concrete floor, they quickly agreed that celebrating Losar was inappropriate given Tibet's turmoil.

A few weeks before Losar, posters appeared in Dharamsala. Bulletin spaces normally plastered with flyers advertising talks on Buddhism, Tibetan films, concerts, yoga, meditation classes, and "past life regression" courses were filled instead with large jet-black posters. They read: "No Losar Celebrations, to Express Our Solidarity with Tibetan Martyrs." The word "Losar" appeared in a red circle cut through with a slash.

Tibetans in Dharamsala were following the lead of compatriots in Tibet who vowed to boycott Losar even though Chinese officials offered money to encourage festivities, according to Chinese-language blogs posted in Tibet.

The Dalai Lama said in a statement, "The occasion of this New Year is certainly not a period when we can have the usual celebrations and gaiety. . . . I admire the determined move by Tibetans, inside and outside of Tibet, not to indulge in celebratory activities during this New Year." Calls for the boycott came as China declared March 28 "Serf Emancipation Day"—a new "holiday" celebrating abolition of Tibet's government in 1959 and China's liberation of Tibetan "serfs." For Tibetans, the holiday was a cruel insult.

In spite of China's clampdown, news from Tibet eventually reached India via email, mobile phones, digital cameras, and the Internet. Exiles responded in a way that their compatriots in Tibet could not. One winter afternoon I encountered a few Tibetans holding candles as they walked down Temple Road. Moments later, dozens, then hundreds of people snaked down the hill. A monk marching at the front of the human chain carried a large, framed portrait of the Dalai Lama. Another person held a framed photo of a young Tibetan man. A *khata* scarf was draped like a parted curtain over the tops of both pictures.

Amid the crowd walked Sonam, a stout refugee in his forties with wavy, tousled hair who had recently spoken at a café about fleeing Tibet after the March 2008 protests. We chatted briefly in Mandarin as we walked, and Sonam admitted he didn't know what was happening but was just following the march. Candlelight vigils were usually organized by one of the major advocacy groups, such as the Tibetan Youth Congress or Gu Chu Sum. They spread word via people with bullhorns who walked the streets or broadcast announcements from a moving car. In spite of ad hoc publicity, word spread. It was common to stumble upon people in the main square readying for a march or candlelight vigil, shielding flames from the breeze and adjusting paper sleeves around candles to prevent wax from dripping on their hands.

That day, hundreds cradling flickering candles formed a river of light in the descending dusk. In the crowd, I spotted Sonam Dorjee, a twenty-seven-year-old activist with the Tibetan Youth Congress, who wore a blazer over a blue sweater vest. He explained that the vigil was to commemorate Pema Tsepak, a twenty-four-year-old Tibetan man detained by Chinese police on January 20 and beaten to death for participating in a small, nonviolent protest in Kham in eastern Tibet. Pema, a painter by profession, and two friends had taken to the streets carrying banners, distributing fliers, and shouting slogans against Chinese rule. The protest lasted forty minutes before dozens of Chinese police officers arrested the men, according to news reports. Pema was beaten and tortured while in detention, then taken to a hospital, where he died three days later from his injuries. The victim's friends, several young men who had marched carrying Free Tibet banners, were also arrested.

The crowd marched to the *kora*, onto its narrow, tree-lined path, and then the wide clearing where I had walked with Norbu months before. The crowd paused at a shrine, rows of prayer wheels and a large stupa carved into the hillside. Men carrying photos of the Dalai Lama and Pema Tsepak stood alongside a man with a microphone who spoke as a map of Kham flashed on a large video screen next to him. The framed photo of Pema showed him smiling in front of some shrubs, wearing an olive T-shirt and a bomber-style jacket. Longish bangs hung across his forehead.

In spite of the somber occasion, Tibetans from all walks of life chattered, babies cried, and toddlers scooted about as the man with the microphone spoke in Tibetan. After speeches, the audience quieted, rose to their feet, and sang loudly in Tibetan as candlelight illuminated their faces in a rosy glow. Tibetans sing the same song at the end of nearly every candlelight vigil in Dharamsala. Everyone knew the words by heart. When they finished, the crowd dispersed and walked along the *kora* back to the temple gate. The atmosphere turned informal, even casually jovial. I walked behind a mother with two small children who squealed and chased each other, as though they had been at a parade. Such was the dual nature of life in Dharamsala where, after another day of work, a mother might bring her children to a vigil to remember a man murdered in their homeland.

. . .

On the morning of Losar, I heard loud chanting emanating from the nunnery's prayer room on the top floor. About a dozen nuns were inside. Without breaking their chant, one of them beckoned to me, so I slipped in and sat on a floor cushion. The prayer room was the same simple two-windowed box as the other nunnery rooms. But against one wall stood a colorful altar with portraits of the Dalai Lama, plastic flowers, and flickering electric candles. Cushions rested on the floor. Another layperson who lived in the nunnery, a Japanese woman, sat in the prayer room too. The musical drone filled my head, and I slipped in and out of a hazy doze, sometimes jerking my head up when it lolled against my neck, but no one seemed to notice. After nearly an hour, the chanting subsided, and the nuns threw a handful of rice in the air and passed around sweets.

Tenzin Deden, one of the nuns, recalled past Losar celebrations in Kinnaur, her hometown, as a happy time of horse races; wearing new clothes, gold and silver jewelry, and "flowers on head"; debates among monks; and making torma—sculptures of *tsampa* (kneaded barley) and butter—and treats of apricot, apple, barley, and rice.

"Are you celebrating Losar this year?" I asked Tenzin Zangmo, a nun who sat next to me in the prayer room.

Tenzin Zangmo smiled and shrugged. "No celebrating this year," she said. Modest religious ceremonies would take place, but the pageantry and merrymaking of Losar would not. The shops on Temple Road were closed with metal shutters pulled down over storefronts. Just a few people walked through uncharacteristically quiet and empty streets. A new white *khata* tied to the nunnery's metal gate rippled serenely in the wind that sunny, cold morning.

On Temple Road I bumped into the activist Tenzin Tsundue, who wore his signature red bandana over his forehead and a black Tibetan shirt. He was talking to a tiny, elderly Tibetan woman wearing a dark blue *chupa*. Tsundue waved me over and translated her words. Her name was Soma, and she was eighty years old. "This is the first time I have not celebrated Losar," she said without hesitation as Tsundue nodded, listening attentively before translating. "But there is so much pressure and tension for His Holiness. When His Holiness is undergoing this, how can we celebrate Losar? There was no audience with His Holiness today, so there is no excitement." She went on, "Losar is a time to see family, to come together to celebrate. No one should go hungry at Losar, but there is a hunger strike."

Indeed, in front of Nowrojee's general store, more than fifty Tibetans sat cross-legged on the ground. The Tibetan Youth Congress had organized a three-day hunger strike in McLeod Ganj's main square. Most of the hunger strikers were monks and nuns who over their red robes wore yellow vests similar to bibs worn by construction workers. They tied black headbands over their foreheads. Many of them fingered wooden prayer beads. Instead of a black headband, one monk wore a Tibetan flag scarf so that red, white, and blue sun rays radiated across his forehead. The hunger strikers sat quietly on thin cotton mattresses within a makeshift corral flanked by bright Tibetan flags and fenced in by barriers covered with banners that read, "United Nations, Monks and Nuns Are Killed. Where Is Humanity?" Above their heads hung more large signs. One said, "Hunger Strike for Tibet by 50 Tibetans to Express Solidarity to Tibetan Martyrs."

It was only midmorning, but already intense mountain sunshine pierced the air. To shade themselves, some monks and nuns folded their red shawls and placed them on top of shaved heads. Warm blankets covered their laps. At one end of the corral, a few laypeople joined the hunger strike. An elderly Tibetan man wearing a knockoff North Face jacket and knit cap with the word "Power" sat cross-legged in the February chill. There were also some young Tibetan men, one with long hair flowing over his shoulders and another with puffy, eighties-style hair and a goatee, as well as a Caucasian woman with wild gray hair who sat barefoot. When a decrepit bus pulled into the square belching plumes of black exhaust, some hunger strikers covered their faces with shawls or tried to fan the fumes away. One nun had come prepared with a white face mask over her nose and mouth.

Dhondup Lhadhar, the thirty-something general secretary of the Tibetan Youth Congress, stood talking to people near a glass case at the Pastry Den that flagrantly displayed cakes just a few feet from the hunger strikers. Petite Indian women carrying concrete slabs on their heads walked past to reach the construction site behind the bakery. Overhead, a hairy monkey scampered on a web of black wires. "For the first time in exile we are sitting in hunger strike on new year," Dhondup told me. "The situation in Tibet is getting worse. Tibetans in Tibet are also taking up action. We are remembering the deaths of Tibetan freedom fighters."

A yellow street dog named Tashi trotted past and sat down amid the hunger strikers, his pink tongue lolling from his mouth. Tashi was a frequent participant in marches and demonstrations, Dhondup noted. In fact, the dog had joined members of the Tibetan Youth Congress on a march all the way from Dharamsala to Delhi in 2004 in the weeks before March 10.

"I think he was Tibetan in his past life," Dhondup observed.

Tashi politely crossed his paws and continued to sit patiently with the crowd.

. . .

During Losar, the Dalai Lama normally leads a packed prayer ceremony to start the new year. This year, at first light, monks from Namgyal Monastery, attached to the main temple, performed cursory prayers, but there was no appearance by the Dalai Lama. In the main temple just a few dozen people wandered about, turning prayer wheels, circumambulating, or lingering in the nearly empty courtyard. Outside a prayer hall stood a table covered with about a hundred brass oil lamps whose flames shimmered in the breeze. A banner behind it showed a photo collage of wounded Tibetans. The banner read, "UN!!! Innocent Tibetans are being killed in TIBET, Where is HUMAN DIGNITY? If justice for all, then why not TIBET?" and "Support us in the promotion of peaceful dialogue on the issue to regain Tibet freedom (Regional Tibetan Women's Association)."

Another table flanked by Tibetan flags held about twenty framed pictures, small brass oil lamps, and pots of plastic flowers. Above, a white banner in Tibetan script read, "Tibetans who have sacrificed their lives for Tibet and Tibetan people." The photos were of Tibetans killed over the past year, their portraits collected by the Tibetan Centre for Human Rights and Democracy and other organizations tracking casualties. Glossy portraits and grainy snapshots featured Tibetans of all ages and all walks of life: monks and nuns with bright red cheeks, smiling youths, and weathered older men and women. I noticed a pleasant-looking monk, a young woman in a wool pea coat, a young man crouching with elbow on knee. One face against a background of shrubs looked familiar. It was Pema, the twenty-four-year-old painter commemorated in Dharamsala at the recent candlelight vigil.

Outside the temple a crowd gathered for a far less solemn spectacle, and a palpable buzz of excitement filled the air. To one side stood a large wooden signboard with a painted caricature of China's president Hu Jin Tao and the words, "Shoe Jin Tao" above his oversized head. Shoe Jin Tao wore large glasses, black suit, and a red tie. One hand covered the mouth of a boy monk below him while his other hand pushed down the head of a shouting Tibetan man. Words painted around Hu in bold letters read,

Dictator Cultural genocide

Oppression

No freedom of speech

Military occupation

Shoe Jin Tao also had big black eyebrows, and a large hole was cut into his wide grin. The point was to throw a shoe through Hu's mouth, like a carnival game. An emcee, a young Tibetan man with a bullhorn, called to the crowd in English and Tibetan, "Today is an auspicious day! If you have something inside, just let it out!"

People chattered and laughed. Children trussed up in silk brocade jackets, their Losar best, squealed and watched in wide-eyed anticipation. Finally, a Tibetan man picked up an old shoe from a pile on the ground, wound up his arm like a cricket bowler, and hurled it. The shoe thudded loudly against the signboard and the crowd erupted in shrieks and laughter. Soon another Tibetan strode up, grabbed a shoe, threw it, and managed to thwack the signboard.

More Tibetans queued up and soon the crowd was thick with enthusiastic boys. A few with better aim sent shoes sailing through Hu's mouth, and eager children raced to retrieve them. Some people stood to one side, leaning against or sitting on parked motorbikes to watch the action, including Tenzin Choeying, head of Students for a Free Tibet (SFT) in Dharamsala, which had organized the Shoe Jin Tao event. A few weeks before, I interviewed Choeying about teaching nonviolent activism to Tibetans. This might seem redundant, but nonviolence requires much more than murmuring prayers. Effective nonviolent resistance requires training, methodology and planning, marketing, public and media relations, and tech savvy, whether live videos streamed over the Internet or using Facebook and Twitter. Lhadon Tethong, then executive director of SFT based in New York, emphasized that Rosa Parks did not spontaneously refuse to give up her seat on that bus in Alabama in 1955: "She was trained. She had attended training institutes and learned some brilliant strategies and methodology. Just because we have this strong Buddhist culture . . . doesn't mean we just know how to wage a battle against a powerful force."

Tibetan activists looked to Mohandas Gandhi and other leaders of non-violent resistance as role models. After its meetings, the Tibetan Youth Congress sings "We Shall Overcome." Nonviolent movements have historically overlapped across continents and cultures. In 1959, Martin Luther King Jr. studied Gandhi's legacy on a monthlong journey to India and brought influential lessons back to the United States for the civil rights movement. "I have returned to America with a greater determination to achieve freedom for my people through nonviolent means," King wrote in a letter after his trip. "As a result of my visit to India, I believe that my understanding of nonviolence is greater and my commitment is deeper."

While the Dalai Lama drew on principles inherent in Tibetan Buddhism, he often cited Gandhi, King, and Nelson Mandela when discussing non-violence and peace. On a 2009 tour of the Civil Rights Museum in Memphis, Tennessee, and a visit to the motel where King was assassinated, the Dalai Lama said the leader was a "freedom fighter of true nonviolence like Mahatma Gandhi. . . . We should follow these great people's method."

While the Dalai Lama espouses nonviolence as a spiritual leader, most Tibetans are regular human beings. And humans express frustration, anxiety, anger, and grief in a range of ways. Choeying calmly watched the Shoe Jin Tao throwing frenzy in front of us. An art teacher Tibetan friend of SFT had finished painting the signboard just the night before. Choeying, sported a goatee, black jacket, and jeans, just as he had during my previous visit with him at the SFT office. At that meeting he sat on a sofa beneath a whiteboard that listed DVD Tibetan documentaries for sale. He described how far pro-Tibet activism had come since his days at Delhi University. Back then, just a handful of Tibetans showed up to protest visits by Chinese leaders. In contrast, a 2007 rally in Delhi organized by the Tibetan Youth Congress drew an estimated 25,000 Tibetans from across India.

How did they come up with the idea of Shoe Jin Tao? "We got inspired by the guy at Cambridge," Choeying told me. Weeks earlier, a student had thrown his shoe at China's premier, Wen Jiabao, during an event at Cambridge University. It was one incident in a spate of shoe-throwing after an Iraqi journalist hurled his shoes at US president George W. Bush during a Baghdad press conference in December 2008. The Iraqi shouted in Arabic, "This is a farewell . . . you dog!" And while pinned on the ground by security personnel, he screamed, "You killed the Iraqis!"

In Iraq and other parts of the world, especially in Arab countries, showing one's feet is a deep insult. The simple but contemptuous act of shoe-throwing struck a chord. In the weeks after the incident, the Turkish manufacturer of the sturdy leather brogue received orders from around the world for more than 100,000 pairs of the "Ducati Model 271."

The Iraq incident sparked several copycats, such as Wen Jiabao's heckling at Cambridge. The protester demanded to know why the university had invited Wen. "How can this university prostitute itself with this dictator?" the man shouted. "How can you listen to the lies he is telling? Stand up and protest." He threw a sneaker at Wen, which landed near the podium. Internet searches in China appeared to block reports about the premier's near brush with a shoe, though China's media had widely showed Bush ducking the Ducati Model 271s aimed at his head.

Throwing shoes at a signboard caricature was fairly tame in India, where protesters sometimes burned effigies, staged riots, burned trucks, and smashed storefronts. Yet shoes flying through the air to smack Shoe Jin Tao's leering grin were provocative. One passerby, an older European woman, caught the contradiction between the aggressive shoe-throwing and the peaceful nature associated with Tibetans. "Don't wish ill on others," the woman called out. "Bad karma!"

Her comments didn't stop the crowd from throwing shoes, and the thuds, thwacks, and laughter continued. "If you have something inside, just let it out!" called the Tibetan man with the bullhorn.

. . .

Nonviolent protest among Tibetan exiles didn't happen spontaneously. In addition to the Tibetan Youth Congress and Students for a Free Tibet, several other groups fostered active resistance. Everett Gendler, an eighty-year-old rabbi from Massachusetts, and his psychologist wife Mary founded the Active Nonviolence Education Center (ANEC) in Dharamsala in 2007. The Gendlers and ANEC's staff held workshops and trainings for Tibetans across India in schools, monasteries, and exile government offices.

That winter they led a two-week workshop at a Tibetan school near Dharamsala for refugees in their late teens and twenties where Norbu had studied after arriving in India. The Gendlers and ANEC staff led part of the workshop based on the teachings of Gene Sharp, a Boston-based intellectual in his eighties who outlined 198 methods of nonviolent action in his 1973 book, *The Politics of Nonviolent Action*. The list included, among other methods,

COMMUNICATIONS WITH A WIDER AUDIENCE:

7. Slogans, caricatures, and symbols

8. Banners, posters, and displayed communications

SYMBOLIC PUBLIC ACTS:

18. Displays of flags and symbolic colors

19. Wearing of symbols

PROCESSIONS:

38. Marches

39. Parades

40. Religious processions

41. Pilgrimages

HONORING THE DEAD:

43. Political mourning

44. Mock funerals

Sharp's methods inspired many nonviolent uprisings around the world. His ninety-three-page guide *From Dictatorship to Democracy*, was available in twenty-four languages and guided protests worldwide, including in Serbia, Burma, Bosnia, Estonia, and Zimbabwe. In 2011, in Egypt, Gene Sharp's writings were widely read by activists in the largely nonviolent resistance that toppled the thirty-year rule of President Hosni Mubarak.

After studying leaders like Gandhi, nonviolent uprisings, civil rights struggles, and economic boycotts, Sharp himself said in a 2011 *New York Times* interview that "advancing freedom takes careful strategy and meticulous planning." Peaceful protest is best, he says—not for any moral reason, but because violence provokes autocrats to crack down. "If you fight with violence," Sharp said, "you are fighting with your enemy's best weapon, and you may be a brave but dead hero."

One cold winter day white-haired Everett Gendler, dressed in a plaid flannel shirt, corduroy pants, and sturdy hiking shoes, led a classroom discussion of twenty young Tibetans who sat in chairs arranged in a circle. I observed while he asked what the word "power" meant to them. The students were silent and shy at first. Many of them were from farming or nomadic communities, and even those from Tibetan cities had limited education. But the students warmed up as one by one they went around the circle and shared telling responses. Power means "something frightening," said one young woman in soft English. Power means "bad or evil"; it means "violence" and "someone who monitors things," other students offered.

At the start of the workshop, it wasn't clear how much the students would get out of the discussions. Did Gene Sharp's lessons on teach-ins and walkouts really matter when protests in Tibet were violently snuffed out? Would talking about power shake a powerful establishment armed with guns and soldiers? Cynics would say no, it didn't promote freedom in Tibet, and in fact, repression had worsened in recent months. But training helped promote resistance in exile, and the Tibet in this parallel existence in India had an impact on the world, judging from media coverage and the discussions and passions it sparked.

It was easy to take protests in Dharamsala for granted, but coordinated action was a relatively new phenomenon. At the ANEC office in lower Dharamsala, decorated with portraits of the Dalai Lama and Gandhi, executive director Tenpa Samkhar acknowledged that Tibetans know that the "Buddha advocated nonviolence for all sentient beings." But peacefulness can also lead to passivity. Samkhar, a former official in the exile government, laughed at the idea of "waiting for karma after thousands of years" and letting your enemies be the victor: "You have to do something. You can't just wait patiently!"

The documentary *What Remains of Us* echoes this idea. It features Kalsang Dolma, a Tibetan Canadian woman who visits Tibet with a short video message of encouragement from the Dalai Lama. The filmmaker clandestinely shows his greeting on a portable DVD player to ordinary Tibetan people: nomads in huts on grasslands as well as young hipsters in Lhasa. Kalsang films their faces as they watch the Dalai Lama's five-minute message. Some of them, whether middle-aged nomads or elderly women or urban youth, wept immediately. I imagine it was the first time many of them had seen videos of their revered spiritual leader. Their faces had a look of stunned gravity, tearful awe, and sometimes rekindled determination. Kalsang quietly observes, "Some people thought we lost Tibet because we didn't pray hard enough. But maybe we lost Tibet because all we did was pray."

Even young people in the film who have only patchy knowledge of Tibet's modern history and current affairs grow sober and respectful at mention of the Dalai Lama. One young woman in Lhasa looked befuddled when asked about the situation in Tibet. At an open-air film screening I attended one evening in Dharamsala, the audience laughed at her innocent ignorance but became thoughtfully sober at the next exchange. "What should you not forget?" the interviewer asks from behind the camera. The girl looks puzzled for a moment, but then her face becomes composed. "So we don't forget our Tibet," she says decisively.

· · ·

In the evenings, the hunger strikers remained in the main square surrounded by flickering candles. On my way home from dinner I walked past the grimy pavement where they slept on thin cotton mattresses, just eerie lumps beneath blankets huddled together against the frigid night. During the day, they remained impassive, their faces vacant and solemn. After three days, when the noncelebration of Losar ended, shops reopened and daily commerce resumed. The hunger strikers left the main square and the corral they had occupied seemed naked without its cluster of bodies.

Conditions were tense in Tibet but remained tightly controlled except for one incident. On February 27, 2009, in Amdo Ngaba in China's Sichuan Province, a monk in his twenties named Tapey doused himself with kerosene, unfurled a Tibetan flag, and set himself on fire in the street. Chinese police shot him as he burned, said the International Campaign for Tibet, the Washington-based advocacy group. The deeper aftershock of that self-immolation would continue for well over a decade. Frustration and despair deepened, and two years later a wave of self-immolations claimed dozens of lives. By February 2013, more than 100 people had set themselves on fire in Tibet, China, Nepal, and India. By January 2015 the number exceeded 130. As of April 2022, 159 Tibetans had self-immolated.

· · ·

With nerves still raw after the first self-immolation in Amdo Ngaba, thousands gathered in Dharamsala to watch an outdoor screening of a documentary called *Murder in the Snow*. The film features until-far unpublished footage from September 2006, when Chinese soldiers shot at an unarmed group of seventy-four Tibetans fleeing over a mountain pass to Nepal. Four hundred meters from the border, shots crackle in the air and the last figure, a seventeen-year-old nun named Kelsang Namtso, falls dying in the snow. A Romanian mountain-climber filmed the incident by chance and smuggled the footage out of China.

At the screening in the main temple's courtyard, the audience watched the film while standing or sitting on the cold concrete floor. Some held candles that flickered in the dark. Tibetans murmured at scenes of the grueling foot journey out of Tibet. People clicked their tongues as shots rang out.

Sally Ingleton, the Australian filmmaker who produced *Murder in the Snow*, was in Dharamsala for the premiere. She heard about the footage when it aired on Romanian television. "I saw the footage and immediately thought, this is it, this is the film," Ingleton told me. "I felt very strongly that that girl's life had to be remembered so she didn't die in vain. I thought the story might expose the situation inside Tibet and that the atrocities continue."

Nearly all of the Tibetans trying to escape over the pass that day were caught by Chinese security and brought back to Tibet, including children. The film showed photos of young, olive-clad Chinese soldiers moving from tent to tent in climbers' camps, searching for the Tibetans.

A British mountain-climber, a police officer in the United Kingdom, was part of the expedition that witnessed the shooting. "In the UK if you shoot someone who is going away in the back, posing no threat to you whatsoever— even if they just burgled your home—that is going to be murder," he says in the film.

After the documentary, Ingleton and director Mark Gould stood beneath the screen and greeted long lines of Tibetans who thanked them for their work. Among them were a few Tibetans from the film who had managed to escape after another attempt months or years later. They included Lobsang Samten, an eighteen-year-old nun scarcely five feet tall from rural central Tibet. Even after viewing the dramatic attempt to escape Tibet, Lobsang remained calm. Why had she, at age sixteen, paid a guide $1,000 to try something so dangerous?

"We have no access to education, whether religious or normal schools," she explained to me through an interpreter. "If we try to say some prayers, the Chinese will accuse us of praying for the Dalai Lama. If you do, you could be taken to prison."

The temperature that evening was in the high thirties. I shivered in my wool hat and North Face jacket, one hand ungloved as I took notes. Lobsang seemed unaffected by the chill. One bare arm protruded from her crimson robes, hinting at her physical toughness. How did this petite woman climb the 19,680-foot Nangpa Pass after ten days of walking in regular clothes, fueled only by barley and bits of dried meat? In contrast, the foreign mountaineers in the film bundled up in Gore-Tex and high-tech winter gear, with sherpas to prepare their meals. They inched along the ice with crampons on their heavy boots while some Tibetans wore cloth sneakers.

Lobsang answered, "We kept thinking we should make it to India, we should have an audience with the Dalai Lama. Finally, I made it to India. I feel like it's a dream come true."

Now she was studying at a nunnery near Dharamsala. Other refugees in her group who managed to later escape had enrolled in Tibetan schools in India or were working.

Freedom in exile was immeasurably better for Lobsang than repression in Tibet, she said. Yet the young woman still longed for the home and family she had left behind. "I have no choice but to stay here considering what's happening inside Tibet, where there's no freedom at all," said Lobsang, pulling her shawl over her bare shoulder. "Every day I dream of going back."

And how did Lobsang feel after watching the film among thousands of other Tibetans? It was a sober conclusion to Losar, but there was also a sense of poignancy that her plight was spotlighted for audiences in Dharamsala and around the world. "What we suffered and what we've been through is not a lie," Lobsang said softly. "It's true. I'm happy it's known to the world."

[8]

Fifty Years

We Have Not Wasted the Past Fifty Years

MARCH 10, 2009

. . .

In the days before March 10, 2009, Jigmey Tsultrim, director of the Tibet Museum, put the final touches on a photo exhibition about Tibetan exiles in India. The photos were culled from some 20,000 images from the Library of Tibetan Works and Archives in Dharamsala, and from various exile government departments. The exhibition featured nearly 100 six-foot-tall panels on metal stands with printed photos. It would go on to travel packed in cases, by train and car, to Delhi and then Tibetan settlements across India, from Ladakh in the far north to Karnataka in the south. The exhibition would give "people a glimpse of what Tibetans went through when they lost their land," said Jigmey, a loquacious forty-something born in Darjeeling in northeast India. He mused that there should have been a Hindi translation, in addition to English and Tibetan. "Some people, especially local Indians, don't know about the history of Tibet. It is eye-opening," he told me.

Indian families and small groups, many from neighboring Punjab State, strolled through the Tibet Museum, a small gallery run by the exile government on the grounds of Dharamsala's main temple. I watched as they became uncharacteristically silent, suddenly tourists in their own country. The exhibition was also revealing for Tibetans themselves, some of whom lived isolated in their settlements in India. Jigmey recalled the awed response of one elderly Tibetan man from Spiti Valley, in remote northern India. Before the exhibition, he had little sense of the sprawling monasteries in southern India or the crowded assemblies of the exile government.

The grainy black-and-white photos documented Tibetan exile from its early days through modern times. Images showed how Tibetans had built a home in India from the ground up—literally—and how far they had come in fifty years. A photo from 1959 showed a youthful Dalai Lama crossing the border into India through an archway made of flowers and leaves, looking deceptively fresh despite a grueling journey marked by dysentery, terror, exhaustion, and grief after he fled Tibet on horseback and foot. More 1959 photos showed India's first Tibetan monastery in exile—low shacks with corrugated roofs—in Buxar, in the poor eastern state of Bihar. It later reopened in Karnataka where it now boasts enormous, majestic prayer halls in the settlement of Bylakuppe, about five hours drive from Bangalore, India's tech hub. In total, about 40,000 Tibetans called Karnataka home, the most in any Indian state. Bylakuppe, India's largest Tibetan settlement, claimed more than 16,000. Bylakuppe boasted expansive cornfields, handicraft centers, large, ornate monasteries, and small factories that make cement, bricks, incense, and oil. Those who built that first humble monastery in Buxar or raised steel girders on ramshackle construction sites in forests could never have imagined that in 2009 there would be more than 230 monasteries in India, with 35,000 members. Bylakuppe's Sera Monastery counted more than 3,500 monks while nearby Namdroling Monastery claimed 5,600.

The numbers are especially remarkable considering that the first 660 Tibetan settlers sent to Bylakuppe in 1960 thought they had been banished to some kind of hell. They suffered due to the heat, dense jungle, and fearsome wild elephants that attacked settlers who tried to clear the forest. Unlike Dharamsala, where a town already existed, Bylakuppe was untamed land. "We all felt so frightened and forlorn that no one could speak," said Lobsang Chonzin, an early settler, in John Avedon's book *In Exile from the Land of Snows*. "Many people sat helplessly on the ground crying to themselves. We could hear the calls of wild animals in the jungle and, unlike in Tibet, you couldn't see a thing. Wherever you looked there was nothing but trees."

How did Tibetans end up there? In the early 1960s, as tens of thousands of Tibetans fled and poured into India, it became clear they needed space beyond the small northern hill towns. Prime Minister Nehru solicited state leaders to give vacant land to the refugees. Over the years Tibetans established settlements in more than a dozen states across India, from Orissa and Chhattisgarh in the east to Maharashtra in the west, many parcels originally inhospitable wilderness.

The photo exhibition documented the dramatic changes in the conditions of Tibetan refugees over five decades. Photos from the 1960s show the Dalai Lama overseeing the community as it was literally built from the ground up; one captured him watching Tibetans plowing an expanse of unbroken soil in Bylakuppe. Another image showed a young Dalai Lama with heavy black Buddy Holly glasses observing a philosophy debate on the edge of what looks like a field. In yet another, he squats and has lunch with uniformed Tibetan schoolchildren. Back then "His Holiness had time. People really felt that His Holiness was very near to them," Jigmey reminisced. "Today how rare it is for Tibetans to see His Holiness so close."

Photos from the 1980s and 1990s were less intimately candid. More formal photo ops documented the Dalai Lama's transformation from obscure Himalayan religious leader to renowned international figure. In a 1987 image, the Dalai Lama addresses members of the US Congress. Another from 1999 shows him accepting the Nobel Peace Prize.

Fifty years of exile seems like a long, tortuous expanse of time. But a walk through the photo exhibition, where time had been telescoped into a digestible chronology, made the five decades more comprehensible. And history was still in the making. Outside the museum, demonstrations clamored almost daily in a constant reminder that the story of Tibet and its exiles was still unfolding.

. . .

In the days before March 10, hordes of visitors—journalists, activists, members of Chinese democracy groups, and Tibetan parliamentarians— descended on Dharamsala. The town had the atmosphere of a jamboree with a colorful hodgepodge of attendees.

I accompanied an international advocacy group on a visit to Dharamsala's Reception Center, where we spoke to some recently arrived refugees, including Samden Thuntsok, a forty-year-old monk who had joined March 2008 protests in Qinghai in western China. Samden, rail thin with an amiable smile, spoke to us on a terrace that overlooked bustling Jogiwara Road and looming snow peaks. The smell of burning paper prayer offerings filled the air. "It is suffocating in Tibet," he declared. "They just opened fire on protesters like animals," Samden said of the violence in Tibet earlier that month. "I couldn't stay like that, with no rights, no respect. I had to go to the streets and protest." Around March 20, 2008, he and a few other monks went to the office of their county district collector, a position akin to a mayor. Outside, monks boldly removed the Chinese flag and replaced it with the Tibet one, an act sure to evoke a harsh response. Soon, military trucks arrived in the village. A few days later, Chinese authorities started detaining Tibetans suspected of protesting. They had already put Samden on a wanted list, so escape was urgent. He fled and hid in nearby mountains. After hiding for a time, Samden walked twenty-eight days from his hometown to reach the Nepal border.

We also spoke to Ama Adhe, the septuagenarian Reception Center house mother who cared for newly arrived children. She wore an orange silk shirt beneath her *chupa*, layered with a woolen vest and striped *pangden*. With her thick glasses, long gray braids, and sunny smile she looked like a prototypical granny, not the survivor of twenty-eight years in a Chinese prison. After China's takeover in 1959, Ama Adhe was accused of helping Tibetan rebels by giving them food. She was forcibly separated from her two young children and imprisoned with 300 women, young and old. By the time Ama Adhe was released in 1987, only 4 of the original 300 prisoners had survived. Many died of starvation or injuries, or they lost their minds because they missed their children so much, she recalled.

In jail, Ama Adhe and other prisoners survived by singing, even though they were often tortured afterward as punishment. "Whenever I was tortured I tried to remember every detail so I could tell His Holiness about it. I still remember screams of pain before prisoners died," she said in *Women of Tibet: A Quiet Revolution*, a documentary film.

When Ama Adhe was finally released, her son was already dead. Her daughter, grown with her own two children, did not recognize her. "The day I was released I went home and no one was there. They had all died," she recalls in the film of her neighbors and friends. "My daughter was just a couple months old when I was taken away. She was now a grown woman like you. My son had already died. During my twenty-eight years of imprisonment my daughter had grown up, raised two children. When I was introduced as her mother, she could not relate to me. It was the same for me when I was told she was my daughter. I could not believe it."

It was difficult to move past this dark part of her life, Ama Adhe confessed. "I had enormous anger against the Chinese, but His Holiness told me it wasn't Chinese people who were responsible, but the Chinese Communist government. Ordinary Chinese people are also seeking rights and happiness. For many years I received teachings from him about anger and forgiveness. His Holiness taught me not to feel anger towards all Chinese. And now, I don't feel anger anymore." When she came to India, the Dalai Lama urged her to forgive her Chinese captors and to defuse her anger by helping children at the Reception Center.

"Even though I am not educated, I can teach with my words," she says in the film. "I remember my children crying behind me when I was arrested by the Chinese. So I feel great compassion for these children who still have parents in Tibet."

That day, when we said goodbye at the Reception Center, Ama Adhe held our hands and hugged us affectionately, wholeheartedly. On our way out we paused to talk with a seventy-four-year-old woman and her grown son who was mentally disabled and walked with a labored gait. The two of them walked arm in arm around Dharamsala. To flee Tibet, the woman and her son walked for three months to Nepal. She was eligible to live in Dharamsala's nursing home, but her son was not allowed to stay with her. They didn't want to be separated so were living in the Reception Center until a solution appeared. Why did she leave Tibet? The woman had a straightforward answer. She squinted through thick glasses and replied, "I didn't feel like living in Tibet under Chinese rule."

. . .

A few days before March 10, I ran into Topden in the main square. To get out of the honking traffic and choking exhaust, we stood near a water tank that dribbled water onto the ground. Topden talked excitedly about the four-week-long training session he had just attended at Help in Suffering, a veterinary hospital in Jaipur, Rajasthan's capital. He had observed operations, learned new procedures, and watched vets work with sick or injured dogs, donkeys, cows, horses, and even camels. "I learned so much," he gushed.

It had been an eventful few months for him. He could now drive the new pickup truck the vet clinic bought to transport sick animals. Driving stick shift up mountain roads was very challenging even for an experienced driver, but Topden apparently had learned to do so within weeks. After Shimmy died I no longer went to the clinic every day, but I sometimes dropped in to visit animals and chat with Topden. When I bumped into him in the main square, he invited me for lunch at his room before the busy days of the Dalai Lama's long-life prayer and Tibetan Uprising Day on March 10. So on Sunday morning we met at a vegetable stand off the road to Bagsu Falls. Topden wore jeans, a pullover, and sneakers while perusing bins for carrots, potatoes, and cabbage.

We walked down a path that wound through the grass to a cluster of concrete buildings. Topden proudly let me into his room: a tidy space with bright windows that looked down onto the green hillside. On the walls hung posters of the Dalai Lama wearing a bright yellow headdress curved like a bird's giant bill. There were two twin beds where he and his cousin slept. The cousin, also a monk, disapproved of Topden wearing layperson's clothes instead of his robes. This weekend, though, he was in Delhi.

I asked Topden how long his cousin would stay there, and he looked flustered for a moment before replying, a little sheepishly, "I do not ask him these things." I had been much too direct even on such a mundane question. Chagrined, I changed the subject and remarked on Topden's collection of plants. His face lit up. A flimsy wooden shelf held several potted plants whose tendrils were carefully arranged along the slats. "I love my plants very much," said Topden as he tenderly fingered a tendril. Glittery stickers of Tigger, Piglet, and Owl decorated another shelf; Winnie the Pooh was missing. A slim bookmark-sized piece of paper pasted to the side of the shelf read, "If possible, you should help others. If that is not possible, at least you should do no harm."

Along with pictures of the Dalai Lama on the wall hung posters of NBA basketball players in mid-dribble or jumping near the hoop. What was his favorite team and player again?

"Kobe Bryant. Lakers," Topden responded without hesitation. "Boston Celtics is quite fine too," he added.

On top of a low table was an antique pedal-powered sewing machine that Topden borrowed from his Indian neighbor. He proudly showed me the "drops" he had made: dark green cloth with holes cut out to lay over animals during operations at the clinic. Topden explained, "I can give them to Indian tailors, but they can't make what I think." I was impressed with his initiative and skill. Whether learning to drive or to stitch wounds on animals, Topden picked things up quickly.

He busied himself in his kitchen, which consisted of a hot plate in a corner closed off with a partition. Topden chopped carrots and cabbage and boiled rice. Through the window black-and-white cows grazed on the hillside, an Indian boy chased a pink ball, and an Indian woman emerged from one doorway with a head of dripping wet hair.

"Indians' life looks very easy but it is very difficult," Topden observed. "They have a lot of work from morning to night." Topden came to India as a teen and Hindi was his second language; he was very comfortable among Indians. Not only did he like his neighbors, but he later admitted he thought Indian women were beautiful, more so than Tibetan women.

Topden finished making lunch and heaped two plates with rice and stir-fried vegetables. We ate with plastic chopsticks and talked about basketball games on television and the coming week's events. The clinic would be closed on and ahead of March 10, so he planned to attend the Dalai Lama's long-life ceremony. Then Topden mentioned how he missed his home in

Tibet; he could not call his family to see how they were doing amid all the strife.

Suddenly I asked a question that rose in my mind whenever I heard what a refugee had given up by leaving Tibet. "Do you think it was worth it to come to India?"

Topden stopped mid-bite and looked at me wordlessly. This question was far too probing, and I regretted my American directness. Embarrassment clouded his face. He didn't answer, just looked away until his frozen expression slowly thawed.

• • •

After lunch with Topden I hurried down Bagsu Road back to town. A small group of journalists were to meet the Oracle. For 1,300 years, Tibet's leaders had consulted the state Oracle, called Nechung in Tibetan, who gives predictions while in a trance state on "virtually every key decision of state." Until recently the "inner workings of his monastery, the nature of the possession . . . had been kept strictly secret." So I was surprised that we could readily meet the Oracle's medium, also known as Kuten, or "receiving body." We spoke to him in a small reception room at the Nechung Monastery, a compact building just off the *kora*.

The title of Oracle is passed on to a new monk each generation. In 1987, three years after the death of the previous intermediary, a young monk in Dharamsala named Thupten Ngodup was verified as the next Kuten of the Oracle. Now Kuten was nearly fifty, moonfaced with a shiny pate. When he met us, he wore red robes and had a welcoming, down-to-earth demeanor as he spoke calmly through an interpreter. A tray with a small pyramid of fried pastries sat on the coffee table along with a vase of pink fabric flowers. Kuten politely offered Tibetan cookies and chocolates before answering questions about his trance state, as well as opining optimistically about changing attitudes in China.

Kuten began by warning he couldn't say anything about the annual consultation that he had recently given a few days ahead of March 10. Even if Kuten wanted to discuss it he couldn't; he was unconscious when Nechung spoke through his body from an otherworldly realm. He spoke about Nechung in the third person, like a well-regarded colleague he had worked with for a long time. What did Kuten do in his spare time when he wasn't channeling Nechung? He answered that he liked to play with his dogs and enjoyed watching Animal Planet and National Geographic programs on television.

He was a nature-lover, he confessed. Suddenly Kuten asked in perfect English, "Would you like some tea?" Apparently, he had a good understanding of English but was more confident using an interpreter.

Nechung has a rank in the exile government though he doesn't do political work, and his consultations are forwarded to the *kashag* (cabinet) and the Dalai Lama himself. In 1956, the previous Oracle instructed the Dalai Lama to go to India to establish first contacts with Nehru and the Indian government. Then in 1958, a year before the Dalai Lama's exile from Tibet, the Oracle prophesied, "In this great river where there is no ford, I, Spirit, have the method to place a wooden boat." He predicted that the Dalai Lama would have to flee Tibet.

At the Dalai Lama's long-life ceremony the next day, mild-mannered Kuten would transform into a whirling deity with bulging eyes who spat and hissed as he delivered predictions. During formal ceremonies, Kuten wore a heavy headdress and elaborate costume weighing about ninety pounds. But that didn't keep him from bending and jumping with supernatural strength during the possession, as though the ornate outfit were weightless gossamer.

What did it feel like when the Oracle channeled through his body? Kuten told us that when it first happened in 1987 it felt like electricity shot through him. Before going into trance he admitted feeling very nervous and uncomfortable. He described the sensation like turbulence on a plane, but in the next breath also as a numbness, "slowly, slowly, just like sleep. Sometimes it feels like you had a dream. It's not clear, like a different world." Sometimes the trance lasted for forty-five minutes, sometimes for ten. "Heart beats too much and there is pain here," he said in Tibetan, touching his forehead. "Afterward, I feel like the happiest man in the world."

Kuten didn't see any contradiction between his mystical vocation and modern science and education, both of which the Dalai Lama strongly supports. And when he spoke about Tibet, Kuten was practical and optimistic. "At one point, the situation in Tibet was very, very critical," he explained. "But with increasing support of people who love peace and justice and an increasing desire of Chinese people for democracy, I feel there is definitely change." He added, "The issue of Tibet is about the future of this ethnic group. It's not just about His Holiness. It's a struggle for our future. We Tibetans believe in cause and effect. This will turn around sooner or later. The Chinese government is run by a Communist system. Just in five minutes it could change! What the leader says, he can't say no to this. In America, even the president can't just decide. Maybe the day after tomorrow is good news."

Kuten recounted meeting a Chinese man from Beijing on a flight from Hong Kong during one of his trips. The man asked, "Are you staying with Dalai?" Kuten was not angry or irritated at this impolite way of referring to the Dalai Lama. After chatting with him, Kuten offered a book about the Tibetan spiritual leader that he happened to have with him. The man declined, saying the book was not allowed in China. "That's the kind of country you live in," Kuten told him patiently. "You should read it and find out for yourself."

. . .

At dawn the following day, March 9, a loud drone of chanted prayers, clanging cymbals, and bellowing trumpets burst forth from the main temple for the Dalai Lama's long-life ceremony. The courtyard and areas outside prayer halls were packed with monks and nuns, Tibetan laypeople, and a few foreigners. The Dalai Lama sat cross-legged on a platform-like "throne" at the head of the crowded central prayer hall. He had a serious expression, wore a peaked yellow hat, and tipped back and forth, rocking in his seated position while clasping his hands in prayer. The Karmapa and heads of other schools of Tibetan Buddhism sat in the front rows facing the Dalai Lama. I watched from outside the prayer hall, peering between shoulders for a glimpse of what was happening.

Eventually, the crowd stirred and the Oracle entered wearing a tall purple brocade outfit and a headdress topped with white plumes. Kuten was unrecognizable in his transformation. I couldn't see the circular mirror studded with amethyst and turquoise that he wears on his chest during ceremonies. Nor could I see his three-foot-long silver sheath and sword. But Nechung flopped backward and lurched forward as horns blasted and cymbals crashed. His jerky motions propelled him toward the front of the room. Nechung thrashed near the Dalai Lama and started to fall backward but attendants caught him and carried him out of the hall.

Noisy music continued as Tibetans lined up to make offerings of golden sculptures and books wrapped in white *khatas*. Finally the room quieted and from his seat on the marigold-laden platform the Dalai Lama said a few words in Tibetan into a microphone. Kalden Lodoe, a journalist for Radio Free Asia, translated for me: "Thank you to everyone, especially the people in Tibet, the international community, and Chinese friends who always wish me good luck. I pray that I can live long especially in times of crisis."

It was an understated reference to the simmering turmoil in Tibet. An estimated 1,200 Tibetans remained unaccounted for since China's crackdown a year ago in March 2008, according to a report from the International Campaign for Tibet. It included a list of more than 600 names of prisoners detained in the past year. Tibetans continue to "disappear," often taken from their homes in the middle of the night to "black jails." Cover-ups of tortures and killings were unprecedented, retaliation especially harsh. China's "Smash Mischievous Rumors" campaign, launched in late 2008, targeted anyone who listened to Tibet news; computers and cell phones were seized. "When you have Tibetans sentenced to five years in prison for making a phone call, that is not an indication of a strong state," said Kate Saunders, spokesperson for International Campaign for Tibet. "China presents itself on a world stage as emerging superpower . . . but genuine stability doesn't come under the barrel of a gun."

Chanting and prayers continued, but only the Dalai Lama knew what the Oracle saw in his trance that morning as he looked into an embattled future.

. . .

After months of anticipation, it was finally March 10. Well before dawn, people flocked to the main temple. The Dalai Lama and other religious leaders, exile government officials, and guests entered the courtyard and sat on the makeshift stage in a roped off area at the top of a short staircase. The ceremony began when a troupe of young men and women in traditional Tibetan dress—fur boots, fur hats, and embroidered tunics—sang and danced. A young man held the Tibetan flag while marching to bagpipes and beating drums. Musicians played a new song composed by the Tibetan Institute of Performing Arts for the fiftieth anniversary of the Tibetan Uprising and exile, followed by the Tibetan anthem.

The Dalai Lama wore his familiar crimson robes and brown oxfords. He sat with his feet crossed at the ankles and swayed and bobbed his head in time to the drums and music. When the music finished, Samdhong Rinpoche, prime minister of the exile government, addressed the crowd in Tibetan for a few moments. Then the Dalai Lama walked to the podium. He immediately turned his focus to Chinese people.

"It is a pleasure to welcome our Chinese friends who have traveled a long way," he said. Sitting next to him were at least thirty Chinese, nearly all middle-aged men, some from Taiwan and others from mainland China who had emigrated to Australia, Hong Kong, and elsewhere. They wore white *khatas* around their necks, over their suit jackets, and applauded loudly when the Dalai Lama spoke. Chin Jin, then vice chairman of the Federation for a Democratic China (FDC) whom I had met in November 2008, sat among them, near the Dalai Lama.

"We are not anti–Chinese people," the Dalai Lama began. "We still have hope and faith toward Chinese people. Many Chinese are protesting against me but some Chinese scholars still support me. There are 300 Chinese scholars and writers who have written articles in support. Most understand the Middle Way. I've met with Chinese in every part of the world who show huge concern for the Tibetan cause. . . . There is a true need for fact-finding." Although the Dalai Lama said in the past that his faith in the Chinese government was "thinning," he insisted that his faith in Chinese people was "never shaken." In a written statement from that day, the Dalai Lama appealed to "Chinese brothers and sisters" and urged them "not to be swayed by propaganda but, instead, to try to discover the facts about Tibet impartially, so as to prevent divisions among us."

When the Dalai Lama finished his speech, Chin Jin took the podium and spoke loudly into the microphone. A British accent tinged his words, perhaps from years of listening to the BBC.

"This is full acknowledgment of our Tibetan brothers and sisters. We are here to give our full support to your expectations!" he nearly shouted, as though addressing a rock concert. In contrast to the Dalai Lama's calm tones, Chin Jin spoke in a frenzied pitch. He was also less diplomatic and more forceful in his accusations and condemnations. "The CCP [Chinese Communist Party] is the root of all problems in China, including Tibet. Democracy is the only solution to solving all the problems in China." Soon the fevered timber of his voice whipped up the audience's mood. It was a familiar style in China, where public addresses were often melodramatic rallying calls. Even the Tibetan translating Chin Jin's words into Tibetan started to raise the pitch of his voice.

Chin Jin continued. "We call on Chinese people to support Tibetan people. It is for not only the freedom of Tibetan people but also Chinese people. Free Tibet can come only when democratic China is established," he cried. The audience cheered and clapped enthusiastically. After the ceremony finished and dignitaries filed off the stage, journalists rushed upstairs to a press conference in the chilly prayer hall. The Dalai Lama appeared and warmly shook the hand of an Indian cameraman. As he settled himself on a chair he disarmingly asked the audience, "Have you had lunch?"

In spite of the tensions in Tibet, the Dalai Lama faced the audience, smiled, and spread his hands out as if to innocently ask, "Now what?" He had no agenda and opened the floor to questions. A foreigner asked the first one, something to do with esoteric Buddhist philosophy. The Dalai Lama happily delved into an explanation for more than ten minutes, as though there were no pressing matters at hand.

Finally, someone asked about the significance of the fiftieth anniversary of the Tibetan exile. "There are many reasons to be thankful," the Dalai Lama began.

> Tibetan people's spirit and determination is very strong. Fifty, sixty years passed. Entirely new generation. But these young generation carry the same Tibetan spirit. Communists used various methods to distort information, brutality and imprisonment, torture, but Tibetan spirit never eliminate.
>
> More and more Chinese starting to acknowledge there is a problem. In order to have more active role in the planet, Chinese need respect and trust from the rest of the world. There are Chinese intellectuals and thinkers who totally disagree with what Chinese government does. There have been 300 articles in China since last March about this. Among Chinese there are many Buddhists. They are eager to learn from Tibetan tradition. We Tibetans are younger students of Buddha.
>
> Chinese government always accuses us of internationalizing issue. Wherever I go they always protest, so that draws attention from the media. So that's tremendously helpful to internationalize the issue. So we are grateful to the Chinese government. I constantly look back since 1959. Fifty years have passed. Where Tibetan Buddhism is today, carried continuously with full freedom. India is our spiritual hope. Buddha comes from India. Now this is home. India-Tibet relationship like guru [teacher] and *chela* [disciple].

A Taiwanese asked about the Dalai Lama's plans for Taiwan. He answered,

> I'm always eager to visit Taiwan. I want to show Han people we are not anti-Chinese. No opportunity to show my face in mainland China. So I will show my face in Taiwan. That's the right place to show my face and sincerity. In Taiwan, big number of Buddhist population. Sometimes Taiwanese ask, "Did you forget us?" with tears. But politically I always make clear: I always have responsibility

to take care of Tibet properly. If things in Tibet show improvement, if Chinese government makes improvement, then my visit to Taiwan is very different.

China deserves respect from rest of the world. Really hope new generation of leadership who are better educated in foreign countries and tasted the values of democracy. With help from these people, I think there could be a more democratic process. Then China could be a respected superpower. China has population, military, and economy. One thing lacking is moral authority. These are very bad for image of China.

The Dalai Lama paused to read from a sheet of paper that quoted the Chinese foreign minister, who accused him of pushing for Tibet's separation from China. When he finished, he looked up with an incredulous expression. Outrage filled his voice. "I am totally committed to Middle Way, not seeking separation. You are now witness. It is our long-term strategy since 1974. Since then our position is clear. Ask him!" he said, referring to the Chinese foreign minister. "These are questions of truth. I never said non-Tibetans should be removed from Tibet. Where I state? He should bring evidence!"

And what would he say to Tibetans inside Tibet? The Dalai Lama reiterated, "The feeling is understandable, but we must restrain from some crisis. Local Chinese authorities want more crisis so they can crush easily. Must keep calm."

. . .

That afternoon there was another press conference with Samdhong Rinpoche, the prime minister of the exile government. I arrived after it ended, just in time to see him walking slowly in his dark red robes toward the Dalai Lama's residence and offices. It was a sunny day and Tibetans and children filled the courtyard and romped as though on a playground.

In contrast to the crowds that always surround the Dalai Lama, Samdhong Rinpoche walked across the courtyard without attracting much attention. A lone bodyguard with a crew cut hovered a few feet from the prime minister, as though ready to catch him if he fell. I approached Samdhong Rinpoche to ask a few questions. The bodyguard didn't stop me and kept a distance as I introduced myself. Samdhong Rinpoche simply signaled to follow him. We passed through the security checkpoint of the Dalai Lama's compound into the reception area. Sometimes this room was full of people waiting to enter or to have an audience with the Dalai Lama, but that day it was empty.

The bodyguard disappeared behind a curtained doorway, and Samdhong Rinpoche and I sat down on a cushioned bench.

The prime minister was a thin man with an angular face, a hawkish nose, and a head of salt-and-pepper stubble. Nearly seventy, he had a PhD in Buddhist studies and was formerly head of the Central Institute of Higher Tibetan Studies in Sarnath.

Samdhong Rinpoche was more serious than the ebullient Dalai Lama and had an air of weariness about him. What did he think about the current situation in Tibet? The Dalai Lama had skirted around this pressing issue during the morning press conference.

With traces of fatigue in his voice, Samdhong Rinpoche sounded a cautious but ominous note. "We are very much concerned that the heavy repressiveness undertaken by the PRC might lead to some disturbances," he said. "The last more than five days, we had no news from inside Tibet. It is absolutely impossible to make contact. Yesterday, entire Tibetan areas shut down for any communication—mobile, Internet, email. Everything is completely blocked."

Days before the communication blackout, they had some news from Gyantse, one of Tibet's largest cities.

> For the whole day Gyantse was on undeclared curfew. No shops allowed to open. No vehicles. No public transportation. No one allowed to come out of homes. If Gyantse was like this, other places might be like this. Not a single journalist is left inside Tibet. There is no way to know what's happening. We heard that PRC wants disturbance so they might try repressive means. Such provocative works are not in favor of peace and stability. We are asking Tibetans to remain calm, asking PRC authorities to restrain. Asking international community not to resort to dramatic measures.

I asked Samdhong Rinpoche if he would run for prime minister again when his term ended in 2011. He replied quickly and firmly. "No, I'm too old now. Political leadership should be a secular person, a young layperson. Someone young in age would do better. Fortunately, our constitution does not allow me to be prime minister again." Tibetan exiles were now in their third generation, and someone in their forties or late thirties would be an ideal age, he explained. "I very much hope there will be lots of candidates."

Samdhong Rinpoche seemed to visibly relax when I asked what the fiftieth anniversary of Tibetan exile meant to him. He sat up a little straighter and, for a moment, his fatigue vanished. In the exhibition at the Tibet Museum, there were photos of Samdhong Rinpoche from over the decades. One showed him as a much younger man, his face not yet gaunt and strained. Some of that vitality returned for a moment.

"My memories of my life spent in Tibet are more clear than memories of yesterday," he declared nostalgically. Samdhong Rinpoche looked into the distance and smiled. "I remember the colors and shapes of trees in our monastery and the friends we debated with. The last fifty years have seen tremendous change, unbelievable change. So I'm satisfied in many ways. The last fifty years have been the darkest in our history. But Tibetan culture has spread to all corners of the world. His Holiness is respected all over the world. That is a great achievement. We have modern education and at the same time traditional education. We must be satisfied."

In spite of his weariness, Samdhong Rinpoche was hopeful about the future. "The rigidness of Chinese leadership will also change. I hope the next leadership will be more open and transparent," he explained. "Sooner or later, China will have to be more democratic. Then the Tibet issue will be properly resolved. We have not wasted the past fifty years. We have used them properly."

. . .

Later that afternoon at McCllo's, the seedy restaurant-pub above the bus station in the main square, I met with Lhadar, a young Tibetan in his twenties. Lhadar was from Dharamsala but had immigrated with his family to Australia as a teenager. He'd recently graduated from Australian National University in Canberra and was back in town to visit relatives. Lhadar wore jeans, sneakers, and an olive canvas jacket, and he spoke with broad Australian vowels. He had a mellow, congenial manner even as he recounted his tense experience in the summer of 2008 at a demonstration in Canberra against the Olympic torch.

Lhadar recalled that a few hundred Tibetans came to Canberra to protest when the Olympic torch passed through the capital en route to Beijing. Their numbers were dwarfed by the thousands of Chinese who flocked to the Australian capital in support. It was believed that many of them came on buses organized by the Chinese government.

"When you were there, you felt like you were caught up in the Cultural Revolution. There were red flags everywhere," said Lhadar, whose mother and brother also participated in the pro-Tibet demonstration. "It was extremely hostile. It was a cross between a war and a mob of hooligans. It was like they were preparing for war or something," Lhadar recounted. "They were swearing at us in English and throwing stuff. It was kind of sad right from the start. They called us scum and running dogs. It was clear that they absolutely hated us. They were pretty worked up and some Tibetans were beaten up. There is television footage of Tibetans being beaten with the Chinese flag. I was shocked. I didn't expect them to behave that way. They must have been caught up in the frenzy. I read on blogs some Chinese saying Tibetans should be eliminated."

Lhadar was remarkably composed and his voice lacked anger. He explained, "We don't think of ourselves as anti-Chinese. When we meet Chinese, we don't think of them as the enemy. We're taught to think in terms of the interests of everyone. Our parents told us we should be friends with Chinese people. At the end of the day, I was proud of Tibetans. I was proud that we were able to keep self-control."

Tibetans stayed composed despite incendiary comments shouted at them. "The Chinese were saying, 'You've never been in Tibet. You don't know what the real situation is,'" he recalled. Yet among the Tibetans were those who had indeed grown up in Tibet. To add insult to injury, some had been political prisoners tortured in China's prisons.

How did they manage to remain calm? "We know by acting in a reckless way we are disrespecting His Holiness," explained Lhadar. "That's the only reason why the event didn't escalate into something more violent. We had to comfort a lot of Tibetans who broke down and started crying. We needed a police escort to leave." He paused and shifted from the grim memory. "Hopefully over the long run, Chinese will have access to free media and will realize that there's another side to the story."

Yet Chinese in Australia did have access to free media. Many of them were likely graduate students studying abroad and part of an educated elite. The troubling situation had seeped into Lhadar's core. It was all extremely sad, he admitted as sipped his Coke. "I'm Australian but there's a certain side of me that is always in pain."

[9]

I Still Have Faith in Chinese People

Just an Ordinary Chinese Democracy Campaigner

MARCH 10, 2009

. . .

Hotel Tibet had a worn, nondescript restaurant that was nonetheless favored by Tibetans and members of the exile administration. They especially liked the bar, a dim lounge with tumblers of whiskey, heavy chairs, and a menu of fried Indian snacks like *pakoras*—battered fried lumps that were once vegetables. Close to the main square in McLeod Ganj, the hotel was a convenient spot to meet Chin Jin, the Chinese democracy activist, on the evening of March 10. As usual, Chin Jin bubbled with energy even after a full day of meetings and events that began onstage with the Dalai Lama on a historic anniversary. After talking for a couple of hours, we were the last patrons when the bar closed.

Although it was Tibetan Uprising Day, our far-ranging conversation gravitated toward China and then eventually to the Dalai Lama's ardent outreach to Chinese people. That underscored why the Dalai Lama had singled me out, hugged me during my first visit to Dharamsala, and said that Tibet and China must talk.

Chin Jin gestured effusively as he explained that many Chinese who oppose his work ask him, "Chin Jin, do you support independence for Tibet?" His standard reply: "The majority of Tibetans do not claim independence for Tibet though they have the right to ask for independence." He clarified his own view in his typically frank manner. "I'm not a separatist. I wish China becomes bigger. We could claim territory back from Russia. The most important thing to me is to make China more democratic. I hope Taiwan can be a beacon, a model for the process of democratization of mainland China. If China collapses, only ordinary people will suffer, not the officials in power.

They are prepared to flee. High officials have prepared foreign passports and foreign reserves so they can still enjoy their lives for many generations."

Although China's government has oppressed Tibet for more than half a century, Chinese people have also been repressed during decades of turmoil and tragedy. China weathered civil war from 1927 until 1949 when the Communist Party and Chairman Mao took control. More chaos ensued through the 1970s. From 1958 to 1962, during Mao's ill-fated Great Leap Forward, at least 45 million people died of starvation, including 2.5 million tortured or summarily killed, according to some estimates. Then during the infamously brutal Cultural Revolution from 1966 until Mao's death in 1977, between 500,000 and 2 million people were killed in China.

Context about China is important, and for Tibet's future it is of course essential. Chin Jin offered that perspective, albeit one as a Chinese dissident. I first met him in November 2008 when a group of Chinese democracy activists visited Dharamsala during a special summit of Tibetan exile leaders. In his mid-forties, he spoke with an earnest air tempered by unabashed, sometimes biting, candor. Chin Jin's tone switched from amused and brash irreverence to respect when he talked about the Dalai Lama. "His Holiness is always encouraging. This is my sixth meeting with him. This is another time to be inspired by his patience, forbearance, and wisdom," he said sincerely. "I'm really, really lucky."

Then Chin Jin laughingly recounted that some Chinese "supporters" advised him to "make use of close contact with the Dalai Lama and borrow money from him. 'If Chin Jin is not selfish, he should do that.'" they lectured. It was peculiar advice, but, Chin Jin insisted, "It's not a joke!"

Chin Jin was born in Shanghai and happened be studying English in Australia in 1989 when the Tiananmen Square protests broke out in Beijing. Australia's government offered asylum to Chin Jin and other stranded Chinese nationals. "The Australian government—they are so nice!" he exclaimed. He became interested in China's democracy movement even though he hadn't paid attention to those issues before. In 1992, he heard the Dalai Lama speak in Australia and was so inspired that he also became involved with the Tibet movement. Meanwhile, Chin Jin studied English, read books on politics and history, and wrote opinion pieces for Chinese-language newspapers in Australia. As vice chairman of the activist group Federation for a Democratic China, he wanted to work with the Dalai Lama to form a broader coalition between the Chinese democracy movement and four other groups at odds with China's government: Tibetans, Mongolians, Taiwanese, and Uyghurs—Muslim minorities from the western province of Xinjiang.

Of course, his dissenting views made him radioactive in China. On a 1997 visit home to Shanghai, authorities stopped Chin Jin when he arrived at the airport. "They said, 'Chin Jin, you are so bold. You still have a Chinese passport.' They blamed me as a traitor. For forty-eight hours they questioned me. No torture," he clarified. The detention didn't scare him. Chin Jin shrugged. "The worst they could do is put me in jail. Or capital punishment," he said without a trace of irony. Authorities allowed him to stay in China, but he was followed by secret police wherever he went for the next month. "They tried to use the 'unity' policy to make me give up what I was doing," he scoffed.

In 2005, Chin Jin visited China again. He had a two-month visa, but when he arrived in Shanghai, authorities canceled it and interrogated him for nine hours. They let him go with a much shorter visa, and minders followed him for eight days. Was he afraid for his family who remained in China? "No," Chin Jin replied without hesitation. In Australia he sometimes spoke by phone to his brother who begged him to stop his political work. "I tell him, 'Okay, you did your job. Now you can stop. Whoever is listening to our conversation heard you say it. Now you can stop,'" said Chin Jin nonchalantly.

During Chin Jin's first encounter with the Dalai Lama in Australia in 1992, he was surprised at the spiritual leader's openness and encouragement. "I was just an ordinary Chinese democracy campaigner," he recalled, still amazed. After that, Chin Jin's activism work grew in earnest with a focus on Tibet. When the Dalai Lama visited Sydney in 2007, Chin Jin helped organize a talk attended by 230 Chinese people. In June 2008, more than 300 Chinese came to a similar discussion. Chin Jin felt a rapport with the Dalai Lama and took his advice to heart. "Twelve years ago, he held my hand and said, 'Never lose hope.' Twelve years on, I am still wholeheartedly working for the movement," he told me.

I first saw Chin Jin interact with the Dalai Lama in November 2008 during the Dharamsala summit that drew Tibetan exile leaders from around the world to discuss Tibet's crisis. At a press conference, Chin Jin boldly stood up and asked the spiritual leader whether there was any possibility for Tibetans and Chinese to work together for democracy. That offered the Dalai Lama a chance to give a long reply about the relationship between Tibetans and Chinese.

"After Tiananmen, a number of Han people often came to see me," recalled the Dalai Lama. "We have long talk with some of the Chinese who are really concerned about democracy. By nature, it is the individual's right to be free. Every human desire is for freedom. Even in China it is getting stronger and stronger. *Wo wangquan tongyi*," he said in Mandarin. *I totally agree.*

"After 10 March, we really felt Chinese leadership might have the courage to face reality. They missed out on a realistic approach. . . . I really hope things may change. If they really accept reality, we are ready to cooperate. We are not seeking independence. We are not seeking separation. But they simply suppressed. Now the Tibetan nation is almost passing through a death sentence. They are trying to eliminate Tibetan spirit and culture. Once a country's spirit is gone, that's death, isn't it?

"Any Chinese reporters here?" called out the Dalai Lama, searching the audience in the main temple's prayer hall. Again he reached out to Chinese people, but he was met with silence. "I am willing to extend an invitation. Stay here for one week as my guest to conduct a thorough investigation. Before, I said they can come examine my stool." He reminded the audience of his irreverent jest earlier in March 2008, explaining, "Some Chinese leaders say Dalai Lama has Hepatitis B. Cancer patient." He became serious again. "My faith in Chinese government is getting thinner and thinner but I still have faith in Chinese people."

As the Dalai Lama traveled the world to talk about Buddhism and interfaith dialogue in the aftermath of March 2008, Chinese demonstrators showed up to rally against him, but he often met them for talks. "In Rochester, I met some Chinese protestors. I explained that we are not anti-Chinese. We are supportive of the Olympics. Only two people were listening to my explanation. Five did not listen. Too much emotion! Too much anger! Luckily there was a big table or they would slap me! . . . I try my best to meet Chinese media people, Chinese-language newspaper. My faith in Chinese people is never shaken."

Tenzing Sonam and Ritu Sarin, a husband-wife and Tibetan-Indian filmmaking team based near Dharamsala, followed the Dalai Lama around the world for a year throughout 2008 for their documentary *The Sun behind the Clouds*. Tenzing told me that the Dalai Lama was almost obsessive in trying to meet with Chinese people wherever he went. Although the Dalai Lama had been doing this for years, his outreach to Chinese people intensified after March 2008. He regularly gave special teachings to people from Taiwan, Singapore, and Malaysia. When home in Dharamsala, he eagerly gave intimate audiences to ethnic Chinese people from China, Taiwan, and elsewhere.

The Tibetan exile administration always warmly welcomed Chin Jin and other Chinese democracy activists. Indeed, they were special guests onstage for the fiftieth anniversary of March 10 that morning. The previous November after I serendipitously met Chin Jin on the street, I accompanied him and other Chinese activists to a meeting with Sonam Dagpo, the exile administration's secretary of international relations. At Chin Jin's invitation I jumped into their minivan taxi and rode with him down a winding road to the cluster of government buildings a mile from McLeod Ganj.

"We have always believed we need to outreach to our Chinese brothers and sisters," said Sonam, a thin bespectacled man in his forties, in his office during the meeting. In 1994 the exile administration established a China desk to produce Chinese-language magazines for overseas Chinese, and later a website in Chinese. "We must have nonviolence so we won't have bad relations with Chinese in the future. Hatred is very dangerous. Nonviolence is mutually beneficial."

Chin Jin chimed in. "The best chance is to resolve the Tibetan issue in the Dalai Lama's lifetime. If the Chinese government waits for the demise of the Dalai Lama, it will be very dangerous. Tibetans have universal respect for the Dalai Lama. Otherwise there is the danger of pockets of violence in Tibet."

Sonam agreed. "It is frightening to whip up anti-Tibet feelings of young Chinese, so we have an added responsibility to reach out to Chinese who are interested in Tibet. Our quarrel is with the Chinese government. We have no quarrel with ordinary Chinese. To use young Chinese nationalists to crush Tibet is very dangerous and not responsible. It leads to retaliation. How can government create such hatred between two countries?"

The free-ranging banter between the government official and Chinese activists continued. "There have been three decades of economic growth in China," Chin Jin remarked. "It's a miracle, but the Chinese government can't sustain it for all. China's economy booming is fantastic, but it can't last long. Disillusionment will come. Totalitarianism is sunset politics. Democracy is sunrise politics. We are on the right side of history. I want to use this phrase!" Chin Jin grinned. "Their days are numbered."

David Chien, a businessman from Taiwan and part of the Federation for a Democratic China, spoke up. David warned that China should not "take advantage of Tibetan's peace-loving habit. If the Chinese government doesn't take advantage of the opportunity to negotiate with His Holiness—" his voice trailed off. "I don't want to see Tibet becoming Palestine, using violence. That would be disaster. Tibetans are running out of patience."

Chin Jin added, "The Chinese government should treasure this opportunity that the Dalai Lama is still alive and willing to take this peaceful route."

Near the end of the meeting Chin Jin cheerfully told an anecdote about protesting the Chinese president Jiang Zemin's visit to Australia in 1999. A motley crew of demonstrators gathered outside the Intercontinental Hotel in Sydney representing what China calls the *Wu Du*, or "Five Poisons": Chinese pro-democracy activists, Muslim Uyghurs from Xinjiang, Taiwanese, Tibetans, and Falun Gong, the spiritual group that China considers a cult. Just three Chinese pro-democracy demonstrators, including Chin Jin, showed up. He decided to stand next to the Falun Gong protesters, but they shouted at him, "No keep away! We are not a political group!"

"There was no place for me to stand," Chin Jin chuckled.

David had the final word. Homonyms abound in the Chinese language, and the word *du* meaning "poison" sounds like another more auspicious word. "We don't mind if they call us Wu Du," David said, amused. He traced the air with a finger to write the strokes of its homonym Chinese character. "*Du* can also be the word for independence."

. . .

Back at Hotel Tibet as the last hours of the March 10 anniversary approached, Chin Jin was still surprisingly optimistic about China's opening up and democratizing. "In the next three to five years, change will start. Next twenty years will be change for sure. I'm very confident. I believe in destiny. Someone said to me, when you are seventy-one, you can happily see the big change already."

What could the Federation for a Democratic China do for Tibet? I asked. Chin Jin rattled off a well-rehearsed though sincere summary.

> We are here to give Tibetans our support. We want to form a coalition in Europe that could give inspiration to people. We want people inside China to fight for their rights, to fight for democracy. Freedom of Tibet is part of our movement. Democracy means everyone has freedom to think, speak, move around and choose their government. So free Tibet. We should treat them equally, invite them to keep their own language, culture, and religion. Tibetans and His Holiness do not claim for independence. They just want meaningful autonomy. Chinese people should not be brainwashed. Chinese people should open their eyes and ears to see the truth.

I thought of Lhakdar's experience in Australia in 2008 with the crowd of hostile pro-China protestors. Chin Jin had also been in Canberra for those Olympic torch protests. "It was a vast sea of red flags," he remembered. "Nationalism is the trump card that China is playing. I hope nationalism will be the last trump card. The Chinese government masterminded the protests in Canberra. They provided the buses so people came from different parts of Australia."

Last call at Hotel Tibet came and went and staff began to tidy the lounge. We left the bar and emerged onto a darkened street. Street dogs trotted down the middle of the road then shadowed us as we walked.

The next morning, I met Chin Jin to resume our conversation in his budget guesthouse restaurant. Backpackers ate breakfast as sunlight streamed through windows. Chin Jin was chipper as ever as he dove into a discussion about China. Protests were on the rise across the country, he pointed out. There were 80,000 mass protests in China in 2005 alone, mostly by peasants, migrant workers, or laid-off workers asking for basic livelihood rights. Ordinary people need more awareness that they had rights to fight for, said Chin Jin.

What about people who said that democracy was an alien form of government that could not be adopted in China? I asked. Chin Jin grinned. "Democracy? My advice is: 'Taste it.' Chinese people *can* enjoy democracy but people in China don't have this awareness. They accept the status quo. We are trying our best to spread these ideas." This was no easy task in China, where challenging ideas was broadly discouraged. Plus, the younger generation was increasingly removed from the profound hardship experienced by their forebears during China's tumultuous decades of war, famine, and bitter political upheaval. They were satisfied with the upward mobility of their lives, he opined.

"Very few young people have ideas that China needs change because they benefited from the regime. People in coastal cities have no idea about democracy. In remote areas, they have no idea what is democracy and human rights." This absence of young people interested in a democratic China greatly concerned Chin Jin. "In ten years who will take over our job? Young people don't care. We encourage young people inside China to wake up. We need mass movement. It is hopeless to wait for the Chinese government to change their mind."

In spite of its grand name, the Federation for a Democratic China had little support from Chinese or foreigners; there was not enough interest from the masses, Chin Jin acknowledged. Chinese democracy "celebrities" don't have the vision to breathe life into the movement, and he derided their "five minutes of enthusiasm." The numbers were telling. After the 1989 Tiananmen Square protests in Beijing, the FDC had 3,000 members, but in successive years, the group's base shrunk. In 2009 there were just a few dozen members. The FDC is headquartered in Australia because Chin Jin lives there; it lacks bases in other countries. "After Tiananmen Square in 1989, people were so frustrated and angry at the Chinese government. Now overseas Chinese want to live quietly, happily outside China. Chinese people don't have the guts," Chin Jin remarked with disgust.

He wondered why Tibet got so much international support while the issue of a democratic China remained overlooked. "There is no free Tibet without free China," he insisted. "How much effort did it take for the Tibet activists to raise that Free Tibet banner?" He was referring to a protest at Everest Base Camp by Students for a Free Tibet ahead of the 2008 Olympics. The activists unfurled a banner at the foot of Mount Everest and did a live webcast before authorities intervened and eventually kicked them out of China. A huge amount of planning, coordination, and risk must have gone into that high-profile protest.

"But they are actually hurting their own cause!" Chin Jin cried. A Free Tibet banner antagonized Chinese people. Why didn't those activists hang a banner that read, "Human Rights? Democracy in China? Or simply, Freedom?" he asked. Those were concepts that a Chinese person could align with, whereas "Free Tibet" angered them and fired up defensive nationalistic sentiments. "A Free Tibet banner *helps* the Chinese government. These Westerners don't understand that if we have democracy in China we will have free Tibet. Free Tibet and free China could be born at the same time."

. . .

On March 31, 1959, after a harrowing escape from Tibet during China's siege, after an arduous journey over snowy mountain passes, the Dalai Lama crossed into India and into exile riding a yak. On March 31, 2009, the fiftieth anniversary of that momentous day, the Dalai Lama crisscrossed Delhi to visit a mosque, a Hindu temple, a Christian church, a Jewish synagogue, a Buddhist temple, and Gandhi's last residence during a morning marathon of prayer with leaders and followers of different spiritual faiths. Finally, in the afternoon he addressed the media at a luxury hotel in Delhi while sitting cross-legged on an armless Queen Anne chair. He took a moment to wiggle out of his sandals first. The weather had warmed, and his footwear changed with the seasons.

Energized and alert despite the day's hectic schedule, the Dalai Lama scanned the audience as though looking for familiar faces. He still had a *tilak*, a saffron-colored dot on his forehead, that had been bestowed on him at the Hindu temple, and he chuckled that he would leave it on. The Dalai Lama's face creased into a familiar amused expression as he laughed. Then he grew sober as he spoke. Tibet was in the midst of crisis and people were suffering deeply, he said. Tibet was under unofficial martial law, with foreign journalists kicked out and barred from entering weeks before the fiftieth anniversary of the Tibetan Uprising on March 10.

A Chinese reporter for one of China's government newspapers asked the final question and repeated what a couple of other journalists had already asked: What could be done to revive stalled talks with China and Tibet? The Dalai Lama had answered the earlier questions by saying his envoys were prepared to talk so long as China was serious about negotiations. This time, though, he bluntly stated that the world knew his stance already. The press conference ended, and the Dalai Lama departed with the usual horde of photographers, cameramen, and reporters hustling after him.

I got up and made a beeline for the Chinese reporter. I didn't want to argue with him. I had never met a journalist from China at any of the Dalai Lama's press conferences, so I genuinely wanted to know what he thought. The reporter was young, articulate, and spoke English confidently. He also argued with an assurance that teetered on cockiness. The Chinese journalist assured me that the picture of suffering and despair in Tibet was not true, that things were fine there. I could go there myself and see, he suggested. He did not budge when I said foreign journalists were barred from entering Tibet; just a couple of weeks before, reporters from US and UK media were turned away by Chinese police when they tried driving into Tibet.

"Well, they are Western media," he explained matter-of-factly. "They are biased and if they go to Tibet they will create trouble."

"So all Western media is biased," I said.

"Yes."

"And you don't think there's a problem in Tibet? You think everything is fine?"

"Definitely," he replied, almost laughing at my question.

I repeated my question.

"Definitely everything is fine," he stated again.

We calmly continued our exchange and a couple of young Indian reporters joined us.

One earnestly asked whether there were really concentration camps in China, which sent the Chinese reporter into peals of laughter. "China is a modern country!" he cried in disbelief. "How can these things happen in a modern country?" He looked at us with a serious expression. "China is not different from your countries except we can't vote and don't have freedom of speech."

"That's a pretty big difference," commented the Indian reporter, whose frankness reminded me why I loved India.

What about political prisoners in Tibet and long lists compiled by advocacy groups of Tibetans arrested after China's 2008 crackdown? The reporter scoffed, saying there wasn't enough space to put all the prisoners. One group listed 6,700 Tibetans arrested and included names, ages, and the cities and villages they hailed from. "How about those lists?" I asked. "Why doesn't China just produce those people and say, 'Here they are, they're fine,' if they haven't really been arrested?" He looked at me and paused. "So? Those lists are fake?"

"Yes, they are fake," he said decisively.

"And all these stories that people have about their time in prison, those are fake?"

"Yes. They are fake."

With China's crackdown, it was not easy to get or verify information from Tibet. Still, 6,700 names would be a vast number to falsify. As best they could, advocacy groups cross-checked information from multiple sources. Cell phone photos, and videos were electronically sent out of Tibet at great risk.

I recalled that cold day in Dharamsala when I sat next to Norbu to watch the rehearsal of the play staged by former prisoners and the abnormal sight of Tibetan monks and nuns marching in perfect military formation. What would the Chinese reporter have said about that surreal and sobering scene? What would he say when years later, photos emerged of prisons and internment camps where at least 1 million Uyghurs were detained? After 2018, more photos and evidence of those camps continued to surface. Would he say that reports about China's shocking repression of its Muslim minorities were fabricated? Perhaps he would simply have said that aerial photos of vast prisons and detention centers in Xinjiang were fake too.

[10]

Women of Tibet

I'm Fighting a Sort of War

MARCH 12 TO APRIL 2009

. . .

In the days after March 10, wariness and anxiety lingered about what could still happen in locked-down Tibet. Rallies and vigils continued in Dharamsala, and soon small posters of a stylized drawing of a Tibetan woman in a striped *pangden* appeared, plastered on walls and bulletin boards. The woman held a fist aloft in the air and tilted her head resolutely, like a Tibetan version of Rosie the Riveter. On March 12, crowds gathered at the main temple to commemorate the fiftieth anniversary of Tibetan Women's Uprising Day, a lesser-known but significant milestone when on March 12, 1959, thousands of Tibetan women gathered outside the Potala Palace in Lhasa to protest China's siege of Tibet.

Decades later, March 12 remained vivid in the Dalai Lama's memory, and he called the women who gathered at the Potala Palace that day "heroines." In the documentary *Women of Tibet: A Quiet Revolution*, he reminisced that "they carried the struggle not just for political reasons but to defend the Buddha Dharma. They had the courage to face the consequences." It was "as if they already knew the feminist movement!" the Dalai Lama chortled, knowing that the Tibet of 1959 was closed off from the world, and that Tibetan women had no inkling of feminist movements brewing in other parts of the globe. "But of course, they had no idea. . . . I think that is perhaps in Tibetan history the first time. Women's movement—that's, I think, very remarkable."

The Tibetan Women's Association, an activist group in Dharamsala, organized a day of anniversary events for Tibetan Women's Uprising Day. A morning ceremony took place in the main temple courtyard, complete with speeches by several female Tibetan leaders in front of a packed audience, and the release of a caged dove. Afterward, people perused a photo exhibition documenting the role of women in Tibet and in exile. A grainy black-and-white photo from March 12, 1959, showed a sea of women, many with long braids, dressed in *chupas* and *pangdens*, standing at the foot of the Potala Palace.

A startling photo from September 26, 1969, documented a dramatic example of Tibetan women's resistance: a woman with a shaved head bent over, pain contorting her face as two Chinese policemen held her down. The caption read, "Thinley Chodon, nun that emerged as a guerrilla leader in a large-scale rebellion of 1969, minutes before her execution. Over thirty others were also executed." Chodon was said to have killed many Chinese soldiers through the guerrilla movement she organized.

Among the crowd of Tibetans looking at the exhibition was Tsering Deckyi, a petite seventy-year-old with a deeply wrinkled face and rheumy bluish eyes. Over her brown *chupa* she wore a maroon cardigan embroidered with flowers. A khaki sun hat perched on top of silver hair. Tsering studied the photo of Thinley Chodon for a moment and then said, "I was there."

A Tibetan friend translated the older woman's Tibetan words into English for me. We learned that Tsering and her elder sister were in the crowd with thousands who witnessed Chodon's public execution in Lhasa. "It was shocking. I felt very sad. Afterward, every day I was crying with my sister," Tsering recalled.

Chinese authorities imposed a curfew on Lhasa and the sisters huddled at home in terror. They were convinced that the Chinese would "wipe away the Tibetan people." As her eyes welled up with tears, Tsering told me, "From that day onward, I knew the Chinese are killing Tibetans. It is only His Holiness who can save Tibetans. We prayed for his long life. We had this hope because His Holiness is still alive." Tsering blew her nose loudly into a handkerchief, and tears rolled freely down her face.

Tsering lived in Lhasa all her life until she got a Chinese passport and came to India in 2000 on a bus from Nepal. How did she feel after decades of living in Lhasa under China's rule? Was she frustrated that there was no real progress toward religious and cultural freedom in Tibet? "I'm not at all frustrated," she replied. "With the presence of His Holiness and coming to a different country, I'm not at all depressed. I have not lost my hope."

Every day, Tsering walked the *kora* in Dharamsala and came to the main temple to do prostrations, clasping her hands in prayer before her chest, bending down, laying the full length of her wizened body on the ground, over and over again. Wood planks for prostration in front of the temple were worn to a silky softness from the touch of so many bodies.

"I have suffered so much under the Chinese government. Prostrations are not at all a hardship for me." Tsering admitted that due to duress she had become mentally unstable in Tibet, but here in exile she was happy. "It is because of His Holiness," she said. "I don't need anything because His Holiness is here."

More recent photos showed the contemporary resistance of Tibetan women in exile. A March 12, 1989, image showed Tibetan women in Dharamsala burning pictures of Chinese government officials to protest martial law in Lhasa. Another iconic image showed a row of Tibetan women wearing *chupa* and *pangden*, hands clenched together to form a human chain, standing with gags over their mouths at the UN Conference on Women in Beijing in 1995.

Bymo Tsering, the bespectacled president of Tibetan Women's Association and a former biology teacher, was also in the courtyard after the morning's anniversary ceremony. Before 1959, Tibetan women had mostly been excluded from politics and activism, and typically only well-to-do families sent girls to school. Bymo explained, "Tibetan women were outspoken, but not in public. The Tibetan Women's Uprising was a historical event. I feel proud because Tibetan women didn't participate in government, but when the nation was at risk they just came out onto the streets."

· · ·

That evening, after a candlelight march to commemorate Tibetan Women's Uprising Day, the documentary *Women of Tibet* had its debut screening in the temple courtyard. Nuns, mothers, young women in jeans, schoolgirls, and grandmothers packed the courtyard in equal numbers as men and boys. The audience alternated between laughter and solemn silence as they listened to Tibetan women, ranging in age from their twenties to seventies, who had been interviewed in the film. People chuckled when Ama Adhe from the Reception Center appeared onscreen and fondly described her early years in Tibet. "We rode horses a lot and tried to impress each other with our riding skills," the septuagenarian recalled, bobbing her long gray braids. Her memories darkened when she recalled the twenty-eight years she spent in prison for helping Tibetan rebels.

The audience laughed at footage of the Tibetan filmmaker's toddlers playing with each other at the Tibetan Children's Village. In the 1960s, a woman named Kelsang Takla helped run the nursery for refugee children that would become TCV. "One hundred and fifty [children] would come and, in a week, ten would be dead of dysentery," Kelsang recalled in the film.

Other Tibetan women, from exile administration officials to young women just starting their careers, also appeared. Tenzin Peldon talked about her work as a radio journalist at the Voice of Tibet, which operates from Dharamsala but is aired over shortwave into Tibet if signals are not blocked. Peldon, in her twenties, spoke earnestly to the camera. "I'm proud that though I've never been to Tibet, my voice is heard every day there. I think I'm doing exactly what the women in the 1959 Tibetan Uprising did. Even though I'm not directly face to face with the Chinese people—I'm not shooting against anything—but I'm fighting a sort of war."

A former education minister in the exile government and previous president of the Tibetan Women's Association, Rinchen Khando Choegyal also spoke in the film. Khando, looking refined with her silver hair swept into a bun, recalled her early memories when she came to India in 1959 as a child. "We thought that at the most we would be here for ten years and then would go back to Tibet." She helped revive the Tibetan Women's Association in the 1980s after the group's original incarnation, established in Tibet in 1959, dissolved with China's takeover. She also happened to be married to the Dalai Lama's youngest brother, Tenzin Choegyal.

A few weeks earlier, I had interviewed Khando at her office in Dolma Ling, a new nunnery about a twenty-minute drive from Dharamsala. She told me that in the early years of exile, she would never have predicted that Tibetan women would take such an active political role. Yet with the Dalai Lama's encouragement, the influence and status of Tibetan women steadily increased over the years, and they became more involved in the politics, activism, and religious life of Tibet's exile community. In 2009, the forty-six-member Tibetan exile parliament had a quota of at least six women; eleven female members served in parliament that year, though Khando said that was not enough. There had been several female cabinet ministers since 1990, but men still far outnumbered women in the exile government's high ranks.

"Everywhere half of population is women," said the Dalai Lama in *Women of Tibet*. "Women's participation in building up society is very important, especially in the preservation of Tibetan culture. Preservation of Tibetan culture is not in a museum, not in a school, but in the family. That's very important."

The Dalai Lama formed his vision for women early on. Shortly after fleeing to India, the Dalai Lama's first priority was to set up Tibetan schools for children. Girls should attend these schools in equal numbers as boys, he decreed. Then, when he established an exile government in the 1960s, he went out of his way to include women in his "experiment with democracy." This radical step pushed against history: Tibetan women were traditionally seen as the "jewel of the home" and did not usually participate in politics.

"Some of us used to sit and talk and say we should be more active as women," Khando told me of a period in the 1980s. "Then His Holiness [the Dalai Lama] said, 'By the way, what happened to Tibetan women?' This made us say, 'Oh, this is really the time. . . . Without him I don't think we could have done as much as we've done as women.'"

. . .

By late spring, the sun warmed Dharamsala during the day, though nights were still chilly. I packed up my wool blankets but kept the duvet folded on my bed where Wangmo, the nunnery cat, languidly napped. Mosquitoes still found their way into my third-floor bedroom.

The nunnery was quiet since residents stayed in their rooms most of the time except for meals, which divided the day into neat sections. At 7:00 a.m., noon, and 6:00 p.m., the cook, a tiny, wizened woman, clanged a bell to signal that food was ready. On cue, doors opened down the hallway as nuns headed to the kitchen, bowls and utensils (usually a spoon) in hand. In the kitchen, from battered pots and a wok, each person heaped a bowl with rice, dal, and vegetables such as mushy eggplant or overcooked green beans.

Sometimes there were Tibetan meals such as *thukpa* noodle stew, or *tingmo*, coiled lumps of steamed dough; and occasionally vegetable *momos*. Breakfast usually consisted of freshly made chapatis, which the nuns ate with peanut butter or fruit jam, and sweet milky Indian tea.

The nuns usually went back to their rooms to eat, but if the weather was pleasant they sat on the terrace down the hall from the kitchen with plastic chairs in various states of decay and a plastic patio table. Scraggly geraniums and sprigs of herbs grew in pots. Big, brown-furred monkeys often cavorted on the roof and balconies of adjacent buildings. According to nunnery lore, a gang of monkeys once got tangled up in a clothesline and then raced about the hillside wearing women's underwear.

The nunnery closed at 10:00 p.m. when a nun pulled the steel accordion gate shut with a loud screech and secured it with a padlock. This was a terrible fire and earthquake hazard, but the nuns weren't worried about being trapped in a concrete box on a hill in a high-risk earthquake zone. Eventually I realized I could climb over the balcony railing outside my room and walk on the building's ledge to the hill behind the nunnery. I didn't know whether to be comforted by the knowledge it was possible to escape, or be alarmed it was so easy to get inside. Since I was the only resident who came home after 10:00 p.m., the nuns gave me a padlock key so I wouldn't have to kick and rattle the metal grate with my hiking boot to get someone to let me in.

The nuns and the cook hailed from Kinnaur in Himachal Pradesh close to Tibet. They could speak Kinnauri and Hindi fluently but learned Tibetan only during their studies. The nuns had the same roommate for years on end. Tenzin Deden and Tenzin Zangmo, the two nuns I chatted with most, had been roommates for more than a dozen years. Tenzin Deden was petite with a round face and sunny smile, whereas Tenzin Zangmo was tall with a powerful physique and angular features. She confessed that sometimes people mistook her for a man or asked if she played basketball.

The nuns had specific duties. One shut the gate at night and opened it in the morning. Tenzin Lhadron, a petite thirty-four-year-old with silver glasses, looked after the nunnery's water supply. She checked water levels in the big storage vats on the roof. Frequent shortages in the winter stressed Tenzin, who called the water company daily and implored them to turn on the taps. The perpetual water shortage made it a pain to wash my long hair. I considered shaving it off for pragmatic reasons, especially since living in a nunnery seemed the ideal situation to give it a try, but I never took the leap. Tenzin Lhadron had a forthright manner and brassy way of speaking, which likely made her best suited to hassle the water supplier. Kelsang Wangmo, the German-born nun who lived across from me, took charge of laundry. The nunnery's washing machine—a luxury donated by a foreign supporter—was kept locked in its own little room on the roof. A few times a week Kelsang Wangmo collected dirty clothes (except for socks and underwear), ran them through the washer, then hung them to dry on clotheslines. Kelsang Wangmo was in her late thirties, but her youthful face and ever-pleasant demeanor made her seem younger. Washing clothes gave her a sense of satisfaction, she told me.

For most of the day the nuns studied in their rooms and then went to evening classes at the Institute of Buddhist Dialectics just down the hill by the main temple. After a few months, I gleaned that the nuns were in the thick of studying for their *geshe* degrees, the equivalent of a PhD for Tibetan monastics. Earning the *geshe* degree typically takes eighteen to twenty years. I also learned that, after eighteen years of study, Kelsang Wangmo was on track to be the first nun to earn the degree. She arrived in Dharamsala as a young backpacker thinking she would travel for nine months before heading back to university in Germany. Almost two decades later, she was still in Dharamsala, fluent in Tibetan, and second in her class—one dominated by Tibetan monks, many of whom hailed from Tibet.

Many monks study to be *geshes* in Tibetan monasteries in India. Until the 1990s, nuns were not allowed on that track. Like most of the world's religious institutions, there was a bias against women attaining high ranks in Tibetan Buddhism. While in Tibet nuns have existed for centuries, nunneries were usually poor subbranches of far larger and more powerful monasteries. Nuns did not take part in rigorous religious training, nor did they receive much formal education. That started to change after the Dalai Lama arrived in India and suggested that women be allowed to become *geshes*.

Nevertheless, ambitious nuns did not have an easy road. Some monks— and even Tibetan women—frowned upon the idea of female *geshes*, saying the change threatened the (male-dominated) religious traditions of Tibet. Today, Tibetan Buddhist monks in India still far outnumber nuns. In 2002, there were more than 27,000 monks in exile compared to roughly 1,600 nuns. In 2009, India had 223 monasteries and 23 nunneries, including those under construction, according to the exile administration's Department of Religion.

The Tibetan religious establishment still had to find a way for nuns to officially become *geshes*. Because of a technicality, in 2009 women were still barred from studying an important Buddhist text necessary for the degree. The issue was under discussion within the Tibetan religious establishment, said Tsering Phuntsok, minister of religion in the exile government. In an interview at his Dharamsala office in early 2009, he told me female *geshes* might have been controversial before, but people had accepted the idea. "Nowadays people are more open." Were women now more involved with religious life? I asked. The sixty-one-year-old monk answered, "Younger nuns are getting education. Their contribution will increase."

Uncertainty about full ordination didn't stop nuns from forging ahead. Tenzin Zangmo, the tall nun, was approaching the last year of *geshe* studies that she had begun in 1988, twenty-one years before. She was just thirteen years old when she became a nun in her isolated village in Kinnaur. "No chance to study, therefore we came here," she explained with a nervous smile. "If nuns have education, then equal. Before 1959, nuns not educated. Do *puja* but no debate, don't explain Buddha Dharma, therefore now very lucky. His Holiness gave us the chance to study Buddhist philosophy. He tell us, 'You learn Buddhist philosophy, then one day we make one way to get degree.'"

· · ·

My neighbors in the nunnery had gotten quite far in their studies. So had the nuns at Dolma Ling, a nunnery supported by the Tibetan Nuns Project. Comprised of sleek, airy buildings connected by tidy stone paths, it housed more than 200 nuns on a bucolic campus in a lush valley past lower Dharamsala. At the nunnery's rear, cows grazed on emerald grass despite noisy construction work for a new debate courtyard and solar-powered bathhouse.

One afternoon when I visited, the sky was steely gray and thick mist swirled around distant snow peaks. A mural in the spacious lobby depicted a tree with hundreds of leaves, each one containing the name of a donor, usually from a developed country, who supported the nunnery. An older nun walked briskly past as she gave two tall Caucasian men—Americans by the sound of their accents—a tour of the grounds. Upstairs featured a large library and computer room. A nearby building hosted a prayer hall with smooth wooden floors and colorful *thangkas* lit by dim lamps. Nuns made crafts to sell in a tailoring workshop equipped with sewing machines. In a huge, spotless kitchen, enormous cauldrons boiled on a stove in preparation for dinner. Nuns chopped spinach into enormous mounds of *momo* stuffing.

The nunnery's modernity breathed of ample financial support from donors, mostly in the United States and Europe. Some older monks clucked their tongues in disapproval when I brought up Dolma Ling. They thought the place was too luxurious for a monastic lifestyle. A solar-powered bathhouse? Granted, it had nine showers to serve one hundred nuns each day, but Dolma Ling's spacious campus and modern facilities made some people accustomed to monastic asceticism uneasy.

The nonprofit Tibetan Nuns Project launched in 1991, when the need for facilities and aid for nuns became urgent. In the late 1980s more Tibetan refugee nuns began arriving in Dharamsala. Some had participated in demonstrations in Lhasa. Facing arrest or punishment, hundreds fled Tibet. A group of 66 refugee nuns, ill and exhausted, appeared on the streets of Dharamsala in 1991 with nowhere to go. By 2009, the Tibetan Nuns Project provided education, training, and humanitarian aid for 700 nuns in nunneries across India. Two new nunneries were established, including Dolma Ling, in 1990, and four others received assistance.

About forty nuns in the Tibetan Nuns Project were on the *geshe* track, including Delek Wangmo, a twenty-nine-year-old from Tibet whom I met at Dolma Ling. Wangmo had wide cheekbones and a friendly smile. She was ten years into a roughly eighteen-year course and thrilled about her circumstances. "When I was in Tibet I never thought I could get such a good opportunity as now," Wangmo told me. In Tibet she lived with her family, not in a nunnery. Delek Wangmo set out with a group of forty nuns from Litang in eastern Tibet to prostrate all the way to Lhasa. After their two-year journey,

Chinese police barred them from seeing the Jokhang, the holy temple in Lhasa. The group didn't plan to go to India, but a lama monk who led them continued walking. They walked for twenty days, and eventually the nuns found themselves in India. All eventually joined Dolma Ling.

"My main aim is not only for the degree, but to study and practice the dharma," Wangmo told me through an interpreter. "If I get the degree, then all the better."

Wangmo had just come from an afternoon debating session in Dolma Ling's stone-paved courtyard. Even before entering the courtyard, the unmistakable din of debate filled the air: an insect-like buzz of loud voices punctuated by the sound of clapping hands. Debate is a core part of serious monastic study that exercises logic and tests knowledge of Buddhist philosophy. Its cacophony is common at monasteries, but it was unusual to see Tibetan nuns engaged in these vigorous debates—aggressive exchanges that could be mistaken for arguing. In groups of three, one nun yelled questions at the other two, who sat cross-legged before her. One nun held a rosary, the other bit her fingertips. The interrogator accentuated her questions with a slap of her hands and a foot-stamping lunge. The nuns continued without pause even when cold rain began to drizzle from the dull sky.

Rigorous debate was something new for nuns; they hadn't been able to have this level of training in Tibet. Tsering Phuntsok, the religion minister, acknowledged that in Tibet, nuns' "educational standards are not as good as monks. Nuns only learn practice of religion, don't debate dharma and study hard." When the Dalai Lama arrived in India, he launched many reforms. Phuntsok explained, "His Holiness is a very special person. When he was quite young he studied Buddhist philosophy. But he also studied about democracy. He wanted to change things in Tibetan society."

In addition to her previous roles in the exile government, Rinchen Khando was also director of the Tibetan Nuns Project. Her spacious office had the same modern blond wood furniture found throughout Dolma Ling. Measured and soft-spoken, Khando possessed a quiet authority. In the past, "there was a big difference between monks and nuns," she said. "They never had a system of education. They didn't have colleges, like monasteries did. In India, His Holiness was able to look in every nook of society. He had a reformist attitude on every level."

People never dreamed of nuns getting the *geshe* degree, observed Rinchen Khando. "They thought women were not allowed. The reaction from the community was mixed. Some said, 'They'll never be able to do it.' Some said it was not proper for women to do that length of study. Some said, 'Let's see them try and see where they get.'"

Near the end of our conversation, Khando asked where I was from. I told her I am American of Chinese descent, and she looked at me with renewed interest. What did she think of the situation in Tibet now, I asked. Her voice took on a nostalgic quality and she answered in an unexpected way.

"It's amazing what age does to a person. Over the years, I've become more and more close to the people of China. As a young girl, I used to be against everything Chinese," Khando admitted.

As you age, you see it's not the people of China, but just a handful of people in the government. In the past twenty years, I realize more the interdependence of the whole world. I've come to understand more about human suffering.

I wish China and Tibet could live happily. What does China lose if Tibet can preserve its own culture? That could only add to the benefit of people in the whole world, including China. Tibet will gain more to go into China. There are wonderful things in China.

But it's a very sad situation in Tibet. People are really suffering. Tibet is a tiny country that has no power. I am utterly worried and concerned about suffering of Tibetan people in Tibet. What else can I say but wish for the Chinese government to open their eyes and hearts to human suffering.

True Life

There Is, There Was, There Will

MAY 2009

. . .

By early spring, Dharamsala began to thaw, but only in May did evenings finally become warm, sometimes uncomfortably so. Mosquitoes found their way into my room on the nunnery's third floor and whined shrilly in the cloying dark. Finally, a violent burst of pre-monsoon rain broke the sticky heat and sent dirt, dust, and dung from cows and dogs tumbling downhill in rippling sheets of water.

One morning in the vet clinic, Topden helped Catherine, an Australian vet, as she finished stitching up the bloody belly of an anesthetized dog. The dog was on her back, belly exposed, with front paws tied and raised in the air with a thin rope. A tube ran down her throat, and her tongue lolled limply from her mouth. The dog had been spayed recently but her stitches had broken open. Some frantic nuns spotted the dog dragging her entrails as she walked.

When Topden and Catherine retrieved the dog, they found her intestines blossoming out of her belly "like a flower," as he described. Luckily the dog hadn't trampled her entrails too much, but they were dirty and some were torn. At the clinic, Catherine flushed the dog's intestines with saline before tucking them back inside her belly and sewing her up.

Topden calmly watched as Catherine pulled stitches through the dog's skin with bloody, gloved hands. "Almost finished," he said looking up with a quick smile. The Australian vet was efficient and delegated tasks to Topden. Seeing a spare pair of hands, she instructed me to fill plastic bottles with hot water. Then we transferred the unconscious dog to the floor, piled her with blankets, and nestled hot water bottles next to her. After such trauma, it was uncertain whether the dog would survive.

It was midmorning when the vet finished and left the clinic. Topden and I sat at a small table while the dog lay breathing shallowly in a corner of the room. It had been unsettling to see the bloody canine sprawled on the table, paws trussed up, like a side of meat. But blood and guts didn't bother Topden at all anymore. In fact, he was far less interested in talking about the operation than about the new drama in his life: Topden had fallen in love. "I met a lot of girls. How beautiful! Maybe I marriage," he mused.

That spring, an Israeli vet and the clinic's team held animal welfare camps in nearby towns where they vaccinated and sterilized street dogs. One week-long camp took place in Bir, a town a few hours from Dharamsala known as a hang-gliding hub. Topden no longer wore his monk's robes to the clinic, and he didn't wear them during the vaccination camps, either. When he started talking to a pretty Indian girl in Bir, something unusual happened.

"I had this strange feeling," said Topden, his face lighting up with wonder. "She is beautiful. Her way of talking, moving, and thinking is very good." They talked every day during his week in Bir, snatching time in between their work and in the evenings. She was in her early twenties but already was thinking of marrying. She told Topden she needed a lot of dowry money to marry. In jest, he replied, "Oh, why do you pay money? Come with me!" Then in a moment of candor, he told her, "You are very special for me. You give me a very strange feeling." He recounted, "Then she got very shy and said, 'Me too!' She said, 'I don't talk to any boys but I want to talk to you. Can I contact to you?'"

They spoke in Hindi and conversations covered a lot of ground. "She said, 'Are you a drinker?' I said, 'I'm not a drinker, smoker, not a liar.' Then she said, 'I love you. Are you happy?' I said, 'Yes, you are my girlfriend.'"

Topden beamed as he excitedly recounted these exchanges. Did the woman know he was a monk? I asked. Unbothered, he shook his head and continued. "She's so nice. She loves me. How can I forget it? Morning and evening, just relaxing, I'm thinking about her. I don't know—it's so strange. We speak in Hindi. I told her, 'You must learn Tibetan.' I gave her my phone number. She calls every night."

"Would you really marry her?" I asked.

"I don't think so." Then he said she was related to the wife of his coworker at the clinic, and she vouched that the girl was very nice. "It doesn't matter if she's poor. We just need love. I'm a poor person but my life is very rich. Indian girls love their men very much."

"How do you know that?"

"It is in many Indian movies."

"Life is not like a Bollywood movie," I gently pointed out.

"If I spend my life with her, it will be good," declared Topden. "I don't know, it's not my hand." It was beyond his control, he meant. Then Topden's thinking suddenly did a 180-degree turn. "If she don't love me, it's fine. I don't care. I can stop. I decide not to call her. It's just stress," he sighed, rubbing his face with his hand. "I am tired and I am thinking about her. Then sometimes it makes me angry." Topden told me that the couple who lived next door to him in Dharamsala fought viciously; he could hear their arguments through thin walls, so he knew love could mean trouble too. Nevertheless, there was a second Indian woman who piqued his interest in a village about thirty minutes from Dharamsala where the vets also treated dogs.

Suddenly, the weight of possibility burdened Topden. "I am tired," he repeated. "This is not true life." Did he mean love was not true life? Before I could ask, Topden continued, "I couldn't get true life because I'm a monk."

I empathized with Topden. Everything he expressed was familiar to anyone who had had crushes, fallen in and out of love, experienced the roller coaster of elation and devastation that comes with so many relationships. Lovesickness is a common "affliction" detailed by countless storytellers since time immemorial. But it must have been disorienting for Topden to experience all this for the very first time as an adult in his thirties. And it was jarring to hear this outpouring of emotion from Topden, who as a boy begged his parents to let him become a monk. He risked his life to leave Tibet and left his family so he could study and practice Buddhism freely and wear monk's robes, but now they were folded up and unworn. They had been untouched for some time.

. . .

During my time in Dharamsala I got to know a few other Tibetan monks. Alak Khempo, a young abbot in his thirties, wore his robes with casual but knowing authority. He lived at Kirti Monastery just across from my nunnery. My neighbor, the German nun Kelsang Wangmo, introduced us because he was looking for an English tutor; they were classmates at the Institute of Buddhist Dialectics. At the time, Kelsang was first in her class and Alak Khempo was second, but he did not mind admitting that. He referred to Kelsang Wangmo with respect and spoke with quiet admiration about her flawless Tibetan. The language is notoriously difficult to learn, but she had mastered it along with her Buddhist studies.

The slim abbot wore silver glasses that gave him an intellectual air. Alak Khempo had a mild demeanor yet often had a slightly knowing expression.

He appeared at my room one day with a cloth bag slung over his shoulder containing thin English workbooks. He wore a bright yolk-colored vest beneath his robes that signaled his high rank. We sat at the wobbly table in my room. He understood some English but was still tentative with the language. When I asked what his name meant, Alak Khempo told me in a low voice that he was a *tulku*, a reincarnation—a fourth-generation reincarnation of an abbot in Tibet, in fact. Alak Khempo explained that his mother had some dreams shortly after he was born, and his identity was later confirmed by senior monks.

Before coming to India, Alak Khempo lived at the main Kirti Monastery in Amdo Ngaba in Sichuan Province. He fled to India in his twenties, nearly a decade before, and because of his esteemed status didn't have a treacherous journey like most Tibetan refugees; some Tibetan businessmen drove him to the border.

After China's crackdown on Tibet in March 2008 it was far too risky for Tibetans in India to call or email family and friends back home, especially in Amdo, which was a locus of protest. Alak Khempo confessed he hadn't spoken to his parents in Tibet for nearly a year.

Because Alak Khempo's schedule was packed with Buddhism classes, studies, and his administrative job at the monastery, we practiced English during his lunch break. Knowing English was practical and empowering for daily life in India. Alak Khempo most wanted to learn the language for his office work: he, like some other monks, had duties that ranged from negotiating land purchases for a new wing of the monastery to coordinating travel for senior monks.

For most of the hour we reviewed grammar lessons from his textbook, practiced exercises, and reviewed homework. Alak Khempo swiftly absorbed lessons and completed his homework almost every day by lightly penciling in answers in his textbook. Insights on Tibet popped up during mundane grammar drills, and we often detoured from the textbook. One day we practiced the sentence pattern "going to." The examples were basic at first: "Do you think it is going to rain?" "Do you think the bus is going to be late?" During February 2009, as tensions grew in Tibet, everyone wondered what would happen on March 10, the anniversary of the Tibetan Uprising. Would riots flare up again? Would violence worsen? Or would strong repression force silence?

I asked Alak Khempo, "Do you think something is going to happen in Tibet on March 10?"

He looked pensive as he thought this over. "Yes, I think something is going to happen," he answered.

Another time we practiced tenses: *there is, there was, there will.* Alak Khempo wasn't as familiar with the future tense so we focused on this. I asked several questions: "Will there be a party?" "Will it snow tomorrow?" He had told me about a pilgrimage to Bodh Gaya, the holy site where the Buddha attained enlightenment. There, Alak Khempo stayed in a basic guesthouse. I asked, "Will there be a bed in the hotel in Bodh Gaya?"

Alak Khempo replied, "No, there will not be a bed!"

I pondered other examples, then spotted my sweatshirt hanging on the back of a chair. It was a black zip-up designed by Students for a Free Tibet with the words "Team Tibet 08" on the back. Since Tibet was not represented at the Beijing Olympics, the idea was for Tibet to symbolically have its own team. The sweatshirt's tag featured a miniature logo of Students for a Free Tibet: a white dove flying over the sun of the Tibetan flag. Alak Khempo read the tag aloud: "Tibet will be free." His face lit up when the meaning dawned on him.

Another time we were practicing use of the word "might" to suggest possibility, and I asked Alak Khempo where he would be the following year. After finishing his studies in Dharamsala he might go to Sikkim or Darjeeling in northeast India where there were smaller branches of Kirti Monastery. "I might go there," he said.

"Have you been to Sikkim?" I asked. India annexed the former Himalayan kingdom in 1975.

"Yes," he nodded. "I saw Tibet." I looked at him in surprise. Alak Khempo recounted a trip there in 2002 with the head of the monastery, who knew a police chief in Sikkim. Tibetans are not allowed to go to the border, but the police officer drove to the border so they could see Tibet across a grassy mountainside. He warned the monks not to speak Chinese since Tibetans are not allowed to go to the border.

Alak Khempo could see Chinese police on the other side of the border and in the distance even saw a Chinese post office and some Tibetan people. A Tibetan woman waved at the group on the Indian side, and Alak Khempo waved back. He was amazed that Tibet was right there; no wall or fence separated him from his homeland. Alak Khempo paused to search his dictionary then came up with the word "rope." Only a metal rope, so thin you could step over it, marked the boundary between India and Tibet.

"How did you feel?" I asked.

Alak Khempo cocked his head and smiled. "Happy," he said.

. . .

Dharamsala had high demand for English speakers to tutor Tibetans, so in the early afternoons I worked with Alak Khempo, and in the late afternoons I helped a monk in his twenties named Tenzin Dhonyue. In contrast to the reserved young abbot, Tenzin Dhonyue had a hearty, belly-shaking laugh, a constant smile, and an air of boyish excitement. Born in India, in the poor eastern state of Orissa, Tenzin Dhonyue grew up on the Tibetan settlement there. He spoke English confidently but wanted to expand his vocabulary and have more advanced conversations. I tutored him in his room in the small branch of Gaden Monastery, in a cramped concrete building near the main square. (Gaden's main branch is in Karnataka.) Tenzin Dhonyue shared with another monk a small room cluttered with bedding, books, and personal effects that smelled of butter tea and close male bodies.

Each day, Tenzin Dhonyue woke up before dawn and managed a busy schedule of classes, prayers, and chores. He could meet only for an hour before dinner or after lunch. At one of our first sessions, he excitedly showed me song lyrics that his former tutor, a German woman, had assembled in a notebook. Handwritten lyrics included songs by Britney Spears and the Backstreet Boys, but he was especially fond of a song by the Black-Eyed Peas called "Where Is the Love?" Tenzin Dhonyue read the lyrics aloud with intense concentration as though reciting a sacred mantra. I could see why "Where Is the Love?"—about dealing with the world's strife and turning away from anger to love—would especially appeal to a monk. The song even tells the listener to "meditate."

A few times, Tenzin Dhonyue and I went to one of the many Internet cafés in town. The one next to Gaden Monastery charged only thirty rupees an hour (roughly sixty cents) versus the forty rupees most places charged. Tenzin Dhonyue eagerly checked his Facebook account and asked for help writing a message to his former English tutor. Tenzin Dhonyue had hundreds of friends, including other monks and international friends he met in Dharamsala. In 2009, I didn't yet have a Facebook account so only watched over his shoulder, unsure how "friending" someone or writing on their wall worked. Eventually, I did join Facebook after Tenzin, a Tibetan monk in a Himalayan hill town, introduced me to social media.

. . .

Without a doubt, Dharamsala was home to a colorful community, and I often ran into friends or struck up conversations with people at Moonpeak Café on Temple Road. Midway between the main square and the main temple, it overlooked tree-covered hillsides with views of dramatic, pollution-enhanced pink and orange sunsets. Some friends sipping coffee on the café's terrace swore they once saw a flying squirrel leap across one of those sherbet sunsets. Its walls were covered with framed photos by its owner Ashwini Bhatia, a photographer for Associated Press.

In addition to its delicious homemade bread, fluffy omelets, hardwood floors, and funky, carefully curated music, Moonpeak had one of the best locations in town for people-watching. Eating al fresco at the café offered a front row seat for watching the comings and goings of town despite the fetid, garbage-clogged drain along Temple Road. One frequent passerby, an enormous black-and-white bull, plodded up and down the road, each hoof heavy as a discus. The bull and a herd of brown cows found wandering the streets of Dharamsala belonged to Namgyal Monastery near the main temple. One day, the bull walked slowly but purposefully uphill until he paused in front of the café and terrace. Then he practically nosed his way onto a Frenchman's breakfast plate until the man good-naturedly handed the bovine a piece of buttered toast. Another time, the bull was no less persistent. He eyed the café and parked himself firmly on the pavement. Finally Tenzin, Moonpeak's chef, came out with handfuls of vegetables and some bread. He fed withered carrots and handfuls of lettuce into the bull's munching mouth. Tenzin smoothed its dirty black snout with his hand.

Although he could speak English, Tenzin usually spoke to me in Mandarin. His stout arms, beefy chest, and crew cut contrasted with his gentle manner and his ability to bake crusty loaves of bread, carve a blossom from a carrot slice, and build a frosted Christmas gingerbread house for display in the café. When he made my omelets and sandwiches, they were accompanied by an artful sprig of parsley or a flower carrot carefully arranged on the plate. Tenzin had fled Tibet twelve years before—and after years of English classes and vocational training, worked as a chef at a hotel in Goa before returning to Dharamsala.

"Is that your regular customer?" I called. Tenzin grinned and kept feeding the bull until the handouts disappeared. But the bull wasn't satisfied and continued to stand with a penetrating stare. Eventually Tenzin returned with a basket of vegetables and leafy greens that toppled to the ground after the bull lunged to gobble his next course. When he finished, the bovine remained standing in front of the café, occasionally turning his head to lick his flank like a grooming cat. A few moments later an old Tibetan man appeared on the street and stuffed some bread into the bull's mouth as though spoon-feeding a child.

I watched the animal's antics while eating a delicious carrot-ginger soup inside the café. It was nearly closing time, and I was the only customer until a few of Tenzin's friends walked in. He introduced a woman in her thirties as his cousin; the man next to her was her husband. This was how I met Deckyi and Dhondup. They had arrived in Dharamsala from Tibet months before, and they seemed shy and uncertain. When Tenzin told me they could speak Mandarin, I greeted them and asked if they were used to Dharamsala now.

"Bu xiguan." *Not used to it*, the woman exclaimed in Mandarin and shook her head for emphasis.

I didn't run into the couple again after our initial meeting, but one day Tenzin asked if I might tutor Deckyi in English. His inquiry was polite, almost timid: "If you have time."

[12]

Deckyi's Journey
I Did Something Good for Tibet

· · ·

Deckyi wasn't tall but her frame suggested a steady solidity. She had a plump face and appeared calm, reserved, shyly serious. Although she could understand only a few words in English, her eyes had a knowing alertness. Many Tibetan women are named Deckyi, after the Dalai Lama's mother, just as many Tibetan men are named Tenzin, the Dalai Lama's given name. In contrast to Deckyi's roundness, Dhondup was tall and thin, also in his early thirties, with a few wispy hairs on his upper lip that passed for a mustache. Dhondup had a gentle air and spoke slowly as though pondering his words.

After I first met the couple at Moonpeak Café, we met many times in Dharamsala to practice English, and they told me their story. Deckyi and Dhondup fled from Tibet in the fall of 2008 and arrived in Dharamsala that December. They couldn't speak English or Hindi so they couldn't find any work. For their first several months of life as refugees in India, they were helpless, like a "new baby," Dhondup said. When I met them in May 2009 Deckyi was adamant about being unused to India—and I would learn more about challenges they had encountered.

After their stay in Dharamsala's Reception Center, Deckyi and Dhondup slept on the floor in Tenzin's room, already crowded with two other Tibetans. They didn't know anyone in India when they arrived, but they met other Tibetans through a broad, informal network of refugees and exiles. Tenzin wasn't really Deckyi's cousin; they had some mutual friends from Tibet. They stayed with him for a week before finding another room in McLeod Ganj occupied by a Tibetan woman who was moving to France. For 15,000 rupees (about $330) she sold them everything in the room: furniture, cooking utensils, cutlery, electronics, bedding.

The many Tibetans walking the winding streets of Dharamsala stunned Deckyi and Dhondup when they first arrived. Old and young; people from the west and east, their origins recognizable from their knee-length *chupa* and how they wore and tied them; spiky-haired urban youth from Lhasa; former nomads with weathered faces; teachers and journalists; shop owners and traders; monks and nuns.

Who were all these Tibetans and how did they get to this place? Deckyi and Dhondup wondered. The answers were as diverse as the Tibetan exiles themselves. Some had been born in India, but many had fled their homeland, some driven by pragmatic choice and some forced by desperation. Like Deckyi and Dhondup, the newest refugees were pushed across the border by the events that Chinese-speaking Tibetans refer to as *San Shisi* in Mandarin, or "three fourteen." China refers to significant events by their dates; for example, *Liu Si*, or "six four," indicates the June 4, 1989, Tiananmen Square protests in Beijing. *San Shisi* is March 14, 2008, when protests and demonstrations across Tibet erupted in violence. Deckyi and Dhondup didn't participate in the protests, but they did do something—a seemingly trivial act that shattered the upward trajectory of their lives.

When they arrived in Dharamsala, through word of mouth Deckyi ferreted out housing and job leads. They lived in McLeod Ganj for three months until someone put Deckyi in touch with a Tibetan man named Lobsang. He and more than a dozen other Tibetans were working at a call center in Delhi, making calls in Mandarin to China. Deckyi and Dhondup had brought their life savings with them when they fled Tibet, but that wouldn't last long, so they jumped at the opportunity. Their salary from the call center would have been a much-needed lifeline—if only their boss had paid them.

Deckyi and Dhondup arranged to sublet their room and at the end of March took an overnight bus from Dharamsala to Delhi. The bus wound its way down mountain roads and around gut-clenching hairpin turns until twelve hours later it deposited them in Delhi's teeming sprawl. They went to the call center for a brief interview in Mandarin and were hired the next day. Deckyi was surprised they got work so easily; securing an office job in Lhasa, at least for a Tibetan, took years of perseverance or connections or both.

The work environment at the Delhi call center was familiar to the couple. Deckyi once had a coveted office job in Lhasa working for an electronics company, while Dhondup managed an accounting firm. On March 22, they started at the call center, as recorded in Deckyi's diary—a flimsy school notebook where she documented her days with brief entries in Chinese. After that first day, she felt a pale glimmer of relief—a rare moment of brightness in a year darkened by turmoil. "We are actually happy here," she wrote in her diary. Her happiness proved to be fleeting.

Hundreds of call center workers chattered away inside a cavernous office about thirty minutes' drive from Majnu Ka Tilla, the Tibetan colony in north Delhi. Most were Indians but Africans, Chinese, and Tibetans worked there, too. Some Indians made calls in halting Mandarin and frantically waved Deckyi over to help when they couldn't understand the Chinese person on the other end of the line. Deckyi didn't ask how the Indians had learned Chinese; it was another one of the mysteries of life in India. Looking for answers and explanations in the daunting crevasse between two languages and cultures was too much trouble.

The work wasn't hard: calling hospitals in China, asking them a list of questions that appeared on a computer screen, and recording the answers. *What kind of medical equipment are you using? Does your hospital plan to buy new equipment in the next few years?* Deckyi repeated the questions over and over. She could read and write Mandarin better than her mother tongue since she hadn't learned Tibetan in school and only spoke it at home.

Even Tibetans in exile in India knew the practical value of Mandarin, and Mandarin fluency was an advantage for Deckyi. It had helped her find work in Lhasa and prosper, and at first it seemed to offer unexpected opportunities in India. In Dharamsala she had begun teaching basic Chinese to neighbors and friends: monks and a young Tibetan man taking a break from his studies in England to volunteer. Perhaps some Tibetans hoped to one day return home, and they thought Mandarin would help them get a job, find better opportunities, or navigate society. Others were unlikely to go back but were learning because the Dalai Lama urged Tibetans to learn Mandarin so they could communicate with their "Chinese brothers and sisters."

Many Tibetans took the Dalai Lama's words to heart. In Dharamsala, Tibetan refugees crowded not only into free English classes offered by non-profits but also the few Chinese classes. I attended one held in a small room where Tibetans sat on floor cushions, eyes fixed on their Chinese-speaking Tibetan teacher as they sounded out tones and words in sing-song unison. I was the object of excited attention in the class as a potential teacher until I quickly clarified I was merely an observer.

On workdays, Deckyi and Dhondup woke up early to be ready when a company van picked up the Tibetan workers at 5 a.m. from Majnu Ka Tilla. The cool respite of Delhi's early spring faded with each passing day. Through April the heat grew oppressive and stirred mosquitoes, lice, and red ants. For 3,500 rupees a month, about $70, Deckyi and Dhondup rented a windowless box of a room across from Majnu Ka Tilla that was entirely bare except for a single bed and a light bulb. Eventually they added a small table.

At night, when Deckyi lay in bed with mosquitoes whining in her ear, memories of what they had left behind in Tibet gnawed her mind. In 2006 they had bought an eight-room house in Lhasa for 280,000 yuan (about $35,000). It was two stories high and they had two TVs, all of which seemed impossibly extravagant as Deckyi caressed memories in the dark. When Dhondup described the house, he mournfully sketched in his notebook a large structure with several rooms layered like cubes. They never imagined they would leave behind their hard-earned home and middle-class lives to become refugees in a foreign country living in a one-room box.

. . .

At first the Delhi call center seemed like an oasis. It was spacious, brightly lit, and as soon as they stepped inside, they were swathed in the decadent silk of air conditioning that gave relief from the city's stultifying heat. Three shifts worked around the clock, so the room had the unblinking feel of a place suspended in time. For lunch a canteen served Indian food that even Deckyi conceded wasn't bad. They could take breaks from the computer monitors and phones, but apart from lunch, Deckyi and Dhondup worked nonstop to finish as many questionnaires as possible before their day ended at 3:30 p.m. Each completed project fetched 500 rupees, about $10. Deckyi worked quickly and in the first five weeks finished thirty-three projects. Between Deckyi and her husband, they earned 33,000 rupees, just shy of $700. That was more than three months' wages for a well-paid chauffeur in Delhi, or more than a year's rent for their room in Dharamsala.

The promise of payment took tantalizing shape in Deckyi's mind, and it sustained her through predawn wake-ups in the stifling dark, long hours under fluorescent lights, and restless nights scratching mosquito bites. With the money, perhaps they could buy plane tickets to another country, if they could get visas. Thoughts of the future fluttered in Deckyi's sleepless mind like the moths that knocked themselves loudly against the lone bulb in their room.

Adjusting to India had been difficult. Deckyi wasn't used to Indian food, slimy lentil dal and vegetables overcooked into unrecognizable lumps, the dirty streets of Dharamsala where cows plodded alongside people, or the stray dogs that disrupted her sleep with frenzied barking. She and her husband felt helpless, even in Dharamsala, where thousands of Tibetans lived alongside Indians. Deckyi wasn't used to asking people for help with mundane tasks like buying vegetables at the market where Indian vendors spoke Hindi and English. She felt like a child, Deckyi repeated.

In their first months in India, the enormity of the events in Tibet that had forced them to leave weighed heavily on Deckyi and Dhondup. They had been fortunate enough to save money in Tibet, but they had paid hefty fees for permits and a guide who led them across the border to Nepal. When they finally arrived in Dharamsala, the expenses added up: bedding, winter clothes, kitchenware for the small room they rented for 2,400 rupees ($50) a month, food, and toiletries. A decision to help someone led to them fleeing Tibet, but it had cost them so much. Was it worth it?

. . .

The first time I went to their room in Dharamsala to tutor them in English, Deckyi and Dhondup regarded me quietly like frightened cats until I took the lead and asked them something, anything, in English. Deckyi looked older than her years, even when wearing a teal-colored T-shirt emblazoned with a surfer and the words "Newport Beach, California." She had a small, pert nose in a chubby face, yet wrinkles pulled at her eyes.

Deckyi showed me a textbook from her English class at a nonprofit and looked at me without comprehension when I asked in English: *When did you come to India? Why did you come here?* We switched back to Mandarin and my questions elicited sobering answers. Deckyi had a smart phone from China that had an electronic Chinese-English dictionary. With one fingernail coated in chipped nail polish, she wrote a Chinese character on the touchpad screen. A word in English popped up and she tilted it toward me. *Zhengzhifan.* "State criminal." When she finally told me what she had done in March 2008, I shook my head. They had not killed or harmed anyone or damaged property or divulged state secrets, so they were not state criminals. I thumbed through Deckyi's red Chinese-English dictionary and found the word I would grow too familiar with: *naming.* "Political refugee," I wrote in English in her notebook.

Even in an English lesson we couldn't avoid the weight of their misfortune. I learned more new Chinese vocabulary when Deckyi told me about how she had come to India. *Zhua, bianjie, tongxingzheng* (catch, border, permit). I jotted down the words in *pinyin* romanization in my notebook for future reference.

One morning, after a few of our lessons, Deckyi took the lead. She had prepared a list of questions and phrases written in her notebook in English and she wanted me to verify them. The first one was puzzling. "Our life is very knotty." I looked at the words blankly. "Where did you get that word?" I asked.

Deckyi pointed at the smart phone. She explained in Mandarin what she meant, and I unfurrowed my brow. "Here. This is better," I said. I took her notebook and wrote a sentence. "Our life is very hard." Deckyi repeated this in a soft voice and surprisingly good pronunciation.

Then she showed me another sentence she had copied into her book: "Can you help feed at the public trough?" I was baffled. Her phone was not so smart after all. After some back and forth, I deciphered the proper translation and was instantly sobered. "Can you help us get our salary?" I wrote in her notebook.

Next she announced that she wanted to sell her calligraphy. "You know calligraphy?" I exclaimed. *Shufa*—I did remember this word in Mandarin. Now was her turn to look puzzled. What she meant was jewelry, *shoushi*. The smart phone had given her the wrong word again. I pointed to a gold ring with a large jade on her finger. *Jiezhe*, ring. *Shouzhuo*, bracelet. She nodded. That's what Deckyi had been doing that morning: trying to sell her jewelry.

After I asked what they had been doing since arriving in India, Deckyi told me about the call center. She added matter-of-factly that they had worked there about five weeks but were never paid so had returned to Dharamsala, their hopes in tatters.

Suddenly Deckyi asked if I would call Samir, their former Indian call center boss. I didn't like the thought of confronting this stranger—but with Deckyi looking at me expectantly it was hard to refuse.

While sitting in her tiny room in Dharamsala one Sunday morning, I called Samir's cell phone and he answered after a few rings. Traffic roared in the background. I explained that I was calling on Deckyi's behalf and bluntly asked when she could expect her salary. Candor was something I appreciated in India, where people seemed remarkably unfazed by upfront talk. When trying to get something you want, I had learned bluntness, even melodrama, is normal, even expected.

Samir sounded surprisingly unsurprised to get a call out of the blue from a stranger asking about the salary of two former Tibetan employees. "The client hasn't paid yet," he explained hurriedly. "They haven't paid me, so how can I pay them?"

"When will the client give you the money?" I replied.

"Soon. I will give them the money soon."

"When?"

"Maybe next month."

"We will call you again in a week to get an update," I told Samir, who didn't object to the suggestion.

When I hung up and told Deckyi about the conversation, she made a face. "He keeps saying the money is coming," she said. "That's what he's been saying for months."

. . .

In Dharamsala, Deckyi and Dhondup lived near the main Buddhist temple in a building surrounded by construction. Several senior monks lived in their building, and sometimes chanting and murmured prayers drifted down the dim, cement-floored corridor. Usually, the sound was drowned out by construction from the adjacent building. Power tools shrieked and sparks flew. Puddles of wet cement dripped onto the stairwell.

In Deckyi and Dhondup's room, two single beds formed an *L* along the walls. Quilts were piled on top, folded lengthwise so the beds could be used as sofas during the day. A television sat in a cluttered cupboard topped with small silver cups. On the wall above, several *thangka* tapestries depicted seated Buddhas. Large photos of the Dalai Lama and the Karmapa, the twenty-something head of another school of Tibetan Buddhism, also hung above Deckyi and Dhondup. The Karmapa fled Tibet in 1999 when he was a teenager, much to the embarrassment of China. In the photo the Karmapa peered knowingly over his round sunglasses, as if monitoring the room. In one corner stood a table heavy with books and papers and an old desktop computer covered by a bedsheet. In order to use the computer, someone would have to sit on the bed. Two doorways led to a small kitchenette and a bathroom. A window looked out onto an overgrown patch of grass that hosted a rubbish heap littered with discards from the construction site—plastic bags, wood shavings. It was a far cry from the eight-room house the couple had owned in Lhasa.

One gray afternoon, the electricity winked off in the middle of our English lessons. We continued as though nothing had happened; in India power outages are as routine as clouds passing over the sun. In the hazy half-light, Dhondup repeated several English words over and over, almost to himself. Then, without thinking, he stretched out in repose on the bed where he had been sitting, as though lulling himself to sleep with the mantra of new words from this new land.

. . .

Dhondup and Deckyi told me the story of their escape from Tibet as we sat on their beds and the Dalai Lama and Karmapa watched over us from their glossy portraits on the wall.

When they lived in Tibet, Deckyi and Dhondup were not very interested in politics. "Life was not bad in Lhasa," Dhondup explained. "Life was getting better." They had jobs, a house, and even a new black Volkswagen they bought for 90,000 yuan, nearly $10,000. That all changed on March 10, 2008, the forty-ninth anniversary of the Tibetan Uprising. Within Tibet, commemoration is normally clandestine. But of course, 2008 was not a normal year. On the outskirts of Lhasa, Chinese police stopped about 300 monks from Drepung Monastery as they began a peaceful protest. In Lhasa itself, fifteen monks from Sera Monastery marched near Jokhang, the sacred temple. They carried the banned Tibetan flag and were quickly arrested. Most of the demonstrations were peaceful, but on March 14 protests in Lhasa erupted into violence.

Deckyi and Dhondup stayed glued to the television to glean any information they could. The news was censored, but they heard from friends about monks marching, carrying signs, and shouting slogans. They heard that such protests were happening not just in Lhasa but all over Tibet and western China—in Qinghai, Sichuan, and Gansu. In the aftermath, Chinese troops raided and surrounded monasteries, in some cases cutting off food and water. Deckyi and Dhondup had extra reason to be nervous. Before March 10, two monks they knew gave them flyers that read "Long live the Dalai Lama," "We want basic human rights," and "We want the Dalai Lama to return to Tibet." Those slogans may seem innocuous, but in Tibet it was illegal and dangerous to distribute such material. Flyers couldn't be made at local photocopy shops lest the owners report them to authorities.

One night after her colleagues went home, Deckyi made photocopies on the machine in her office. She gave the flyers to the monks who hid fifty copies inside their robes. Deckyi never saw the monks again. In the days after March 14, the implications of those flyers began to dawn on Deckyi and Dhondup. Tension was thick in the uneasy quietude after the Chinese clampdown. Even Tibetans who stayed cloistered inside their homes "were shaking with fear," Deckyi remembered. "Even the sky was changed." After the protests and the crackdown, the sky was dark, discolored like rotten fruit from the smoke of burned shops, smoldering vehicles, and tear gas.

In April 2008, some normalcy returned to their lives, and they resumed work even though Lhasa resembled a war zone. Barricades had been erected throughout the city, and soldiers and trucks were stationed everywhere. Deckyi and Dhondup heard more and more reports of Tibetans being detained, and they feared the day when loud banging would sound on their own door. They lived in constant fear and both had trouble sleeping and eating. The anxiety took such a toll on Dhondup that he had to take time off from work.

The unbearable tension reached a crescendo in September 2008. One night when they were getting ready to eat dinner and watch TV, Dhondup began sighing incessantly. He had gotten word that the two monks who gave them the flyers had been arrested. A monk warned Dhondup that the detainees might reveal who had photocopied the contraband. "The Chinese police may have found out we were doing this," Dhondup said, his voice heavy with despair. "If we don't leave right away then once they arrest us, not only will we lose our jobs, but we will be arrested. They will beat us mercilessly or sentence us. And we could also get our colleagues and family in trouble."

Was the decision to leave home agonizing and drawn out? For Deckyi and Dhondup, it was just the opposite. "The decision was so instant because of our fear," Deckyi told me. "The following day we asked through some connections at a hospital to sign a medical excuse so we could request one week sick leave from our work unit."

Next they paid 2,000 yuan, about $220 (though the fee was normally 15 yuan), to get a permit that allowed them to travel near the Nepal border. The high premium, paid to an intermediary, allowed Deckyi to get the permit almost immediately with no questions asked. For another 10,000 yuan ($1,100) they arranged for a car and guide to take them to the border. This service normally cost 4,000 yuan, but security had become so tight that guides charged more than double for risking their own lives. Deckyi and Dhondup padded their clothes with their life's savings. They decided not to tell their family about their plans to flee, so that they "wouldn't suffer so much" and to protect them in case police came looking for information about the couple's whereabouts.

For half a day they drove to Shigatse where they stayed one night in a hotel registered under someone else's name. The next day the car drove eight hours to Dham, a city near the Nepal border.

Deckyi and Dhondup didn't know what to expect next and spent a sleepless night imagining what lay ahead of them. "That night we discussed how far we would have to travel, how many days we would have no food or water, if we should be pursued by Chinese soldiers and if they fired then what?" Deckyi recalled. "What if something happened that neither of us dared talk about and couldn't bear to imagine?"

Money cushioned the journey considerably. Because they could hire a car and guide, Deckyi and Dhondup were fortunate to drive close enough to the border that they walked just four hours in temperate weather, climbed one "snow mountain," and crossed a bridge to reach the border. Dhondup was exhausted from anxiety and walking but "we were so terrified that we forgot our fatigue," he said. His face was slick with sweat and his mind became blank.

In a meadow near the border they stopped at a small wooden house. A woman came outside and offered the travelers some water. Deckyi could see inside the house and was startled to see a forbidden photo of the Dalai Lama on the wall, ostensibly because it was in a remote location. His smiling face beamed at them. It was the first time she had seen a big portrait of the Dalai Lama displayed openly, and Deckyi stared at it in amazement and reverence.

A bittersweet mixture of emotions washed over Deckyi as she sipped water that the woman poured for her. It was cold and delicious, better than anything she had ever tasted. On that grassy mountainside, Deckyi and Dhondup had a last taste of their homeland. The unknown of a new country awaited, but at least the Dalai Lama's warm gaze comforted them as they prepared for the final steps into exile.

· · ·

Deckyi longingly remembered that clear, sweet water of Tibet during their first days in Nepal. At first, they were excited to arrive in Kathmandu. Portraits of the Dalai Lama hung everywhere, along with the snow lions of the Tibetan flag now fluttering freely outside shops. Then the poverty of Kathmandu sank in. The dirty streets, rundown buildings, congested traffic, and piles of garbage disappointed Deckyi and Dhondup. They were used to Lhasa's wide, clean streets and new houses like the one they owned.

For one month they stayed in a Reception Center in Kathmandu run by the Tibetan exile administration. Men and women slept in separate dorm rooms filled with simple cots arranged side by side. They were given blankets, clothes, food, and even aid money, one batch from foreign donors and one from the Dalai Lama's fund. Ironically, it was when Dhondup received the money that he truly felt like a refugee. He and Deckyi had been lucky— they fled Tibet with little hardship compared to others who trekked for weeks, were tortured in prison, crippled by frostbite, or robbed along the way to Kathmandu. But now, the reality of exile began to set in.

There was no question that they had had to leave Tibet, yet a hollow sense of loss consumed Deckyi. At night, sandwiched between other refugees on narrow cots, she shed her stoicism and cried into her blanket. "We spent our whole life in Tibet under Chinese control," she said. "We had worked so hard to get jobs in an office where we could work like Chinese people. We got all these opportunities and then we lost them all."

Deckyi's loss was literal too. In Nepal she lost the baby that had been growing inside of her for nearly two months, conceived in Tibet but lost during their escape. Later, she shared with me a letter she wrote in Chinese that recounted their flight from Tibet. It described emotions Deckyi didn't articulate when we talked in person. "We lost our first family member during our escape," she wrote. "We had given him or her so much hope. We had hope that in the future, even if we ended up in a place where we had no other family, we would not end up being alone even if one of us should die. We had thought that we would try our best to raise the child to be a useful talent for Tibet. But in the blink of an eye everything fell apart."

. . .

That was not the first time Deckyi experienced loss. She pragmatically and euphemistically called those tragic events "social experiences" that she learned from. Her father was a construction worker who moved the family with him as he traveled from site to site in her early years. It was a harsh and hazardous environment for a young family. When Deckyi was seven, her five-year-old sister was crushed at a construction site by a roller used to flatten roads. Did Deckyi remember the accident? She nodded but did not say more.

After 1983, Deckyi's father was able to keep the family in Lhasa because his construction company established itself there. Deckyi went to a Chinese school through high school. Under Deng Xiao Ping's administration, schools in China were inexpensive and almost anyone could attend—different from the current situation when Chinese parents were often expected to pay bribes or "key money" to get their children into good schools. If Deckyi didn't learn Tibetan in school, did she speak it at home with her family? I asked. Did they practice Tibetan traditions at home? "Of course," she answered quietly but firmly. "We know we are Tibetan." Although they were not allowed to have pictures of the Dalai Lama, "every Tibetan has his picture in their heart."

The toil of construction work took its toll on her father. When Deckyi was twenty, he died from a stomach illness attributed to malnourishment during hard labor. Her mother died two years later, of grief and harsh conditions, Deckyi said. After that, she was on her own and managed to find a series of jobs: cashier at a disco, liquor store clerk, translator for Chinese medical equipment companies, and finally at the electronics company. Deckyi took an exam in Chinese for the latter job, and she was overjoyed when she passed.

Although she and Dhondup gradually prospered, they felt that Tibetans were still second-class citizens. It was harder for them to get jobs and they faced more barriers, even when they enjoyed the fruits of a better life, like having enough money to take vacations. Every two years they flew to Chongqing or Chengdu in Sichuan where they had medical checkups, visited their Chinese friends, and ate out, enjoying Deckyi's favorite dish: Sichuan hotpot.

Deckyi and Dhondup had many Chinese friends, which didn't seem strange to them. They had no problem with Chinese people, they told me, and their Chinese friends knew their views as Tibetans. The feeling of being second-class citizens came from the government. For example, on their way back to Tibet from Sichuan, they had to stand in a separate line at the airport where Tibetans were singled out, searched, and questioned before they were allowed to proceed.

Even though they both missed Tibet terribly and vowed to return home one day, Deckyi and Dhondup were well aware of the problems in their homeland. Prostitution was rampant. "This will be Tibet's doom," Deckyi said somberly as Dhondup nodded in agreement. They described entire stretches of Lhasa filled with brothels that Chinese authorities encouraged by turning a blind eye. Chinese soldiers stationed in Tibet also frequented them. "When Tibetan girls come to the city they can't find any jobs," Deckyi explained. "They have no choice." Dhondup swirled a jar of tea leaves floating in hot water. The worst thing, he said, was that Tibetans have no freedom of speech.

On many evenings in Dharamsala, just outside Deckyi and Dhondup's building, candlelight vigils snaked down Temple Road to commemorate important days on the Tibetan calendar or mourn others—a documentary filmmaker sentenced, young Tibetans carrying banners shot. Those nights, one could hear people chanting and singing as they marched into the temple courtyard to listen to speeches and exhortations.

When they first arrived in Dharamsala, Deckyi and Dhondup were shocked by these open displays of protest; they would have been swiftly and brutally snuffed out in Tibet. They were also puzzled. What good did these marches and demonstrations do? The real troubles were happening in Tibet. Eventually Deckyi realized their importance. She understood how Tibetans in exile could express their solidarity with those in Tibet. She also saw that journalists, whether from India or foreign countries, filmed, wrote about, photographed, and kept the issues in Tibet alive in a way that was impossible in her homeland.

The world depicted on television in Tibet and in China offered a version of reality. Deckyi and Dhondup usually watched a Sichuan channel that somehow aired on their Indian cable network. It broadcast familiar programs watched by both Tibetans and Chinese in southwest China and neighboring Tibet. During conversations with Deckyi and Dhondup, I glimpsed muted Chinese programs and commercials out of the corner of my eye: a state-of-the-art factory stamping out instant noodles on a conveyor belt; a dewy-skinned woman extolling the virtues of her air conditioner; a young man trying to tame an unruly blue-eyed Husky dog. Grim aspects of real life in Tibet were omitted. The television relayed a bizarre collage of fantasy, aspiration, and promises attainable only by some. Those left out could only watch from the other side of a beveled piece of glass.

· · ·

After they left Tibet, Deckyi and Dhondup's stay in Kathmandu stretched on while they waited for their "white passport"—the document that would allow them into India. Dhondup showed me an oversized white booklet that he extracted from a folder on the cluttered desk. The front bore the emblem of India: three lions with ruffled manes perched on a pillar. "Ministry of External Affairs, Government of India," it read. "Special Entry for People of Tibetan Origin." Dhondup's personal information was handwritten on the pages inside. "Small tattoo on [left] arm," noted one box. Dhondup pushed up a sleeve to show me what looked like the puckered flesh of a small pox vaccination on his forearm. In a box marked "Occupation," someone had wrongly written "Lorry driver"—easier to understand than "manager in accounting firm."

Finally, after they received their white passports, they boarded a bus in Kathmandu filled with Tibetan refugees bound for Delhi. Two days later, they arrived in India's capital and boarded another bus for the twelve-hour journey to Dharamsala. This time, they stayed two days in Dharamsala's Reception Center. Fortunately for Deckyi and Dhondup, the Dalai Lama

was home and they didn't have to wait long for their welcome audience. On a
winter morning Deckyi and Dhondup joined a hundred or so other Tibetans
with the Dalai Lama in his tranquil residential compound.

When they recalled the audience, Deckyi and Dhondup both broke into
bashful smiles. Tears started flowing "automatically" when the Dalai Lama
came into the room to speak to them, Deckyi said. The audience lasted nearly
half an hour, but at the end Dhondup couldn't remember what the Dalai
Lama said. He was too excited and dazed and felt so shy that he couldn't
even look at the spiritual leader. "I regret that I didn't hear him or remember
his advice," lamented Dhondup. Many Tibetans describe their first audience
with the Dalai Lama as a waking dream.

Two days after that they left the Reception Center to stay with Tenzin, the
chef at Moonpeak café. While recounting the story of their exile, Dhondup
and Deckyi didn't seem angry or bitter. Did they regret making the photocopies? Was their loss, all for fifty sheets of paper, worth it? I remembered
asking the same question of a Tibetan man imprisoned in a Chinese jail for
seven months. After the prison guards beat him, they left him naked in the
cold so pain seeped deep into his body. His crime? Making photocopies
of the Tibetan flag. He still suffered health problems, and though he had
escaped to India, he could not earn a living. Did he regret making those photocopies? I asked him quietly. Tears slid down his face and he wiped them
away with the flat of his hand. He nodded.

Deckyi and Dhondup lost so much: their home, jobs, relatives, and the
beginnings of a baby. Without hesitation, both she and Dhondup shook their
heads at my question about regret. "Even though we had to leave Tibet, we
don't regret making the photocopies," Deckyi replied firmly. "We did something right, something good for Tibet."

[13]

Money Matters

Principle? No One Does Anything on Principle

. . .

Before you see Delhi High Court you see the lawyers. Their black, billowy robes and crisp, white collars make them stand out on the road, stark as ink splotches across a bright canvas. Amid the stream of lawyers, Deckyi stood by the main gate, near armed soldiers in khaki uniforms toting machine guns. When I climbed out of the autorickshaw and waved, Deckyi's face lit up in a tentative smile.

It was a cool autumn day, and as we stood on the curb to debrief, the sun felt mild and pleasant—so different from the scorching heat that oppresses Delhi for most of the year. Deckyi wore jeans and a baggy red jacket, and her long hair was held back with a plastic clip. In Mandarin, she introduced me to the man next to her: a former colleague at the call center. A Tibetan in his late thirties, Lobsang had a thin mustache and shaggy black hair tinted slightly maroon. He switched between English and Mandarin, but eventually we relied more on English.

Lobsang had fled to India some fifteen years before, so he was comfortable speaking English. I jotted in my notebook as Lobsang shared his story.

"When did you start working at the call center?" I asked. "How long did you work there? Did you work every day? Did you register when you went to the office? How much should they pay you? How much do you want?"

Lobsang answered effusively, sometimes nudging my arm or shoulder with a flick of his fingers to emphasize his point. He became so excited that he periodically grabbed my notebook and pen with his fleshy hands. Lobsang scrawled calculations about his salary, circling numbers and multiplying and dividing sums so that soon his loose handwriting commandeered any blank space on the paper.

That afternoon I wore my black-rimmed glasses, a blue-collared shirt, and pinstriped trousers. I had never negotiated with a lawyer so figured I should look as serious as possible. As I stood with the two Tibetans outside the court, I began to feel unusually detached and calm. Deckyi didn't seem nervous either, though a court must have seemed an alien place to her.

After a few last questions, I phoned the lawyer who told us to come to the consultation room inside. I shrugged my arms into a black blazer, which was folded to protect it from dust during the autorickshaw ride from home in another corner of Delhi. Unbidden, Deckyi straightened my rumpled lapel and extended a small hand as she offered to hold my bag. It held only a thin sheaf of papers that Vinayak Sharma, the Indian legal aid lawyer in Dharamsala who helped Tibetans, had emailed me the night before. I declined since the bag was practically empty.

We concluded our curbside meeting and walked through the arched entrance, past the armed guards, through the rusty metal detector and security check where a bored-looking woman stroked my chest for hidden weapons, and we joined the flow of black-robed advocates.

Inside, the courthouse had the decrepit feel of other Indian government buildings—smudged walls, dingy floors, a sour smell wafting from a bathroom door—except there was hardly any security. Apart from the initial security check at the entrance, we just walked in, no registration book or signed permission slip to enter. Lawyers milled around and streamed through. Humanity bustled in crowded corridors. Black-robed lawyers congenially stopped mid-conversation to give us directions to the consultation room, which buzzed with chatter; it had the feel of a school cafeteria at lunch. Lawyers in voluminous robes surrounded rectangular tables next to clients. When we walked in, a man stood up from the table and lifted a black sleeve to wave at us.

We sat down with Mohit, the lawyer representing Samir, Deckyi's former boss at the call center. Mohit was in his thirties, clean cut, with freshly trimmed black hair flecked with gray. His white advocate's collar was starched to a crisp stiffness; the two ends of his tie jutted out like miniature arms. He cracked a cursory smile in greeting. I sat at the end of the table with Mohit on my right and Deckyi and Lobsang on my left. Facing me at the opposite end of the long table was an overweight older man in a worn sweater. He sat by himself and gazed vacantly into the distance. As Mohit and I talked, I imagined the man listening to our conversation. In fact, he was too far away to overhear, but I wished someone else could have witnessed the surreal exchange that followed.

· · ·

Months before, in May, after my brief phone call with Deckyi's former boss, I suggested she talk to Vinayak Sharma of Tibet Legal Aid in Dharamsala. Vinayak offered free services to Tibetans after his regular work day at the local Indian court. Tibetans said if they closed their eyes and heard Vinayak speak, they would think he was Tibetan too: he had attended school at the Tibetan Children's Village in Dharamsala for most of his life.

Earlier that spring, I went with Deckyi to see Vinayak at his Dharamsala office—a small room in a gloomy building next to the post office. A flowered synthetic curtain blocked a single window so the only light came from fluorescent lights overhead. Vinayak sat behind a wooden table; clients entered and waited on two hard twin beds that served as sofas. Half a dozen people crowded inside awaiting their turn, including two young women, middle-aged men, and a young man who looked like a student. One woman carried a metal-framed baby carrier on her back. Her curly haired infant had bright apple cheeks and occasionally squawked like a young bird.

Everyone waited silently while Vinayak asked Deckyi questions in Tibetan and scribbled notes in English. If Deckyi was surprised to be speaking to an Indian man fluent in Tibetan, she didn't show it. She responded to his questions in short bursts of Tibetan punctuated by shakes and nods of her head. Vinayak looked up and summarized their conversation in English in his soft, even voice. "I think according to labor laws this is a Delhi case because the company is in Delhi. I will send the boss a legal notice telling him to pay within thirty days. Let's see what response comes," he explained.

"Do you really think he will pay?" I asked.

"Sometimes they do."

"The boss might respond to the legal notice since now there's some pressure, right?"

Vinayak replied, "If she files a complaint she has to do in Delhi. She has to do herself. Then it could take seven to eight months for the court to decide." He added, "We will send the legal notice first. Let's see." He instructed Deckyi to get the names of the six other Tibetans in her group who were not paid, along with contact information for the Indian boss and the call center. Deckyi nodded.

. . .

Later that autumn I was spending most of my time in Delhi after starting a new job at a microfinance company; I thought it was a way to work on reducing social inequities beyond just writing about them. I still had my room

in the nunnery and went to Dharamsala sometimes, but it had been months
since Deckyi and I had seen Vinayak.

One afternoon that fall, Deckyi called me out of the blue. "Where are
you?" she asked after greeting me.

"I'm in Delhi," I replied. "Where are you?"

"I'm in Delhi. Do you have free time?"

"When?"

"Today."

"Today? What's the matter?"

"To meet the lawyer." I was puzzled, so I called Vinayak for a better update. He had sent the legal notice to Samir, the call center boss, and followed
up with a phone call. Samir at first denied the Tibetans had worked for the
call center at all, then said they performed badly so would not be paid, then
said he paid them already. Samir said he would come to Dharamsala and
meet the Tibetans and Vinayak to discuss the situation. Instead, a few days
later Vinayak got a phone call from Mohit, the lawyer Samir had retained.

Going to see a lawyer with Deckyi was not part of my plans for my work
day, or something to be done ad hoc. "We need to prepare," I told her. The
next day Vinayak emailed me the legal notice he sent to Samir and a memo
about the situation. The two-page document began:

> I serve you with the following Legal Notice that my clients ap-
> proached Samir C—[sic] Time and again to pay them balance
> amount of their earned money but he always on one pretext or the
> other avoided the payment of money. . . . That it is brought to your
> notice that Tibetan refugees even though they are foreigner's [sic] in
> India enjoy full protection of laws in India. Your act of not paying the
> amount of money agreed is illegal, contrary to the provisions of law
> and also violation of basic human right as enshrined in several provi-
> sions of our Indian Constitution.

It was enough to spark action from Samir. He called Vinayak to say that he
and his family were upset and did not want to go to court. Through Mohit,
the Delhi lawyer, he agreed to pay Deckyi and the six other Tibetans 70,000
rupees ($1,500) even though they said they were owed 178,000 rupees
($4,000).

"He said these people [the Tibetans] had not done the work correctly,"
Vinayak wrote in his memo to me. "They have asked false questions, had
mis-behaved with his clients. And a result of which he have [sic] received

only half of the amount from his clients and therefore he can give to Tibetans the half of the money only."

When Mohit called Vinayak, the message changed again. Vinayak recalled, "He said that we know these Tibetans are very poor people therefore they want to pay the money i.e. 50 percent on humanitarian ground only. His client i.e. Samir C— is very good person and does not want to do such inhuman work. We want to pay the money because they know that these Tibetans were very poor."

It was highly doubtful that Samir was as compassionate as he professed to be. But once a settlement was proposed, Deckyi took the bus from Dharamsala to Delhi to get the money in person. She called me to accompany her to see the lawyer since she couldn't speak English. Vinayak was satisfied with the settlement of 70,000 rupees, but told me to assess the situation first and refrain from immediately talking about a settlement. "Don't be too rigid in your dealings with them just see the situation and be a bit easy in deciding the matter," he advised in an email. "They are cleaver [*sic*] person so just be attentive."

At first Deckyi wanted me to go see the lawyer on my own, saying that she had to return to Dharamsala. Why did she need to go back? I asked. English classes, Deckyi replied. She was running out of money to stay in Delhi, she offered next. Vinayak said it was common for his Tibetan clients to want to flee confrontation. I was busy with my new job but wanted to help resolve this messy situation, so I told Deckyi to stay in Delhi and that she had to go with me to see the lawyer. Then I called Mohit, who sounded surprised and curious to hear from me. Without much fuss he agreed to meet on Friday afternoon at Delhi High Court. That gave me a few days, so I started to prepare.

· · ·

Back in the court's consultation room, the chatter around us buzzed. I introduced myself, Deckyi, and Lobsang to Mohit, then cut to the chase. After three years in India, I knew that people played hardball during negotiations and didn't bother with niceties.

"These Tibetans worked at Excell [call center] and never got paid. When will they get paid?"

"There's no record they worked there," the lawyer stated firmly.

"The company didn't give them work contracts?" I asked. We stared at each other. "Shouldn't a multinational call center give employees work contracts?"

"If they didn't have work contracts then there's no case."

At that moment my phone rang. A lawyer friend in Delhi was returning my call, and I listened to his quick tips. I hung up, turned back to Mohit, and deliberately dropped the name of the prestigious law firm where my friend worked. "My friend says even if there was no work contract we can show there was a relationship between the company and the Tibetans. They did have to sign in every day when they went to the office. Why don't we just look at the register and prove they did work there?"

"We don't have access to the register. It doesn't exist."

"I doubt that," I said. "It's the norm at Indian companies for employees to sign a register every day. Deckyi and Lobsang said they signed in every day."

Mohit suddenly switched tack. "They didn't do the job correctly. They misbehaved with the clients."

"Really? Where is the documentation of that? And what exactly did they do incorrectly?" I demanded.

"They don't have the records of that."

"If they performed so badly, why would you let them stay with the job for more than a month?"

"It takes a very long time to get feedback from the customer."

"Don't you have recordings? Deckyi says their work was monitored every day." I added, "Even if they performed badly—which you can't prove—you have to pay them for the time they worked. You can terminate them, but you can't withhold pay for the time they worked." I wasn't sure if that was true, but it sounded reasonable to me.

Mohit grew exasperated. "What was the work they were doing anyway?" He turned to the Tibetans with a skeptical look on his face. Lobsang tried to interject but Mohit cut him off before he could explain. "Don't get emotional," he snapped at Lobsang.

I looked at Deckyi and asked her in Mandarin, "He is asking what kind of work you were doing."

She replied in Mandarin, "The computer has a list of questions. We were calling hospitals in China to ask them what kind of equipment they had. It was simple."

I told Mohit what Deckyi said. When he suggested they had done the work badly I insisted on proof. "Who decides their work is good or bad? Isn't there some system, some documentation? Or is it completely arbitrary?"

Next, Mohit claimed that the Tibetans could not really speak Mandarin. "He says you can't speak Chinese," I told Deckyi in Mandarin. Even unflappable Deckyi was perturbed by this remark; her eyes widened in disbelief. "What do you think we're speaking right now?" I asked Mohit.

When Mohit claimed some of the Tibetans were already paid, I asked for receipts and documentation. This back and forth with Mohit continued.

"This is such an interesting situation, isn't it?" I asked. "I think a lot of journalists would be very interested in a story about Tibetan refugees in India and how they are cheated by Indian companies. This would really make a very interesting story."

"A journalist can't write about this. That's defamation!" Mohit spat.

"It's not defamation if we say the Tibetans allege they haven't been paid. Then we go to the company and ask them for their comment," I shot back.

"You can't do that. No newspaper will run such a story without proof."

"Then the journalist can ask the company for proof. And if they don't have any, then what? We can say the company can't back up their claims." I pulled out some information about the call center from their website. "Isn't it strange that a multinational call center with offices in New York, Argentina, and India would have such labor practices? I saw Excell's board of directors is headed by a guy named John C—. John is the CEO of K— Partners, a 'knowledge process outsourcing' company, and I actually interviewed him a couple years ago." This was all true. "Why don't I write to him about this situation? I'm sure he would be very interested in the conduct of a company where he is on the board of directors."

Mohit looked at me humorlessly. "If we go to court, it will take more than a year to resolve this."

"The Tibetans don't have much to lose since they haven't been paid for eight months. And there are other things we can do besides go to court."

"Who will represent them if this goes to court? This takes time."

"Why don't I ask someone at the Human Rights Law Network?" I retorted, dropping the name of the well-known legal advocacy group in Delhi. "They do a lot of pro bono work for Tibetans. We could ask Colin Gonsalves, who does a lot of work for Tibetans." A friend had worked at Human Rights Law Network and suggested mentioning Gonsalves, its founder and famous legal crusader who was particularly interested in Tibetan issues. I didn't know him but dropped his name anyway. "Do you know him?" I asked.

An odd smile creased Mohit's lips. "Yes."

"Then you know he would be very interested in this."

Mohit huffed a bit and pushed himself away from the table. "I don't have time for this. This is such a small amount of money. I'm not getting paid for this. You know what I usually charge? 50,000 rupees."

"Then you know this is a pittance for this boss, Samir, and he should just pay the Tibetans their money. For him this money is nothing. They worked and they should get paid. It's very simple."

"I don't have time for this."

"Do you think I do? Do you think they do?" I indignantly gestured to Lobsang and Deckyi. "This is on principle."

"Principle?" Mohit guffawed. "No one does anything on principle."

His flippant comment irked me. "Yes they do!" I practically shouted.

"Actually in my own life I am straight and honest," he confessed nonsensically.

"Then you know this is wrong," I retorted.

Mohit threw his hands in the air impatiently. "This is India! There is fraud all the time!"

"I don't care. They worked, they should get paid. It's very simple," I repeated, genuinely outraged by this blatant exploitation of vulnerable people. "Just on principle they should get paid." I glanced at my watch; forty-five minutes had passed. I moved on. "So Samir says he is willing to pay them 70,000 rupees. You know that's a fraction of what they're owed. 70,000 rupees is not enough. Here's what would be adequate." I wrote in my notebook "Rs. 120,000" and showed it to Mohit.

He let out a sharp laugh. "That's impossible."

"Why? Actually they should get paid the full amount of 178,000 rupees plus damages—interest, travel, time wasted."

"Damages?" Mohit sneered. "Who is going to determine damages?"

"Why don't we call Human Rights Law Network? I'm sure Colin Gonsalves would help."

He looked at my notebook and shook his head. "120,000 is impossible."

"You know this is nothing for Samir. Discuss it with him. Why waste everyone's time? Tell him 70,000 is not adequate."

Mohit glared at me. "I suggested to my client not to pay anything. That is my advice. Don't pay anything."

"Why is that? Because you think you can screw them?" I glared at him.

"I don't have time for this," Mohit said, beginning to push himself from the table.

"Neither do we! So you will talk to Samir?"

"Yes."

"When can we expect to hear from you?"

"Call me next week." Mohit rose from his seat. He gave me his business card and I gave him mine.

"Wait," I said, asking for my card back. "Tell Samir I think John would be interested in this situation since he is on the board of directors." I wrote the full name of the call center's board member on my card in large letters and handed it back to Mohit. We trailed behind him as he left the consultation room. "Did you understand?" I asked them. Lobsang nodded. Even Deckyi, with her limited English, had gotten the gist of what Mohit had said.

In Mandarin she replied incredulously, "He said that he would not give us even one cent."

"Do you think we have a chance of getting the money?" asked Lobsang in English. Unlike Deckyi, his face betrayed anxiety.

"I don't know. I think so. Now there's pressure so I hope he tells Samir. He must be a little worried now." I shrugged in agitation. "We'll call him next week."

. . .

India's glacial bureaucracy is infamous. Lesser known is just how swiftly things can happen. Later that same evening Deckyi called and told me Jampa, another Tibetan from the call center, told her Samir would pay them the following day. I had no idea who Jampa was, but Deckyi passed the phone to him and he spoke to me in rapid-fire Mandarin. Samir wanted to meet tomorrow near his home to discuss payment, Jampa claimed. He would give me the address later. But Deckyi wasn't clear how much Samir would pay and whether he would really do so.

On Saturday morning Deckyi called me at 11 a.m. "Can you come with us to meet Samir?" she asked anxiously.

"When?"

"12 o'clock."

"12 o'clock?!" I looked at my watch.

"Where?"

"I don't know."

"Deckyi," I said, trying to remain patient. "I need to know the address of where to meet."

"I will tell Jampa to SMS you." She added, "And this Jampa, be careful. He's not honest." Jampa was Samir's Tibetan middleman who took a cut of the money earned by Tibetan workers. Later Lobsang said of Jampa, "His heart is black. How can a Tibetan do this to his own people?"

"We should choose the place to meet," I warned Deckyi. "We should meet in a public place, not Samir's home."

Jampa sent me a text message with Samir's neighborhood and said he would let us know an exact time and address. I had never heard of the area and couldn't pinpoint the location in my detailed Delhi road atlas. I waited but didn't hear anything. Late that afternoon I called Deckyi who informed me that she, Jampa, and Lobsang went to meet Samir at a restaurant near his home but he never showed up. Samir's phone remained switched off.

"I will call Samir myself," I told her. "Don't agree to meet until I speak to him."

On Sunday morning I called Samir and to my surprise, he answered his phone. I didn't bother with niceties and asked why he had failed to meet the Tibetans the previous day.

He protested, "They shouldn't meet me until I tell them to." He started going through the same arguments Mohit used at the courthouse: the Tibetans had done the job badly so he couldn't pay them; they had been paid already. "These Tibetans are very poor," he said defensively. "So I want to help them."

"You can help them by paying them their salary," I replied angrily. "Did Mohit tell you what I said?"

"Yes."

"You understand the situation?" I pressed. Abruptly, Samir hung up. When I called back his phone was switched off.

The rest of the day was consumed with phone calls to Deckyi, Lobsang, and Vinayak. At 10:30 a.m. I called Mohit, who sounded harried and surprisingly contrite as I complained angrily about the runaround. In the background I could hear a baby wailing.

Late in the afternoon as I walked to my neighborhood store for groceries, Samir called me. This time, he amplified his defensiveness and anger and accused me of wasting his time.

I didn't hold back. "Me wasting your time?" I shouted. Cars and mopeds whizzed by on the street. "You're the one who is wasting everyone's time! Why are we wasting time talking now? When are you going to pay them!?"

"Now everyone thinks I am a villain," whined Samir, his voice rising in pitch. "You think you are good in the eyes of god?"

"I'm not worried about what god thinks of me. Maybe you should be worried."

"They misbehaved with the clients," Samir argued. "They abused them! Because of them we lost the client."

"What?" I yelled incredulously even though I was walking down the street. "Let's see some record of that. I'm sure your company has these records."

"Only I have access to these records," Samir retorted.

"You're the only one with access? You're a multinational company and only you have the records? Why? Why don't we ask someone on the company's management team for the records. Is your company a member of Nasscom?" I asked, referring to India's powerful IT and outsourcing industry association.

"I don't know."

"You don't know? I'm sure they are. Why don't I write to the head of Nasscom? I think they would like to know that you are violating labor laws. And how about John, the director of your board. Why don't I send an email to him today?" I said referring to the American CEO I had coincidentally interviewed previously through my journalism.

"Why don't we meet?" Samir suddenly offered. "You, me, and the Tibetans."

"Why? What's the point?" I asked in exasperation. "I don't want to waste any more time. I'm not interested in meeting until you agree on payment. And if we meet, I want to meet with a representative from your company, and I will bring someone from the Human Rights Law Network."

"I am busy and I don't have time for this!"

"Neither do I!"

After the heated exchange we hung up and, without breaking my stride, I continued to my local market to buy light bulbs and bread. As I stepped over a stray dog sleeping on the dirty floor of the small marketplace, my phone rang. It was Mohit. "You see," the lawyer oozed in a conciliatory tone markedly different from his "bad cop" one. "No one has time for such a small amount of money. You calling me, him calling me. Samir will pay 80,000, maybe 90,000."

"No! I told you they want 120,000 rupees." It was a difference of $1,000—a lot of money in India. I stood outside a small tailor shop where a bespectacled man measured cloth with a yellow measuring tape draped over his shoulder. Normal life continued while Mohit and I fought on the phone.

"Ok. 100,000," Mohit smoothly countered.

"Did you talk to Samir? How do you know he will agree to this?"

"He will agree."

"It's not enough. Let me talk to the Tibetans." I knew from years of bargaining in developing countries and haggling in markets that Mohit's quick capitulation meant don't take the first offer.

"Just agree and we can meet tomorrow at my office at one o'clock."

"No! I have to talk to the Tibetans first."

Mohit sighed. "If we go to court it will take a year to settle."

"I have better options than court." It was true, so I spoke with confidence. As the Dalai Lama often said in a different context, truth was on our side. And it was useful to be a journalist and have lawyer and human rights activist friends. I had been exploited and mistreated myself, so now that I could help Deckyi and the other Tibetans, I shed any self-consciousness or decorum to fight back. Conflict in India is routine, so no one batted an eyelash at me yelling into the phone while standing in the marketplace.

"When will you call me back?" Mohit asked.

"Soon."

I went home and called Lobsang, Deckyi, and Vinayak. They were all thrilled about the prospect of a 100,000 rupees settlement.

"Should I ask for more?" I asked Vinayak.

"Don't get too greedy. It is good they will get any money at all," Vinayak told me.

"But this isn't even the full amount of what they should get," I reasoned.

I waited a few hours to text Mohit so I didn't appear too eager. "They will settle for 110,000," I wrote a little after 9 p.m. Within five minutes he called me back, eager to set a time to meet the next day. I suspected my offer was too low, like a haggling customer who finds a vendor abruptly agreeing on a price. Still, the money—around $2,400—was more than anyone expected.

• • •

On Monday afternoon, I met Deckyi and Lobsang at Delhi High Court, a landmark we all knew by then, and from there we went to Mohit's office. It was in the eastern part of the city, not too far from the court but in a neighborhood I had never been to. The taxi stopped at a crowded marketplace with cramped storefronts and a jumble of worn signage; goats stood alert on spindly legs on the curb and small barefoot children played cricket in alleyways. Mohit's office was in a basement through an anonymous doorway marked only by a white sheet of paper with his name and title printed on it. I cautioned Deckyi and Lobsang that we couldn't count on anything until we had the money in hand.

Mohit, wearing a navy V-neck sweater over a crisp, white collared shirt, greeted us with a cool smile. We followed him to a spacious but sparsely furnished glassed-wall office. The only person inside, Mohit sat behind a desk that held a laptop computer and a small printer. We sat on three flimsy chairs facing him. Heavy legal books filled shelves on the wall behind him.

"Is Samir coming?" I asked. The meeting was set for 1 p.m. and it was already a few minutes past the hour.

"Yes, he is coming," Mohit reassured us.

"Are you sure? Because I called his phone this morning and it was switched off."

"He is coming," Mohit said lightly. "I just talked to him fifteen minutes ago." He picked up his mobile phone as if to show us its call history.

Mohit was typing a letter of receipt on his laptop. He asked Deckyi and Lobsang to verify the spelling of their names and the other Tibetans.

"Are they men or women?" he inquired.

Deckyi confirmed she was the only woman. On the computer screen, Mohit added "Mr." before six of the names.

"She is our leader," Lobang said in Mandarin to me, grinning. Deckyi's eyes lit up with pleasure. She had rallied on behalf of herself and six men, including her husband who stayed behind in Dharamsala, while she tried to get their money.

As he typed, Mohit chatted to me in a mild tone. "What province in China are you from?"

"My parents are from Hong Kong."

"When did you move to America?"

"I was born there."

"You did your schooling there?"

I nodded. "Yes."

"Where? Chicago?"

"No, Boston," I said, wondering why he guessed Chicago since I did spend time there. "Where are you from?"

"I belong to Bihar."

The conversation was casual. But I sensed that his queries were more a postmortem of his adversary than interest in me as a person.

Mohit finally printed the letter for us to review. Some forty minutes later, a man entered the room and without introducing himself, plopped onto a chair next to Mohit. An air of restless irritation surrounded him like a ring of gnats.

"Is that him?" I murmured to Deckyi. She gave me a sidelong glance and nodded.

After our verbal sparring by phone, this was Samir in the flesh. I had imagined him as an older man, in his forties or fifties, someone with an air of authority to account for his shameless audacity. Instead, Samir was young and pudgy-faced, in his late twenties or early thirties with long, greasy hair tied back in a ponytail. A scraggly beard rimmed his face although just a few sparse hairs lined his upper lip. Rectangular glasses with purple wire frames—an unsuccessful attempt to look fashionable—perched on his nose. Around his wrist he wore a red holy string, a *rakhi* bracelet, that symbolizes kinship. A gold ring embedded with a blood-colored stone adorned one pinky. It was a chilly day, and even cooler in the basement office, but his striped short-sleeve shirt topped with a puffy blue vest exposed his plump forearms. Despite the facial hair and because of his impatient, impertinent air, Samir resembled an overgrown, petulant baby.

He didn't bother looking at us but started speaking with Mohit in Hindi and chuckling in little airy gasps. Without acknowledging us, the two of them perused the letter in front of them and discussed the names of the Tibetans in the group. Lobsang interjected and reached over the table to point at the document and tried to explain in labored English that he was not paid for another project, how many hours he had worked, and how much he was owed.

Samir brushed his hand aside and shook his head violently. "Leave it, leave it! I know, I know!" he cried.

I interrupted the whining outburst. "He is saying there's another project and you didn't pay him."

"Leave it! I know!" Samir thrashed his head and shoulders. "I understand," he screeched. Mohit let out a nervous laugh and met my gaze with an embarrassed look. I realized then that they probably didn't really know each other. Mohit was probably just doing a favor for Samir through some connection. Then, very calmly, he steered Samir's attention back to the paper, like a parent distracting a toddler from a meltdown.

They insisted on writing the check to me so they could hand off responsibility for the money. Did I have an ID? Mohit sent Deckyi to make a photocopy of my passport from a shop outside. Since I was already familiar with India's mercurial bureaucracy, I had brought all kinds of documents with me.

"How about your ID?" I asked Samir. "Do you have one?"

"My check is my ID, don't worry," he replied. "The cash is there."

"How do I know? I haven't seen it." He and Mohit resumed their discussion about the receipt.

"It will be your responsibility," said Mohit.

"Fine." I told Deckyi about this exchange and asked whether there would be any confusion with the Tibetans seeking payment on their own. "They don't want the others to come to them asking for the money," I explained.

Deckyi piped up in tentative English. "Come and going, costs money."

"I know they do not have money. I know everything about you people. I know your financial condition," Samir declared breezily. "I know each and everything."

"I'm sure you do. Very well," I said, dripping sarcasm.

"There are people from different countries working with me. This is the first time the problem occurred because of these guys. You can ask her." Samir tilted his head toward Deckyi. "Some of them made abusive calls."

This comment unleashed a three-way torrent. It filled me with rage that he was still flagrantly lying about the Tibetans. "Abusive calls? What kind of abusive calls?" I snapped.

Mohit held up his hands in a pleading gesture. "Let's not go back. It's done, it's all over. No, no."

"No no no no no no," cried Samir like a child having a tantrum.

"Why would someone in a call center make abusive calls?" I wondered loudly.

Mohit tried to calm everyone down. "That chapter is over. Please, please. When we sit for settlement we should not go in the past."

I told Deckyi what Samir said. She laughed. "If we scolded people, we couldn't ask so many questions," she told me in Chinese.

Samir took out a long blue check from his jacket and began filling it out while he and Mohit talked in Hindi. Then in English he said to me, "I will speak to the bank manager, ok. If I give it to you—it will go to you and you will be responsible." His pen made a scratching noise on the desk as he filled out the check.

As he wrote, I asked Samir a few casual questions and to my surprise he replied politely, as if pleased by the attention. "Where is this call center?"

"Mathura Road."

"Is it 24 hours?"

"All call centers are 24 hours."

"How many people work there?"

"About 500."

"Mostly Indians?"

"Mostly Indians. Other nationalities work under me. I work as a vendor in the company, as a consultant. And I'm also an employee there."

"So you are an employee there. And a consultant as well?"

"Consultant is my father. He provides language resources." Samir paused.

"So does he recruit people who speak other languages?"

"I recruit them."

"What other languages do people speak?"

"All the languages. Depends on what kinds of projects the company receives." Samir heaved a great sigh. "This is the first time in my life that I've had a question mark over my head that says, 'This is a bad man.'"

"Really? Only the first time?" I asked sarcastically.

"This is the first time in my career."

"Do you think this will be the last time?"

"Obviously it will be the last time." Then he handed me the check for 110,000 rupees.

I glanced at it but kept my no-nonsense attitude. "So where is the bank. You said GK One?"

"I've already told them. I told them yesterday someone will come."

Deckyi and I peered at the check. "Is there money in the account?" she asked quietly. "Let's see," I replied, "We will go to the bank today."

Lobsang started pleading to Samir about other work he had done. "What I did I did complete. All are recorded. I sent emails, they replied. Everything complete."

Samir responded impatiently. "You come by tomorrow and see. Tomorrow you are coming for ARP money. So when you come we will talk about it, don't worry, okay. Come any time after one o'clock."

"Where? Office?" Lobsang sighed. "I am a very poor guy. Not much money for autos."

"There's another project you need to pay him for?" I interjected.

"Yes there is," Samir admitted.

"Can you pay me now?" Lobsang beseeched.

"I cannot. See this?" Samir waved a couple of checks in Lobsang's face. "There are just a few left. I need to go to Defence Colony and pay this guy. So I cannot do it. Come by tomorrow and I will give you a check. I cannot!"

"In order to save money for me," Lobsang began as Samir started laughing. "You are a rich man."

"Okay, take the auto money and come tomorrow. Pukka!"

Lobsang turned toward us. "In AMR I did twenty-eight projects. He paid only five. He paid me only 3,500. Actually it should be 16,000." I didn't know what AMR referred to and could only imagine all the other work Lobsang had never been paid for.

"Did you check your quality?" Samir snapped.

Mohit tried to calm everyone down. "No, no. I have told you. No dispute, nothing. Don't discuss past," he implored quietly. "No, no, no. There is no need, no need. There's no point to fight."

Samir spoke in a loud and frantic tone. "I'm just paying this because of peace. So I don't get calls 'Cacacacaa!' I don't like it!"

"Shouldn't there be some system in this company instead of this haphazard way of paying, not paying?" I demanded in an exasperated tone.

"There is a system!" yelled Samir. "These guys never accept their mistakes. They talk to the project manager and he shows him the details of everything."

"Then why are you still hiring him?" I yelled back.

A four-way free-for-all broke out with all of us hurling comments and Mohit trying to pacify us. Only Deckyi remained silent.

"Please. No. Please, both of you. Silence please. Silence please," Mohit repeated. "Please please please please."

"What do you want me to do? Take out all the money and give it to you?" Samir flapped the checks angrily at Lobsang.

"Lobsang! Please, please," Mohit chimed.

Seeing Samir wave checks in Lobsang's face made my blood boil. "So you will pay him tomorrow, right?" I yelled.

"No no no no no. Tomorrow I will pay him the project money. But he did blunder in one of the projects." Samir's voice rose to a frenzied pitch. "I just hired him for my love. You can ask him what kind of person am I. Though he does mistakes I hire him each time." His speech became even more rapid. "He comes and says, I need work, I need work. I say come again. He works I pay him money. And then he says, 'Blah blah blah you are bad, you are bad.'" He turned to Lobsang, agitated. "What do you want from me? Why are you exploiting me? Did I ever exploit you?"

"You call me, I come to you, and then I worked. We are working," Lobsang said slowly but loudly in English.

"I know, I know! Did I ever exploit you?"

"Let's be peaceful," replied Lobsang. They continued talking about payment for other projects.

"Ask him, ask him, ask him," cried Samir frantically. "He's trying to make me bad or something, I don't know."

Deckyi and I looked at each other. "Lobsang continued to work for Samir?" I asked her quietly.

"Let them to themselves," she murmured. "I don't know what they're talking about."

"You should be honest," Lobsang scolded Samir.

Samir crossed his plump arms across his chest. "It hurts me, you know."

As Samir and Lobsang continued their exchange, Mohit leaned across the desk and showed me the receipt he had typed up. "You have to sign here. You will keep one copy and this will be my copy." He showed me how to sign on top of the pink stamp pasted to the page.

"Everybody has got problems," Samir laughed and slapped Lobsang jovially on the back as he teetered between silliness, anger, and hysteria. "Everybody has got their family, don't worry. I become angry but I am never bad, right," he announced to us. "I call these guys because if I call someone else instead of them it doesn't look good to me because these people are my people. If there's any trouble in the company I take care on their behalf. One mistake—out. These guys—a thousand mistakes, no problem. I will take care of it. They should cooperate that's why I'm saying."

"Why do you keep hiring them if they keep making mistakes?" I pressed. "Maybe that's why your projects aren't working?"

"I don't know." Samir looked at Deckyi. "She worked for the first time with me so I don't know her. Other people who have worked for the first time and things went wrong. So I'm a bad bad bad man." He started cackling madly.

"I think if you don't pay someone for the work they—" I started.

"I am the middleman, so I am caught on this side, that side. What is happening!? Leave me, leave me!" Samir signaled toward Mohit, who shrank from him, then launched into an almost unintelligible hysteria. "I told him, help me my friend. I don't want any call from this guy, that guy. I want to be released. Let me stay happy! He said, 'Okay, okay, I will do something.' Oh shit, man, what's happening? If there's any trouble with the check just ring me at the same time and I will take care of it. I try to stay happy."

Mohit handed me the signed receipts with an official stamp. "Leave immediately or the bank will be closed," he commanded. "What time is it?"

"It's only 2:30."

Lobsang, Deckyi, and I rose from our seats. I took a parting shot at Samir. "It's a strange process where the employees have to come to your home to get paid."

"Leave immediately!" Mohit repeated, not completely unkindly.

The three of us trooped out of the basement office into the afternoon sunshine, where we flagged down an autorickshaw to take us to the bank.

. . .

The Oriental Bank of Commerce was located in an upscale Delhi shopping enclave called Greater Kailash I, commonly known as GK One. The cramped U-shaped cluster of shops was a far cry from the sacred Tibetan mountain that was its namesake. The trendy boutiques in GK One did brisk business selling expensive Ayurvedic soaps, sleek mango wood furniture, embroidered pillow covers, and chic cotton tunics. These shops had a notion of customer service notably absent from Oriental Bank of Commerce, which was a "government of India undertaking," according to its storefront sign.

Deckyi, Lobsang, and I entered the bank and ducked our heads beneath a metal grate half-lowered over the doorway. Inside, the drab room was nearly deserted and desks behind the plexiglass partition that separated the waiting area from offices sat empty. It was 2:40 p.m.; five minutes remained of lunch hour. We sat down on some stiff chairs to wait for the workday to resume. At 2:45 p.m., people filed inside and headed to the office area. Some sat at their desks and bent their heads over stacks of paper like automatons. No one acknowledged our presence or offered to assist us.

A middle-aged man behind the partition busied himself by sifting through paper. Eventually he looked up but kept shuffling his papers as I handed him the check and pulled out my passport. I expected hassles, but the man didn't even bother checking my ID. After taking the check he gave me a metal disc with a number. He nodded his head toward a cashier's window where a man was too busy counting money to look up. "Wait," he intoned.

I sat down, waited a few minutes, inquired again with the first man, then gave my metal token to the cashier. He nonchalantly pushed three bricks of money through the small hole in the scarred plexiglass. The money's solid heft surprised me. When I sat down with Deckyi and Lobsang and handed them each a stack of bills to count, they rifled through the bills quickly, paper moving through their fingers in a blur, while I fumbled with the cash. Deckyi observed my clumsiness and remarked to Lobsang, "She doesn't know how to handle money."

It was true; I had never manually handled so much cash. My salary didn't come in stacks of bills, and I didn't pay people with a paper bag stuffed with money. We finished counting the money, every last brown 500-rupee and blue 100-rupee bill. It was all there.

I heaved a sigh of relief. "Chenggong," I said in Mandarin. Success. The three of us looked at each other and grinned.

· · ·

None of us had eaten so we had a late lunch at the Golden Dragon, a nearby "Chin-jabi" Chinese restaurant with Chinese food for Punjabi palettes: spicy food smothered in starchy sauces. A few years before, Lobsang had worked there as a dishwasher, waiter, and then cook. It was midafternoon so we were the only customers in the restaurant. It had the feel of countless Chinese restaurants around the world, but here, red paper lanterns hung from the ceiling alongside paper stars sold in Indian bazaars. Purple tinsel garlands complete with a small, dangling Santa Claus doll decorated one corner of the room. A tinny Muzak version of "Careless Whisper" by Wham! crooned from a stereo.

Lobsang and Deckyi looked tentatively through the heavy, oversized menu. They shyly urged me to choose some dishes, and finally we ordered spicy pork for Deckyi, spicy tofu that turned out to be paneer (Indian cheese), and vegetables. I hoped they would have Deckyi's favorite dish, Sichuan hotpot, but a large tureen of seafood soup was a poor substitute. Slender Indian waiters brought out steaming platters and served us by pressing a fork and spoon together like tongs to pile food on our plates.

A wistful smile appeared on Lobsang's face. "I used to work here as waiter," he reminded us. As a dishwasher at the Golden Dragon he made 3,000 rupees a month, about $60, working seven days a week. "So many dishes!" he groaned at the memory. Eventually he moved up to become a waiter and then the higher-paid position of cook. He hadn't known how to cook but learned quickly.

The work was hard—the hot kitchen, hours of standing—so when a job came up at the call center with its air conditioning and cushioned chairs, he left the Golden Dragon. Lobsang pieced together work at a few other call centers to support his wife and three young children. He liked Delhi. A bigger city meant more work. It didn't matter that his two older children, ages seven and five, went to an Indian school. Did they speak Tibetan at home? "Of course," Lobsang replied.

We finished our meal of overspiced Chin-jabi food. Deckyi and Lobsang insisted on paying the bill though I tried to decline. They had enough money to treat a guest.

. . .

By the time we left the Golden Dragon, day was fading to dusk. The three of us crammed into an autorickshaw that pushed its way north, through traffic and hazy pollution that obscured the dimming sun. We managed to avoid major traffic, so it took just forty-five minutes to reach Majnu Ka Tilla, in Delhi's northeast corner. We rode in silence the whole way, lost in our own thoughts. Conversation would have been impossible anyway with the roar of buses, autorickshaws, mopeds, and cars around us. In my lap I clutched my purse, stuffed full with rupees worth a couple of thousand dollars.

The autorickshaw deposited us at Majnu Ka Tilla and we walked across a pedestrian bridge above a loud river of traffic. It was dark and there were few streetlights. As we walked down sooty stairs, we stepped around a crouching, wild-haired Tibetan woman who wailed loudly, then past an elderly Tibetan man with one gnarled hand outstretched. He sat surrounded by a pile of trash he had swept up with the broom in his other hand. It was the first time I had seen Tibetans begging in Majnu Ka Tilla. At the bottom of the steps, an androgynous dreadlocked backpacker napped serenely on top of his rucksack, face tilted toward the sky.

It was a relief to slip into the relatively tranquil warren of pedestrian lanes in Majnu Ka Tilla. Deckyi and Lobsang walked easily through the urban village's winding lanes, past small shops, restaurants, cheap guesthouses, and vendors selling trinkets. The path opened into a spacious plaza, an oasis of calm ringed with Buddhist temples. Colorful prayer flags were strung across the paved stone plaza where street dogs trotted after children. A few young Tibetans with tinted, spiky hair sat behind a table covered with pamphlets. More Tibetans of various ages sat on the steps of the temples and chatted with one another.

I followed Deckyi as she turned down another narrow lane. An open doorway interrupted the darkness and revealed men feeding cloth through sewing machines. Then we walked past a table piled high with empty plastic bottles. Deckyi stopped at a small house and opened an unlocked wooden door to step inside her friend's single-room apartment. It had a cluttered table and two single beds forming a familiar *L* shape in front of a television. A teenage Tibetan girl sat cross-legged on one bed watching a Chinese soap opera. She blinked at the sight of us trooping into the room and silently pushed her hair back from her delicate face with a plastic headband.

"My friend's daughter," said Deckyi by way of introduction. Her friend and daughter were sharing one bed so Deckyi could sleep on the other one. The spare bed was covered with a thick-tufted Tibetan carpet. Deckyi and Lobsang sat on each side of me as I took out wads of bills from my purse. On a scrap of paper, they calculated how to split the money among the seven Tibetans in their group. The Tibetan girl watched us for a moment then turned back to the TV, where medieval Chinese warlords with tortoise shell-like armor and pointy beards prepared for battle.

While Deckyi and Lobsang counted, I took in my surroundings. The dingy single room had a stale odor. A dirty patterned cloth covered one window that probably looked out at another house; through it I could hear another television blasting Hindi and the rhythmic clatter of sewing machines. A panoramic poster of the Potala Palace in Lhasa, majestic and colossal against a crisp blue sky, hung above the television, along with pictures of the Dalai Lama and the boy Panchen Lama. The Panchen Lama was one of the most prominent figures in Tibetan Buddhism. In 1995, when he was six years old, Chinese authorities placed him under "protective custody" in Tibet. His status and whereabouts remain unknown. Meanwhile, Chinese authorities identified and appointed another boy as the official reincarnation of the Panchen Lama.

A blue stuffed bear sat in front of a glass case containing brass Buddha statues and books wrapped in orange cloth. The coffee table was littered with plastic mugs, a roll of pink toilet paper, a plastic hot water thermos common in China and ostensibly in Tibet, some scattered playing cards, a plastic headband, and a strand of wooden prayer beads. Except for the blue bear, it looked like many other Tibetan homes in India.

Next to me, Deckyi and Lobsang divided the money into smaller stacks, calculating extra costs for transportation to and from Dharamsala and around Delhi.

"You should give a little bit to Vinayak since he works for free," I suggested. I doubted the legal aid lawyer had much money at all.

Deckyi nodded. "We already discussed this. We will give 300 rupees each."

When the money was sorted into small piles, Lobsang took two 500-rupee notes and extended them to me clasped between both hands, head bowed.

"Please. You have helped us so much."

I shook my head. "Thank you. But no, you keep it."

Deckyi chimed in. "You spent so much time to help us. Please take it. Without you we couldn't get our money."

"Thank you. But I can't take it. You can give it to Vinayak."

This went back and forth for a while. I firmly repeated that I wouldn't take the money. "Really?" asked Deckyi. I nodded. She and Lobsang looked at each other, then reluctantly put the money back.

They walked me back through Majnu Ka Tilla's maze of streets to the main road, through a gated archway where bicycle rickshaws waited for passengers. I was headed to the metro station. I planned to catch the subway, so surreal in its sleek and modern efficiency beneath the chaotic streets of Delhi.

Lobsang bargained with the skinny Indian rickshaw driver, a boy in his late teens, and managed to knock five rupees off the fifteen-rupee (thirty-five-cent) fare. Then he thrust a liter bottle of water at me. He must have just bought it as we walked.

Deckyi and Lobsang watched as I perched on the seat, out of place in my black blazer and pinstriped pants—my legal negotiations outfit—on the bicycle rickshaw, a light contraption of metal tubes and rubber tires so vulnerable in heavy traffic.

"Thank you!" Deckyi called again in Mandarin.

"No need for thanks," I replied in Mandarin.

I waved to Deckyi and Lobsang who watched as the rickshaw driver began pumping the pedals, leaning all his body weight to get the wheels moving. We eased soundlessly into the thrumming traffic and rode away from the bright lights and fluttering prayer flags of Majnu Ka Tilla into the darkness of the city.

· · ·

A couple of weeks later I got a text message from a number I didn't recognize. I read it a few times before I realized it was from Tenzin, the chef in Moonpeak Café in Dharamsala who first introduced me to Deckyi.

It read, "Hi emei how r u? really how I thanks to u. emei without ur help they will never get that money even me. So thanks a lot for help. any how see u soon. ok. 4rom ten zin."

Far from the Rooftop of the World

It Was Hard Work but We Had a Lot of Fun

BYLAKUPPE (KARNATAKA), INDIA, AUGUST 2010

. . .

Nine months after I helped count cash with Deckyi, I found myself well off the beaten track in southern India, some 1,500 miles from Delhi. Indian pop music blasted within the autorickshaw. The flimsy metal buggy chugged to a raucous dance beat as we bumped along the road to Bylakuppe, India's largest Tibetan settlement, about five hours south of Bangalore. Next to me, the plump, middle-aged Tibetan woman squeezed into the back seat wasn't happy. She barked something to the Indian driver in Hindi and he called back over his shoulder as he dodged a jeep roaring at us from the opposite direction. He wore plastic flip-flops but had taken them off so he pressed the pedals with his callused bare feet.

"What's the matter?" I asked her.

"He only has Kannada music," she grumbled, referring to the local language of Karnataka, the southern Indian state that we were in. "I want Hindi music!" I couldn't really tell the difference between the two Indian languages when embedded in fast-paced music—the aural equivalent of sparkly bangles and sequined hot pink polyester. The woman yelled at the driver again until, cowed, he pulled over and rummaged in a compartment under his seat. He spoke to the woman apologetically and she let out another stream of chastising Hindi. Finally, when she accepted that he really did not have any Hindi cassette tapes, she let him blast Kannada music and resume the ride.

We were leaving the noisy, crowded streets of Kushalnagar, the nearest Indian town to Bylakuppe. Throngs of chaotic traffic typical of India disappeared as we turned onto a side road leading toward the settlement. Soon we were one of just a few vehicles on a road flanked by woods. When we passed a concrete shack that was a police checkpoint, I leaned back into the autorickshaw to make myself inconspicuous. Foreigners were supposed to get a "PAP," or a "Protected Area Permit," from the Indian government to enter the Tibetan settlement, and I didn't have one. I was told if you were lucky it took months and reams of paperwork to get it, and I had organized this trip just two days before because of an article I was writing that had suddenly come up for the *International Herald Tribune*. I needn't have worried. The autorickshaw didn't even slow down as we passed the checkpoint. Even if it had, the Indian policeman slumped in a lawn chair probably would have seen my face and waved me along. To an undiscerning, sleepy Indian policeman, my East Asian face could pass as Tibetan. Tibetans, however, knew otherwise.

When the Tibetan woman had first climbed into my autorickshaw with her shopping bags, she had turned and squinted at me. "You belong to Japan?" she had inquired quizzically in English. Her voice was blunt as a mallet.

I had shook my head. Sometimes it seemed too complicated to explain, and I didn't have the energy, so I had supplied an answer that was easier to understand. "I'm from Singapore." I had had to raise my voice over the chopper-like ruckus of the autorickshaw's two-stroke engine.

The woman's face had lit up in comprehension at the strange sight of an Asian passenger sitting next to her. A hirsute Caucasian traveler loaded with a rucksack was foreign enough to do odd things like travel to small towns in India by themselves. But a lone Asian woman—someone who looked similar enough to her so as to be assessed by her standards—was more of an enigma. Of course, I wasn't from Singapore, but I didn't want to go through the more complicated explanation that I'm Chinese American. I figured Singapore explained the Asianness, but was foreign enough that people from there might do things like travel to small towns in India by themselves. In retrospect, I should have said I was from Japan, which was more likely because I have met many adventurous Japanese people traveling solo, rough and off the beaten track. As far as I was concerned, there were far more unusual sights to behold in Bylakuppe than myself, and I was about to encounter some of them.

When we entered the settlement, a surreal vista startled me: vast, pristine cornfields and a red-robed Tibetan monk, complete with crimson trucker's hat, driving a tractor across our path. We were a long way from Tibet, the "rooftop of the world."

· · ·

It was 2010, and I was a year into a very intense job at the Indian microfinance company, yet I still did freelance journalism in my "free time." This meant I was living in Delhi, flying regularly to the southern city of Hyderabad where the microfinance company was based, and occasionally going to Dharamsala. My life and career were unspooling along interesting threads. But the one that included Tibetan exiles had thinned over the past year after interest from a literary agent sputtered out. I tried to keep hope for a book alive, and I jumped at opportunities to write about Tibetan issues.

In 2009, when I was still living in Dharamsala, I published an article about science education for Tibetan monks for the *New York Times*. The science project focused on Dharamsala as well as the big Tibetan monasteries in Bylakuppe. A year later, I was extremely busy at the microfinance company, which was starting its own roller-coaster ride. But in August 2010, I pitched an article about solar energy that would bring me near Bylakuppe. Within a few days I arranged a trip that involved a three-hour flight from Delhi to Bangalore, then a five-hour car ride to Bylakuppe, all on a shoestring budget and pieced together with field visits and interviews for my article. I was eager to see India's largest Tibetan settlement, a place where monasteries were bigger than ones in Tibet and where refugees had carved out sprawling towns from the jungle over decades.

After I finished work for my article, I found myself staying at a guesthouse in Kushalnagar outside Bylakuppe. I didn't want to risk staying in Bylakuppe itself without a permit even though I heard coconuts were the only inhabitants of the local jail. In Kushalnagar, Mahalaxmi Guesthouse was named after the goddess of wealth, not its clean rooms that cost eight dollars a night. It was just a short walk from a bus terminal that received buses from the north. The smooth two-lane road from Bangalore was lined with bright green fields of spiky sugar cane and roadside restaurants with signs declaring themselves as "Pure Veg." The bus station was on Kushalnagar's main road, which was clogged with small shops, clouds of dust, and throngs of noxious traffic. Plumes of the black exhaust that streamed from buses, trucks, and cars looked like lung cancer in gas form. At noon, traffic flowed in a messy ooze, and drivers leaned on their screeching, bleating horns. For fifty rupees, or about one dollar, an autorickshaw driver agreed to take me to Bylakuppe. This wasn't the best price—locals paid thirty rupees or less for the twenty-minute ride—but it was low enough to show I hadn't been rolled over. Plus, I was eager to escape the cacophony. After four years living in India, shrieking traffic still made me grimace, so I jumped into the autorickshaw.

Before we drove more than a couple of hundred meters, the driver pulled over next to someone on the roadside. A moment later, I met the middle-aged Tibetan woman who peered inside. A look of surprise crossed her face when she saw me, but she exchanged some words with the driver in Hindi to settle the fare and gathered up her *chupa* to climb inside. Sometimes drivers picked up extra passengers to make more money. Even though this wouldn't lower my own fare, I let him do it; this was India, where normal rules did not apply. I slid over to make room for her and her shopping bags.

"You alone?" the woman asked. She had long hair and a gap between her teeth.

"Yes."

The woman seemed perturbed. "Alone? No family?" she asked incredulously. "You are afraid?" It wasn't common for Indian or local women to travel alone in India, much less to small towns. The further one got from cities and tourist routes, the more peculiar it was to see a young woman traveling solo, especially one who didn't look obviously foreign.

I smiled and shook my head again. "Akeli," I said, using one of the words in my small Hindi vocabulary. It was a word I learned from mustached taxi drivers in Delhi who turned around to give me befuddled looks when I confirmed that yes, I was alone, *akeli*, though sometimes I hastily clarified that my fictional husband was waiting for me at home. People in India and most of Asia did not seem to understand the concept of being alone, bereft of the bustle and drama of two or three or four generations of extended family crammed together under the same roof. The common misconception was that being alone was something to avoid, a low-grade curse. It was almost unfathomable that someone would willingly choose this for themselves—and enjoy it. And a woman who was *akeli* was especially odd, and sometimes suspicious. I didn't mind being *akeli* when I traveled. In fact, I enjoyed it. I met more people and had more interesting conversations when I was alone. And it was because I was *akeli* that there was enough room in the autorickshaw to pick up this Tibetan woman.

"You live in Bylakuppe?" I asked the woman.

She replied that she had grown up there and lived in "Camp Three." When Bylakuppe was founded in the 1960s, it was a refugee camp for the steady flow of Tibetans who followed the Dalai Lama into exile in India. Some of the old lingo remained, and locals still refer to different sections of Bylakuppe as "camps" even though today the settlement is really a town of 16,000 Tibetans spread over 5,000 acres. It is one of the few inhabited places in India I visited that felt spacious, sprawling, and peaceful. The makeshift tents of the 1960s that sheltered destitute refugees in what was an inhospitable jungle were long gone. They were replaced by tidy clusters of low concrete homes, schools, clinics, enormous monasteries, small factories, and acres and acres of cornfields. Rice and tobacco also grow there, but corn dominates. After struggling Tibetans in the 1960s failed to cultivate a variety of crops, Swiss Technical Co-operation's agricultural advisory recommended grow-ing corn. By 1966, Bylakuppe was self-supporting due to corn—a crop that unexpectedly thrived when transplanted to new soil, tended by people who had never tasted the stuff before.

. . .

Our autorickshaw swooped up and down the rolling hills of Bylakuppe's main road. Fields of shoulder-high cornstalks flashed by, occasionally punc-tuated by a windmill twirling in the breeze. For a few minutes we were the only vehicle on the road and our autorickshaw seemed to chug along with joyful abandon as if enjoying a solitude that was so rare in India. Suddenly the sight of a large golden-roofed temple in the distance emerged from the chartreuse sea of cornstalks, like something out of a dream.

As I stared at the spectacular scenery, the woman told me she had lived in Taiwan for a few years.

"Taiwan?" Now it was my turn to be puzzled. I met Tibetans who traveled on well-worn paths to the United States, Switzerland, Australia, Canada, and England but never to Taiwan. "What were you doing there?"

"Working in a factory," she explained.

"Did you like Taiwan?" I asked. The woman beamed and nodded enthu-siastically. "What do you do now?"

"Not much," she answered. "Wash some clothes. Clean house. Cooking."

"You live with your family?" I asked.

"No." She shook her head. So she was *akeli* too—unusual for a middle-aged Tibetan woman. Before I could learn more or ask how she got to Taiwan, the autorickshaw pulled over and the woman clambered out. She looked back inside at me, concern flashing across her face, as though now she worried about me and my *akeli* state. Before she could impart any words of advice, the driver gunned the motor and the autorickshaw sputtered away down the road.

Roughly 40,000 Tibetans live in Karnataka, alone. Some are recent refu-gees but some, like my fellow passenger, were born and raised in India, are fluent in Hindi, can demand Hindi pop music over Kannada, and have never set foot in Tibet.

Because foreigners need permits to visit official Tibetan settlements, Bylakuppe lacked the touristy feel of Dharamsala. One disappointed visitor
from California, an older woman who lived on an ashram in southern India
for a couple of months, remarked that Dharamsala reminded her of kitschy
ski resort towns in Colorado. Bylakuppe, by contrast, felt like a real town and
an unusual blend of Tibet, and say, Iowa and Maine, seasoned with Indian
masala. Maine came to mind because of the expansive, bucolic landscape and
cool weather. If Tibet is the rooftop of the world to Tibetans, Bylakuppe is
the basement, albeit a refurbished one made surprisingly comfortable over
time.

· · ·

That August, the heat in Delhi was still scorching and relentless. After months
of being pummeled by sweltering temperatures, my body had forgotten what
cold was. I packed hot weather clothes for my trip "down south" to Bylakuppe, along with one long-sleeved shirt and a synthetic shawl suitable for
two hours in airplane air conditioning. I was unprepared for the cold nights
and damp, rainy weather in Bylakuppe at the tail end of a long monsoon. The
chill reminded me more of autumnal New England than India's prototypical
heat. There were also torrential downpours during my visit.

On my second day in Bylakuppe I bought a plaid umbrella made in China
from the Tashi Delek Supermarket, one of the shops in Camp #1 Shopping
Complex, a small commercial area crowded with little shops and grimy
restaurants. (*Tashi delek* is "hello" in Tibetan, more literally "blessings" or
"may all good things come to this environment," according to some translations.) Autorickshaws, their drivers seeking passengers, lined the street. In
a nasal drone, Indian vendors called, "Lama khenpo, lama khenpo! Lama
khenpo, lama khenpo!" Their call translated roughly as "Monk, abbot!
Monk, abbot!" Hand-lettered signs advertised phone calls to "Tibet and
China" for 150 rupees. A poster on one wall declared, "I will vote will you?
Election 2011," in a preview of elections next year for prime minister of the
Tibetan exile government.

A large banner over the road read, "Hearty Welcome to Nobel Laureate His Holiness the Dalai Lama and all the Delegates of the First Tibetan
National Conference 2010." In a few days, on September 2, the spiritual
leader would arrive in Bylakuppe to commemorate the fiftieth anniversary
of Tibetan democracy in exile. There would also be a long-life ceremony for

the Dalai Lama and a conference attended by Tibetan leaders from all over
the world to discuss the state of Tibet and life in exile.

The plaid umbrella I bought from Tashi Delek Supermarket broke on the
first day; I struggled to close it without cutting my fingers on the rough metal.
At night in my room at Mahalaxmi Guesthouse I wore my only long-sleeved
shirt over my summer weight nightshirt and wrapped myself in my shawl. I
still shivered from the damp cold.

It wasn't always so cool in Bylakuppe; in fact, it was normally very hot in
the summer. Many of Bylakuppe's early Tibetan settlers were unused to the
heat and died from tropical diseases and the harsh change in conditions. In
its early days, life on the settlement was downright bleak. In contrast to the
bucolic, peaceful atmosphere of Bylakuppe today, the first 660 settlers sent
there in 1960 thought they were in hell. Unlike Tibet where the sky and wide-
open landscape stretched on as far as the eye could see, they couldn't see
anything in the dense jungle where wild animals lived. The sense of ominous
claustrophobia must have been terrifying.

The Tibetans thought their stay would be temporary and didn't under-
stand why they had to bother cultivating farmland. Harsh years of backbreak-
ing work followed: clearing forest and coaxing alien crops from the ground.
When the Dalai Lama visited the southern settlements in the early 1960s,
he was heartbroken over the early settlers' high death rates and low spirits.
Still, he retained a vision for what the settlement could become. "Whenever
I visited our larger settlements I always promised we would prevail," the
Dalai Lama said in the book *In Exile from the Land of Snows*. "I pushed
and pushed and pushed and finally, year by year, the picture completely
changed."

· · ·

Bylakuppe's dramatic transformation is embodied in its magnificent monasteries. Today they have far more monks than their original counterparts in
Tibet. Namdroling Monastery, known colloquially as the Golden Temple,
attracts crowds of Indian tourists each day, as well as a few foreign visitors. In
1959, Penor Rinpoche of the Nyingma school of Buddhism fled Tibet, resettling to southern India in 1961. The group of 300 he left Tibet with dwindled
to 30 after deaths from disease, harsh weather, and the hardship of fleeing
their homeland. In 1963, with just 300 rupees in his pocket, Penor Rinpoche
built a bamboo temple to train a handful of monks. Today the monastery is
home to roughly 5,000 monks and nuns, a teaching college, and a hospital.

The spectacular Golden Temple, finished in 1999, houses a fifty-eight-foot gold-plated Buddha within walls painted with vibrant, elaborate murals of Buddhas and deities. Nearby, another four-storied temple boasts stunning layers of golden roofs stacked atop each other, pagoda-like. A massive golden arc circles over the topmost roof like a nimbus.

When I visited the Golden Temple, I strolled on its manicured ground and took in the palm trees, a small bridge over a man-made stream, and neat humps of green grass, perfect for sitting on. Unlike most of India, there was no litter and water in the stream was surprisingly clean. I paused near a group of Indian schoolchildren on a field trip dressed in white uniforms and yellow hats so they resembled ducklings. They perched on grassy mounds and stared at me in silence. When I took a photo of them and waved, they erupted into giggles and cheerfully waved back. I was getting hungry, so outside Namdroling's main gate, I bought an ear of corn from an Indian vendor for five rupees, about ten cents. He tended a cart where he laid ears of corn, freshly released from husks, on top of glowing red coals. Then the vendor placed my perfectly roasted corn on a sheaf of pale green husk—nature's version of the paper boats hot dogs are served on.

A couple of miles away down another road lined with cornfields sat Sera Monastery. In 2010, some 3,800 monks were registered there. In contrast, the original Sera in Lhasa established in 1417 has just a few hundred monks. China's repression has resulted in a steady influx of monks fleeing Tibet for India since the early 1980s. Monks also come from Nepal, Bhutan, and all over India to study at Bylakuppe's monasteries.

When I arrived at Sera, its main courtyard hummed with activity. It was all hands on deck to prepare for His Holiness's upcoming visit: monks were busy putting up a large canopy over the courtyard, stringing bright new prayer flags from roofs, painting large Tibetan symbols on the ground, and cleaning a stage where the Dalai Lama would sit. Twenty thousand Tibetans from across India would attend the upcoming democracy commemoration, and security would be very strict, for some reason. Indian policemen toting machine guns would only let people with IDs or special credentials pass through metal barricades set up 100 meters from Sera's entrance.

But that day, I casually walked through the open gates of Sera's main entrance. An acquaintance had suggested I get in touch with a monk they knew, so I called Geshe Ngyima on his cell phone. While I waited for him, I snapped photos of prayer flags strung from the massive three-story building that housed a prayer hall and offices. With its cream-colored walls, trapezoidal windows, and golden roof, the building resembled a gigantic sheet cake spanning a city block.

After a few minutes, Geshe Ngyima, a bespectacled monk in his forties, arrived. Together we strolled around Sera's large campus. The grounds stretched behind the main building to form a village complete with a grocery store, Cyber Cool Internet café, library, outdoor tea stall, dormitories, and cottages where senior monks lived. One bungalow had a sign on its door that indicated a "Chant Master" resided there.

Geshe Ngyima spoke perfect English in a soft-spoken voice. He had studied at Sera for more than twenty years to attain his *geshe* degree. Born in northern India, he had come to Sera more than three decades earlier. He remembered when the monastery was small and struggled in a "difficult financial situation." The monks had to pitch in with farm work to make ends meet. Geshe Ngyima recalled that the monks had to work in the fields one month each year. "It was hard work, but we had a lot of fun," he said, smiling. Nostalgia cracked his reserved exterior.

We passed an administrative building and Geshe Ngyima told me there would be a photo exhibit there during the Dalai Lama's visit. We went inside and met a young Tibetan man named Tashi Phuntsok from the Tibet Museum in Dharamsala who was busy setting up panels to display "Tibet: 50 Years' Experience," the exhibition I had seen in March 2009. It was traveling to various Tibetan settlements across India, just as I had been told, and now here it was at the other end of the country.

I looked again at the black-and-white image that showed the first Tibetan Buddhist monastery in India, established in 1959 in the state of Bihar. The grainy photo depicted a shack-like structure in a scrubby landscape. Another photo from the 1960s showed a youthful Dalai Lama in Bylakuppe observing monks debating in the middle of what looks like a patch of dirt. These reminders of the past offered a sharp contrast to the present day.

One recent photo of Sera Monastery showed thousands of monks lined up on its steps to form a crimson sea. In another image, monks debated in Sera's courtyard, which was as big as a soccer field.

· · ·

After Geshe Ngyima and I said goodbye, I set out to look for dinner. It was drizzling and the sky was dark. The weather made me crave comfort food and I thought of *momos*, particularly fried ones with crispy brown skins. I started salivating at the thought. There were no restaurants at Sera Monastery, so

I exited and followed signs to the guesthouse a couple of hundred meters away. The building looked promising. It had white plaster columns, a small veranda, and a spacious lobby inside. It was early for dinner, and I was one of the only customers at the restaurant, though quite a few monks, as well as Tibetan men and women, stood around, talking casually. A monk at the cash register handed me the menu, a smudged, laminated sheet. *Momos* were nowhere to be found. It offered only the standard list of Indian fare: aloo gobi, paneer, dal, butter chicken. "You don't have *momos*?" I cried in dismay.

The monk shook his head unsympathetically. Disappointed, I scanned the menu and chose "talumein soup," unappetizing instant noodles in an overspiced broth, and paratha, a flaky flat bread.

As I ate my uninspiring meal, an elderly Tibetan woman approached me. When I entered the guesthouse, I had seen her sitting with two older men in the lobby. She smiled at me kindly, creasing her wrinkled face, and sat down opposite me. The woman was small and wizened, had long gray hair, and wore a dark *chupa* with a long sleeve shirt beneath it. She clutched a strand of brown prayer beads in one hand. Without introduction she asked in Mandarin, "Ni yige ren?" The literal translation was, "You one person?" If she spoke Hindi, she would have asked me if I were *akeli*.

"Yes. I'm one person," I replied in Mandarin. I was no longer fazed when Tibetans spoke to me in Mandarin.

"Where are you from?" the woman asked.

"Meiguo." America, I said in Mandarin. "Wo shi meiji huaren." *I am Chinese American.* I didn't gloss over my nationality and ethnicity this time since it was relevant to our conversation. The woman smiled. When Tibetans usually asked where I was from, the question was driven by curiosity, never by animosity, even here in Bylakuppe far from mainstream tourism.

The previous day I had visited the Tibetan school in Bylakuppe, called SOS Tibetan Children's Village. It was a pleasant stone-paved campus dotted with coconut palm trees, classrooms, basic bungalows that served as dormitories, dining halls, and study areas. At last count in 2021, about 800 students were enrolled from kindergarten through high school. Clotheslines hung outside bungalows, strung like prayer flags, except they held small trousers and tiny T-shirts with slogans like, "Soccer is life; The rest is just details." I happened to visit during lunch when a room full of high school girls sat on benches ready to eat rice and mushy vegetable curry. A plastic basin of watermelon slices sat on the floor: dessert. The girls stared at me as I walked in and then to my surprise, before I had said a word, a couple of them

animatedly called out, "Ni hao!" Before eating they raised the bowls over
their heads and sang in Tibetan to bless the food. After lunch I chatted with
one girl, a tall eighteen-year-old from Sichuan with luminous skin and red
cheeks. She was shy but seemed to glow with excitement as she spoke. The
girl came to India eight years ago in 2002 to go to the Tibetan schools in exile.
She bashfully admitted she liked the weather in Tibet better than in India.

· · ·

On my last day in Bylakuppe I visited Sakya Monastery, not far from Camp
#1. It wasn't a big tourist attraction like the Golden Temple, or as big as Sera.
My autorickshaw driver didn't know where it was (or at least he didn't understand me) and had to pause en route to ask for directions. We turned off the
main drag onto a small, unmarked road until we entered the gates. The monastery itself was a compact but beautiful structure painted red and yellow. It
was somewhat trapezoidal in shape and perched on top of a hill, where it
caught afternoon light that brightened its walls into a buttery glow. Palm trees
dotted the grounds, but dark green parasol-shaped conifers lined the hilly
path leading to the monastery—probably another transplant to Bylakuppe.

As I walked up the steep hill, all was quiet except for a few young Tibetans
snapping photos of each other. The guys had spiky hair and the girl wore
skin-tight jeans. When they finished, they all climbed onto a new motorcycle
and rolled off downhill. As I looked at the monastery's enormous doors, a
friendly young monk appeared and asked in fluent English if I wanted to look
inside. He produced a set of keys to let me in and I admired the tidy prayer
hall lined with large ceremonial drums and long, rainbow-hued tapestries
that hung from the ceilings.

The monk's name was Desal and though he looked boyish, he was thirty
years old. He told me he was from another Tibetan settlement in Karnataka
(a poorer one, he said somewhat sheepishly) and was nine when he became
a monk. He came to Bylakuppe twelve years ago. The prayer hall we stood in
was new—just a few years old—and built from funds mostly raised in Taiwan,
he said.

I thanked Desal for the glimpse of the prayer hall then wandered outside
toward the back of the monastery. A large, grassy field stretched behind the
building; strings of colorful prayer flags flapped in the breeze. To one side, a
group of monks crouched in the grass cutting lush green blades with handheld scythes. It was a painstaking task, and they had succeeded in clearing
just a small circle in the large field. Meanwhile, another group of monks were

engaged in a more enjoyable activity, playing soccer. Some wore sneakers but others were barefoot as they chased the ball up and down the field through the grass. Some had discarded their red robes in heaps to one side, while a couple of others rolled them down and tied them around their waists, revealing tank top undershirts. They flattened the grass with their pounding feet, shouted for passes, and shot the ball through makeshift goal posts made with stray shoes. A windmill whirled nearby, and overhead gauzy clouds drifted across the blue sky as the sun descended. The grass-cutting monks gathered up their tools, but the other group continued their soccer game even as darkness began to fall, their shouts and sounds of stampeding feet emanating from growing shadows.

I went to Sakya Monastery guesthouse to say goodbye to Acharya Yeshi, a monk friend who was staying there while attending the big conference at Bylakuppe. He was based in Delhi and was a member of parliament in the exile government. When I found Acharya he was engrossed in a conversation with another conference attendee and could only pause for a moment. By now it was dark out, and Acharya asked the young monk working in the guesthouse's restaurant to walk me to town to find an autorickshaw. He gladly agreed, and we set off down a back road past the monastery, now just a darker lump of black on the hill. It was almost pitch dark and I walked cautiously while my companion confidently strode on. He didn't speak much English, but I gleaned he was from remote Arunachal Pradesh near Tibet. My companion took out his cell phone and shone its feeble light on the path.

"This road is danger," the young monk announced. "Snakes."

I stopped in my tracks.

Then, deciding it was worse to be alone in the dark with any nocturnal or slithering creatures, I trotted after the monk's dim, bobbing light. After minutes of terse silence, we finally reached the main road and I was surprised to find that we were close to Camp #1 Shopping Complex, where I had bought my plaid umbrella. The young monk waved down an autorickshaw and spoke in Hindi to the driver. I hung back and didn't say a word. Thanks to his negotiating, the fare was just twenty rupees. I climbed into the rickshaw, pulling my thin shawl around me for the blustery ride back to town. The monk waved goodbye cheerfully despite his long walk back to the monastery on a dark road populated with snakes. I waved back at him as the autorickshaw's engine coughed to life and we drove off, leaving the Tibetan town of Bylakuppe behind us on our way back to the noisy thrum of India.

. . .

When I was getting ready to return home to Delhi, I wasn't sure how I'd get to the Bangalore airport, five hours drive north. Days before, a car from the Indian solar energy company that I wrote an article about had dropped me off at my guesthouse in Kushalnagar. To get back to Delhi, I was on my own. The helpful owners of Mahalaxmi Guesthouse told me there was a bus to Bangalore that stopped on the roadside in Kushalnagar. Improbably, it went all the way to the Bangalore airport. Adding to my luck was the news that a night bus would get me to the airport in time for my flight to Delhi just after dawn.

On my last night in Kushalnagar, I worked on my laptop in an empty conference room at Mahalaxmi Guesthouse, then left after 10 p.m. As instructed, I stood on the roadside bereft of streetlights with my L.L. Bean backpack and laptop bag wondering if this night bus would really arrive. To my surprise, a bus roared out of the darkness at the appointed time. I waved my arms so the driver wouldn't whiz past, and the bus slowed to let me on. He may have looked even more surprised to pick up a lone female traveler on the roadside, but I got on and found a seat in the nearly empty vehicle. It was unexpectedly new and modern, more like a city transit bus than a coach. I slept for most of the next five hours and woke to a brightening sky as we approached the Bangalore airport. The blazing city lights and wide tarmac roads were a stark contrast to the dark road in a small Indian town where I had caught the bus.

For once, I arrived with plenty of time for my flight, whereas normally I literally run late through airports and get stressed by long security lines. At that early hour there were no queues, and I breezed through to my gate. As I boarded my flight, I marveled at my uncharacteristically relaxed airport experience. It was rather miraculous considering my ad hoc journey from Kushalnagar. Any number of things could have gone wrong, but the smooth end to my trip was one last surprise about my spontaneous journey to Bylak-uppe, a place that had become home to so many Tibetans.

Beyond

2015 to 2021

Australia, Belgium,

United States

New Year, New Land

I Haven't Had My Mum for a Long Time

NORBU: MELBOURNE, 2015

. . .

On New Year's Eve, Flinders Street Station swarmed with people coming into Melbourne for celebrations. With its soaring domes and towers, the massive ochre building is a city landmark whose walls stretch down several city blocks. By late afternoon on that Australian summer day, the station and surrounding streets were even busier than usual as merrymakers flocked downtown to usher in the new year.

The crowds made it hard to find Norbu. He had told me to meet him under the clock at Flinders Street Station, so I stood on the sidewalk at the corner of Flinders and Elizabeth Streets. I didn't spot Norbu anywhere even though he texted me to say he was also waiting under the clock. Finally he called. Unlike me, he wasn't flustered; he patiently told me to meet within the station by one of the platforms. Inside, a rushing river of people buffeted me along and I craned my neck and looked around. Someone approached me from the side—Norbu found me in the crowd.

His chin-length hair was pulled back in a topknot. With his high cheekbones, his face was unmistakable, but it seemed a bit wider, and he was thicker around the waist and chest than when I had met him seven years before at the Japanese restaurant in Dharamsala where he worked. He looked older, the skin around his eyes creased with wrinkles, yet still seemed youthful in his denim shorts, black T-shirt, and backpack. We laughed incredulously as we greeted each other. It was surreal to see him again in summertime Australia, a place that seemed so far away when he'd told me about his plans to go there in his icebox-cold room in Dharamsala years ago.

It had been several years since I'd last seen Norbu in India. I had visited him in Delhi in Majnu Ka Tilla, the Tibetan quarter. It was a stifling hot summer day, well over 100 degrees, and he had come from Dharamsala for an interview at the Australian High Commission and to submit paperwork for his visa as a refugee in Australia.

After Norbu left India in 2010, I wasn't sure how to contact him, and we had lost touch. For a time, my work unexpectedly diverged from Tibetan exiles, and I left India in 2013 to attend graduate school in New York at Columbia University. Then in the fall of 2014 I went to Bangladesh to write articles about climate change and reforming garment factories. By December 2014 I was in a rural Bangladeshi town when the prospect of going to Australia to visit Norbu came up. I decided to try an email address he used years ago. To my surprise, he replied within minutes: "hi Amy how are u? its been a long time. i hope everything is good? i am in Melbourne. wish to I see u soon. take care."

When Norbu confirmed he would be in Melbourne, I quickly made plans to travel to Australia. An Australian friend from Delhi put me in touch with his sister-in-law and brother, who generously invited me to stay at their home in Melbourne even though I had never met them.

Now, on the last day of 2014, I was standing with Norbu in Melbourne.

I smiled at him. "Do I look the same?" I asked.

He hesitated, which I took to mean that I also looked older, maybe more hardened and tired.

But after a pause, he replied, "Yes."

We had no specific plans for the evening, so we joined the crowds flowing out of the train station onto Collins Street. We turned onto Swanston Street, one of Melbourne's main thoroughfares, and paused to watch a crowd gathered around some street performers.

"Maybe there is dancing," said Norbu. The group of young men from New York did some light break dancing, which captivated him. But I was shocked when a member of the hip hop troupe pulled an Asian man into the circle, spoke gibberish into the microphone, and mocked him like an Asian Sambo. To make matters worse, the Asian man, who may even have been Tibetan, laughed awkwardly; he probably didn't know he was being ridiculed. It seemed like his English wasn't fluent when he spoke a few words into the mic. I was shocked; these youths had performed a racist act in front of an ogling crowd. Perhaps it was ignorance that made it grotesquely "normal" to be racist toward someone Asian when it was masked as a joke. The public display normalized racism and made it entertainment. But I wondered how Norbu would feel if I made a scene moments after we were reunited. I don't know if he recognized what happened, but there seemed to be an uncomfortable silence as we watched. For someone like Norbu who had en-dured beatings in prison in Tibet, maybe the exchange was insignificant, or maybe he didn't notice. For lack of better alternative, I suggested we leave. That was the easiest thing to do. But to this day, I still regret that I said and did nothing.

Norbu and I didn't speak about the incident, and I tried to push it aside so it didn't sour the night's celebrations. We continued on Collins Street and passed a group of Falun Gong demonstrators who smiled and pushed flyers and magazines into the hands of passersby. I took one. The glossy magazine cover showed a blonde woman meditating cross-legged in a field of yellow flowers. The title read, "Falun Gong: A peaceful practice for mind and body now persecuted in China." Sandwiched among articles extolling the benefits of Falun Gong was one that described the group's persecution in China. I tucked the magazine into my bag.

Norbu and I made our way to Melbourne's Chinatown a short walk away. Thousands of other people had the same idea and long lines spilled out of restaurants. Finally, on Swanston Street, we found a seat at one of Mel-bourne's ubiquitous Vietnamese restaurants. He still liked *thukpa*, Tibetan noodle stew, the best. There was no Tibetan restaurant in Chinatown at that time, but pho was a good second choice for Norbu. As we ate from our steam-ing bowls of noodles, he told me about his life in Australia.

· · ·

It had been nearly five years since Norbu arrived in Melbourne. For the past couple of years, he had worked as a chef in a nursing home near Albert Park, a pleasant neighborhood with leafy streets. It was a steady job, and "not dif-ficult," said Norbu. Nursing home residents ate mostly soft foods. Earlier that day for lunch he had made pickled pork and onion tarts, sandwiches, and "finger food" such as fish fingers and meat balls. Otherwise, he baked ham and barbecued a lot of chicken, sausage, and burgers. For Christmas dinner, Norbu made roast ham, turkey, and salads. He also learned to bake Anzac cookies, the quintessential Australian oatmeal biscuit. "Old people like this," he told me. Four other white-uniformed chefs—Moroccan, Chinese, Indian, and "Ozzie" (presumably someone Caucasian) joined Norbu in the kitchen.

The nursing home's fifty-five residents came from various backgrounds but were mostly of Italian and German descent. One Greek couple had been close to one hundred years old but looked seventy, Norbu observed. The wife died and shortly afterward, her grieving husband followed.

Norbu rented a room in a Tibetan Buddhist institute in a quiet, upscale neighborhood and rode about thirty minutes to work on a racing bicycle. He said his Tibetan prayers as he cycled. It was a smooth commute since Melbourne's well-marked bike lanes made it easy to get around. But he was thinking of getting a car so that commuting in the rain would be easier. Melbourne's weather was relatively mild but temperamental. Even in summer, temperatures could reach the upper nineties and then plunge thirty degrees a few days later.

Two days each week Norbu worked part time at another nursing home, so most of his week was spent working and then resting. He didn't eat much at home because he didn't feel like eating after cooking all day. Tonight was one of the few times he came into the city for fun. A few hours earlier, Norbu had finished work then cycled home to change before coming into the city to meet me.

I could easily imagine Norbu baking Anzac cookies. In the Japanese restaurant in Dharamsala, I had watched him make homemade miso paste from fermented soybeans and marveled at his adopted culinary skills. In Tibet he had no inkling about miso, not to mention tempura or sushi. Now his work as a cross-cultural epicure was taking the form of onion tarts, Anzac cookies and other Australian fare.

In the Vietnamese restaurant full of rowdy revelers, we slurped our bowls of pho. When we finished, I tried to pay at the cashier, but Norbu insisted while I protested. We jockeyed over the check. He literally pushed me aside and held out some bills, which the bemused woman behind the counter took from him. It reminded me of when Norbu in 2008 insisted on paying for my round Tibetan bread wrapped in newspaper and chai after our morning walk around the *kora* in Dharamsala.

* * *

Back on Swanston Street, we headed toward the Yarra River. We passed a church festooned with a banner that read, "Let's fully welcome refugees," which captured some of the current debate about migrants in Australia. At Federation Square, crowds had gathered on the large plaza to watch Jumbotron screens showing an emcee, singers, acrobats, and other performers on a stage somewhere nearby. We wandered over a bridge spanning the river and paused by the tower-like antenna next to Hamer Theater.

The city had carefully planned the evening so all would remain orderly. A sign politely instructed, "No Fireworks Viewing from the Bridge: Please

Keep Moving." We eventually found a spot to watch fireworks. I sat on one of the Falun Gong magazines I had stuffed into my purse. I offered one to Norbu, but he sheepishly declined, and I realized I was being casually sacrilegious. He wanted to keep anything with words off the ground as a sign of respect. I remembered how Tibetan and foreign devotees touched prayer books to their heads after dharma classes, and how religious texts are wrapped in gold-colored cloth to protect them. I felt slightly guilty for sitting on the Falun Gong magazine—but not bad enough to rest my bottom on the bare pavement.

We settled in to wait for several hours for fireworks over the Yarra River. Norbu took out a bag of Doritos from his backpack and offered some to me. The gesture reminded me of the bag of walnuts he had proffered in his cold basement room in Dharamsala years before.

As midnight approached, the crowd became louder and more animated. Some metal railings were set up to clear the street. The fencing bulged with the weight of people leaning against it, but all remained orderly. I marveled at this seemingly simple phenomenon. In India, such a crowd could quickly snap into chaos. But here in Australia, a place where refugees arrived to escape conflict, calm prevailed. In the minutes before midnight, the crowd whooped while counting down the last seconds of the old year. Then explosions of fireworks blossomed against the sky.

I took a few blurry selfies of Norbu and me with colorful bouquets of light in the background. I smiled wide like an earnest American, while Norbu looked seriously into the camera. Wrinkles around his eyes were visible even in hazy light captured in the first moments of the new year.

• • •

In 2010 Norbu left India on a plane with three other Tibetans who also received humanitarian visas from Australia as political refugees. They were picked up at the airport by Tibetans already living in Melbourne who had arranged temporary accommodations for them. In 2015 about 400 Tibetans lived in Melbourne, community leaders told me. Roughly 700 lived in Sydney, home to Australia's largest population of Tibetans. Norbu had no particular memory of arriving in Australia, just that things were a "little confusing" at first, such as getting around the city and using its trams. Melbourne was "very quiet compared to India," he observed. He and the three Tibetans lived together for a month before he moved to the Buddhist institute.

Tibetan refugees granted asylum have relatively smooth entry into Australia. A small committee from the Tibetan community greets new arrivals and helps them with the first steps of settling in, such as finding a place to live, opening a bank account, and registering them for free government-funded English classes for immigrants. The bank account is essential for receiving biweekly welfare payments that cover day-to-day needs. The refugees are also assigned a government case worker, but Norbu met his only twice: upon his arrival, and again at an exit interview months later. As documented political refugees, Tibetans are eligible for 500 hours of free English classes at AMES, the Australian Migrant Education Services, and then 800 hours after that. AMES, a government-funded private organization, offers English classes, job placement services, skills training, and other services to refugees and immigrants granted visas by the Australian government. Norbu attended classes there for six months. He recalls students from all different countries: China, Ethiopia, Japan, Korea, Iran. "There were so many different people," he recalled. His teacher was Vietnamese but "born here, like Ozzie."

Because he already had a foundation of English from his schooling in Dharamsala and years living in India, Norbu left AMES soon after he arrived. He then enrolled in a Melbourne culinary institute called William Angliss, where he earned a certificate in hospitality. Australians and international students also attended the school. Regular students can pay tens of thousands of dollars, but for Norbu tuition was free.

He had years of experience cooking in Dharamsala, but the culinary institute's coursework was demanding: three classes a day, demonstrations, preparation tests, and lots of homework. Hardest of all were all the papers and written assignments. "Writing is very hard," said Norbu. "I didn't do it before." In Dharamsala, he learned to speak English at the Tibetan Transit School for older refugees, but there was not much emphasis on writing. In Melbourne, an older Australian woman sympathetic to Tibetans tutored Norbu. With this extra support, he passed his course and could look for work as a chef.

· · ·

One evening, I visited Norbu at the Buddhist institute where he lived. We walked across a small verdant park to reach the house. It was a warm summer night and tall trees shrouded us in even darker shadows. All was incredibly quiet—perfectly normal for a suburb, but strange in contrast to the constant cacophony of India. Norbu said that sometimes animals appeared at night and that had startled him at first. He described one animal, and I guessed it was a possum. Australia was so clean, marveled Norbu, but in his new home "the best thing is weather—not hot, not cold."

The Buddhist institute was housed in a stately mansion built in the 1870s. During the twentieth century it had been a hospital, a Catholic home for girls with learning disabilities, then a school for the disadvantaged run by nuns before its latest iteration as a Tibetan Buddhist center founded in 1987. Behind the grand main building that hosted philosophy classes were quarters for students, staff, and four Tibetans, including Norbu.

The room was larger and had far more belongings than his room in Dharamsala. Norbu's new space had a flat screen TV, a small refrigerator, and a shelf filled with binders from the culinary institute. A guitar leaned against the shelf. Clothes hung from a rack covered with an Australian flag. Suitcases and plastic bags from Aldi, the supermarket chain, sat next to it. A leather loveseat rested near a double bed where the duvets were folded into long sausages like in other Tibetan homes I'd seen. Norbu's racing bicycle leaned against a wall.

On the wall hung a map of Tibet, a *thangka* of a green *tara*—a female Buddhist deity—and a poster-sized photo of the Dalai Lama clasping his hands. There was another *thangka* of the twenty-one *taras*. Norbu pointed out that it was blessed by His Holiness. A chocolate bunny in golden foil perched on a shelf. The Tibetan snow lion flag hung on the wall—just as it had in Norbu's room in Dharamsala.

That evening Norbu wore jean shorts again and a T-shirt probably bought randomly at a discount since it read, "Techno is not dead." A fan rippled a gentle breeze as we talked. A clock on the wall was stuck at 4:45 p.m. Norbu showed me his thick culinary school binders. They were full of photos of grilled vegetables and instructions with diagrams demonstrating "How to dice an onion" and "How to make an omelet." There were recipes for black forest cake, dry petits fours, apple strudel, and many other dishes.

He told me he could make food with no problem, but there was other uncharted territory in his classes. Norbu recalled they had writing assignments about "conflict management" at work, a topic he'd never studied. Yet he had experienced work conflict in real life, with his Tibetan ex-boss at the restaurant. Norbu had often railed about his boss's mistreatment of him.

After he earned his certificate from William Angliss, Norbu landed part-time and temporary jobs catering and working as a kitchen hand in expensive restaurants. He catered big corporate functions for the Melbourne

Cup, the annual horse racing extravaganza, and worked at the Melbourne Cricket Ground. At fine restaurants, like one in Melbourne's trendy St. Kilda neighborhood, he cooked seafood for the first time: calamari, oysters, mussels, shrimp, and dreaded lobsters. "I hate lobster," said Norbu, wrinkling his face.

Eventually he found a full-time job at the nursing home. The minimum wage in Australia was almost twenty dollars, and people got paid double on holidays and in some instances, triple. Norbu made a good living, he said.

When Norbu wasn't working, he occasionally met with Tibetan friends to play cards at Brighton Beach not far from where he lived. One of his closest friends was a university student and another was a house cleaner. Sometimes he played soccer and cricket with them. Tibetans also got together to celebrate the Tibetan New Year, the Dalai Lama's birthday, the December day when he won the Nobel Peace Prize, and other holidays on the Tibetan calendar.

Under Australian law, Norbu had four weeks of holiday each year. He had gone camping a few times. Lately he was working seven days a week so didn't have much time for recreation. During the summer holidays, several of his friends were away visiting Australian "villages." One friend had sent him photos of a strange animal with a "body like a camel but face like a deer," Norbu described. He showed me a photo and asked, "What is this animal?"

I peered at the photo on his phone. "Probably a llama or an alpaca."

"Is it for meat?" wondered Norbu.

I thought for a moment. "I think it's for wool," I said, though I later learned that alpacas in Australia are bred for meat too.

Norbu had settled well in Australia, but he also dreamed of finally going home. Earlier in the year, he had applied for a visa to China so he could visit his mother in Tibet. It took four months for the Chinese consulate to deny the request. They gave him no reason but of course they would know he held political refugee status in Australia. When I had last seen Norbu in India, he was also anxious about the possibility of never seeing his mother again. Next time, he would go to another country like Thailand and apply for a Chinese visa from there. He had heard from other Tibetans that one had a better chance of getting one that way, though he didn't know anyone who had succeeded.

Did Norbu miss India? He shook his head, no. "All my friends are gone." However, he did read news about Tibet and India online. He had no plans to visit India, but he still missed Tibet. His "friends, siblings, family" were all there. Norbu admitted one reason he applied for cooking jobs in nursing homes was because of his mother. Working in the nursing home was a kind of proxy for the care he couldn't give to her.

"I haven't had my mum for a long time," he said. That year she was seventy-seven years old. Norbu's father had passed away when he was four. Still, sometimes the nursing home was a strange experience, since such facilities didn't exist in Tibet. In Australia, people who worked in aged care could be brusque with the residents. "Some carers, they don't care. Only money," Norbu told me.

Traditionally, Tibetan families care for the elderly at home. In the nursing home in Melbourne some people "sleep on bed for four or five years," observed Norbu. They "shit—everything in the bed."

In Tibet, an elderly person might be bedridden for one to two months, then they would pass away, he said. In Melbourne, they suffered from dementia. "They take a lot of medicine. I haven't seen like this." When an elderly resident passed away, there was a brisk nonchalance about those deaths that Norbu found strange. The people who worked there were largely unfazed. "No care, no value," Norbu remarked. It was disconcerting to him considering that for Tibetans even "if a bird dies, we can say prayer."

I thought back again to that morning in Dharamsala when I bumped into Norbu on the *kora* as he scattered food scraps for the birds. That was a world away from this suburb in Melbourne, yet he was still the same person sitting next to me. But like the Norbu I knew in Dharamsala, he still longed for his mother and family in Tibet, and was still searching for a way to return to his homeland.

[16]

Australia Day and Losar

It Has Given Me a Sheer Honor

MELBOURNE, JANUARY 2015

. . .

Several weeks after ushering in the New Year with Norbu, I was back on Swanston Street in downtown Melbourne. A Tibetan community leader had invited me to join the Tibetan group marching in the city's annual parade on January 26, and I was pushing my way through even denser crowds for Australia Day celebrations.

Metal barricades along the sidewalks cordoned off the road, which became a dammed-up river of people dressed in a wild variety of clothes. It took a while to find the Tibetans, but wading through the throng offered a glimpse of Melbourne's kaleidoscopic multiculturalism. Calmly clustered next to each other were Vietnamese women in sleek *ao dai* dresses, Scots in tartan kilts and knee socks, and Sikh men with blue turbans and black beards crammed alongside Star Wars Club fans wearing full Storm Trooper body armor. Drums thumped, wooden flutes and bagpipes tooted, and marching bands tuned their instruments in a cacophonous symphony.

Australia Day marks the anniversary of the arrival of British ships in 1788 to Port Jackson, New South Wales. On that day, the British proclaimed sovereignty over Australia's eastern seaboard. Many Australians celebrated the public holiday simply with barbecues and trips to the beach for another leisurely summer day. Or in Melbourne, thousands—like the ones around me—marched in a festive parade stretching from beyond City Hall and Parliament, over the Yarra River, to the parklands of Kings Domain.

But Australia Day had become controversial and contested, much like Columbus Day in the United States, which many consider an offense to Native Americans who were forced from their land and killed by conflict, disease, alcoholism, and poverty over centuries. Like Columbus Day, Australia Day was synonymous with genocide for some.

That Australia Day in Melbourne, the indigenous rights group Warriors of Aboriginal Resistance and First Nations Liberation joined the parade in protest. The group held Aboriginal flags and signs that read "Stop deaths in custody" and "End the NT intervention" to protest conflict in Australia's Northern Territories and police brutality. They chanted "always was, always will be Aboriginal land," and "No pride in genocide."

Earlier that morning, activists laid flowers on the parliament steps to commemorate Aboriginal people killed during white settlement and the Stolen Generation of children taken from their families and forced to live in foster care. One organizer said it was a "day of mourning for Aboriginal people," according to *The Age* newspaper. She added, "We don't celebrate Australia Day, because Australia Day celebrates genocide. Today is Invasion Day for Aboriginal people."

Although January 26 was a dark day for many Aboriginals, Australia had started branding it as a celebration of multiculturalism and new citizenship rather than British arrival. Across the country, new immigrants were granted citizenship in ceremonies officiated by mayors and other civic leaders. At a ceremony at Melbourne Town Hall led by the mayor, more than one hundred people from thirty-one countries became Australian citizens. They pledged allegiance to Australia and received certificates and waved Aussie flags for photos. In 2013, across Australia, more than 17,000 people from 145 countries became citizens on Australia Day.

My Australian friends in Melbourne were sheepishly ashamed of the oppression and colonialism that Australia Day represented. They were surprised when I told them about how the holiday was celebrated at the parade just a couple of miles from their home.

The issue of who gets to enter the country and become Australian was a hot-button issue at the time. Asylum seekers, especially from the Middle East, were detained at islands off Australian shores. Poor conditions and treatment of detainees, especially of children, dominated headlines. Liberals and activists lambasted the Australian government for cruel treatment of asylum seekers, many of whom were displaced by turmoil in the Middle East.

But that day, what I saw of the parade was cheerful. One hundred groups represented a variety of ethnic, cultural, sports, and special interest affiliations. They clustered together and held signs identifying themselves. Around me a group of yellow-robed Hare Krishnas jumped gleefully, Filipinos played harmonica, Southeast Asians wore conical hats, and Australians of Danish descent carried signs that clarified, "The People, Not the Pastry." In a group of Filipino drummers, an older man shimmied his shoulders while blowing a whistle to the drumbeats. Japanese women in kimonos and men from the Sikh Interfaith Council walked next to a group with a banner for the Mainland China Association. A brass marching band in blue and white uniforms played next to members of the Falun Gong. There were Thai dancers in exquisite costumes and the Qui Yi Lion Dance Association whose members stood on each other's shoulders so they towered above the crowd. A Filipino drummer ogled the shapely bare back of a Thai dancer in a slim sparkly skirt.

There were also special interest groups such as the *Doctor Who* Club of Victoria, the Skateboarders' Club of Melbourne, fans of *Planet of the Apes*, members of the Laughter Club and of the Bhutan–Miss Trans-sexual Australia Association. One group cut across race, age, and culture: "The 26ers"—people born on January 26. People who joined the 26 Club received a birthday card from the state government, as well as an invitation to march in the parade.

I weaved among the crowds that filled Swanston Street, unsure how to find the Tibetan contingent amid the sea of traditional ethnic attire and colorful outfits. But as I pushed through Filipino drummers sporting big feathered headdresses, I spotted Tibet's snow lion flag and long *chupa* dresses. More than seventy Tibetans—young and old—waved Tibetan and Australian flags as they readied to march. Little girls wore *chupas* of bright silk brocade, their hair hung in long braids down their backs. A child rode in a toy car festooned with miniature Australian flags. Men wore white traditional shirts or capacious dark Tibetan tunics. Some wore them tied around their waists according to the style of their region in Tibet. There were nuns and monks, one of whom sported an unruly topknot. He twirled a prayer wheel in one hand and had a pinkish complexion, like a fish unexposed to sunlight. Someone later told me he was a practitioner of Tantric Buddhism and was a hermit in Tibet and India, from where he had emigrated. And now here he was, parading among thousands down Melbourne's main commercial boulevard in front of a 7-Eleven convenience store, Lush beauty boutique, and a shop touting tax-free opals mined from Australia's hinterlands. I squeezed myself onto the curb. Next to me, a young Tibetan man helped a friend adjust his shirt.

"Can you hold this?" he asked, then handed me the Tibetan flag on a hefty pole. I obliged and held the roaring snow lions aloft. The day was cool and gray; rain began to fall. Some shielded themselves with the full-sized or miniature Tibetan or Australian flags they held. When the rain began to pelt the parade-goers more vigorously, some fled to nearby bus shelters. At the Bourke Street bus stop, I huddled next to some Tibetans, Filipino drummers, and another group of drummers from Kerala in southern India who held slender *J*-shaped drumsticks. On the street, some women opened umbrellas depicting Tibetan or Australian flags.

The rain subsided just in time for the start of the parade. In a hum of excitement, the river of humanity started walking, drumming, and tooting while carrying musical instruments, banners, flags, and signs. We passed the stores of the Central Business District near Flinders Lane. Go-Go Sushi, Subway, Christian Dior, and Robert Burke Couture all witnessed the sea of humanity heading toward the open sky above the Yarra River.

Along the one-and-a-half-mile parade route, I walked next to a Tibetan in his twenties dressed in a men's robe-like *chupa*, women in *chupas* pushing baby strollers, and young men wearing "Free Tibet" headbands. I chatted with a bespectacled Tibetan man who had only been in Australia six months. We walked past the tall antenna of Hamer Hall theater, close to where Norbu and I had watched New Year's fireworks, then through a green tunnel of trees by the National Gallery. Finally, we spilled into Kings Domain, thirty-six hectares of parklands adjacent to the Royal Botanic Gardens. Thousands of parade-goers settled in among the rolling meadows to lay out picnics. More than 450 classic and vintage cars lined the roads as part of an exhibition. Men on vintage penny-farthing bicycles teetered by on giant tires, past the groups of Storm Troopers, Punjabi men, and silk-clad Thai dancers.

The Tibetans unfolded blankets on the plush grass in a wide circle and set out plates of *tingmo* steamed bread, rice noodles with beef, and *momo*. An older woman nudged me and offered a Digestive biscuit from an open package. I watched as kids in Tibetan dresses and shirts chased each other around a tree. One of them cradled a bag of Smith Cheese and Onion potato chips. A boy in a miniature white tunic pushed a girl onto the grass. Big crocodile tears dripped off her reddened face, and a grandmother set her back on her feet. A Tibetan man in black cowboy boots, crimson shirt, and wide-brimmed hat sipped a cup of milky tea. Women in *chupas* clutched coffee cups and chatted. Another man in a cowboy hat and cream-colored shirt offered me a bag of dried plum candy.

I talked to a few Tibetans involved with the exile community in Melbourne. Thinley Jigme had come to Melbourne from the northern Indian city of Dehra Dun six months before. When I asked him what he thought about marching in the parade, his eyes lit up.

"It has given me a sheer honor to have shared the parade with them, sharing our own traditions, culture, dress. It's way much honor for me," he said. "I'm just hoping something like this [will happen] in Tibet soon." Something else struck Jigme about Australia. "Everyone is equal. Indians can look down on Eastern faces." He was referring to the racism commonly experienced by northeast India's Asian-looking ethnic minorities. Of course, inequity existed in Australia, but for newly arrived Jigme, his adopted home was more equitable and full of opportunities. Marching in the parade was "a very honoring thing," he told me in a radio story I recorded for Voice of America. Being visible and talking about Tibetan issues was important to him. "I have a responsibility of creating the awareness of what goes on in Tibet, the reality situation. I just try to share the real thing that go on in Tibet."

Jigme kept Tibetan identity alive in his family and spoke to his young son in Tibetan. "I'm teaching him at home, trying to tell him what our culture is like although I don't have much reminiscence with my own experience in Tibet." He explained to his son about "why we are away from his grandparents and my parents, why we are staying in a different location so he won't forget, growing in a different environment."

At the picnic, I ate *tingmo* and Digestive biscuits and smiled at the Tibetan children frolicking around me. I wondered how they would one day recall these childhood memories of Australia Day, when they waved flags bearing both Tibetan snow lions and Australia's Southern Cross stars.

. . .

A few days later, I took a commuter train from Melbourne for a short trip to the town of Footscray. Australians describe the town as an "outer suburb," but it sits just four miles from Melbourne's Central Business District. Instead of glossy department stores, boutiques, and fast food chains, storefronts in Footscray had signs in a variety of languages, including Vietnamese, Arabic, and Chinese. On a wide pedestrian boulevard, African men in traditional garb sat chatting on benches. A line of people waited inside Sunny Nguyen Bakery for a woman to make *banh mi* sandwiches behind a glass-topped counter. Entirely in Vietnamese, the menu offered items such as *cac loai banh mgot* (delicious cakes). Although Tibetans live all over Melbourne, hundreds had settled in Footscray. Many had also settled in a Melbourne neighborhood called Prahran that had a Tibetan weekend school for children.

I went to Footscray to meet Tenzin Khangsar, a clean-cut Tibetan in his early thirties and a leader of Melbourne's exile community. He had grown up in India and attended the Tibetan Children's Village in Ladakh, in India's mountainous far north, and Dharamsala. Tenzin went to college in Chennai at the Madras Christian College and then got a master's degree in the north-western state of Gujarat. Unlike most Tibetans in Australia, Tenzin came not as a refugee but as a student to study business at Victoria University. His English was fluent, so he worked part time as a Tibetan-English interpreter for the government, in addition to volunteering to help new Tibetan refugees and organize cultural events. In 2014 Tenzin was the vice president of the Tibetan Community of Victoria, and a few years later he became its president.

After we met, Tenzin invited me to a concert in a packed hall in Melbourne where renowned musician Tenzin Choegyal performed. Before he sang the Tibetan national anthem, Choegyal, an émigré to Brisbane, told the audience, "We are allowed to sing this song in exile. If you sing this song in Tibet, then you can be persecuted. It's to honor the courage of Tibetan people within Tibet."

When we first met in Footscray, Tenzin seemed slightly surprised; perhaps he wasn't expecting someone Asian who looked Chinese, but he didn't probe with personal questions. Instead, we sat by some park benches outside a food court, then went inside to have coffee. That day Tenzin wore a traditional Tibetan shirt with his jeans. Since the 2008 protests in Tibet, some exiled Tibetans began observing "Lha-kar" or "White Wednesday." Each Wednesday, Tibetans wore traditional clothing, ate Tibetan food, and patronized Tibetan businesses as a show of support for Tibet and Tibetan heritage.

Tenzin walked me through what a new refugee could expect when they arrived in Australia. Unlike asylum seekers, Tibetan refugees with humanitarian visas got a lot of support from the Australian government; they were not "boat people" who arrived without documentation. Like Norbu, they arrived by plane with visas granted by the Australian embassy in India. After arrival, a government social worker helped them set up a bank account and connected them to Centrelink, the Australian welfare system. In 2014, every two weeks they received a $570 living allowance electronically deposited in their bank accounts.

Usually, other Tibetans hosted new arrivals while they looked for more permanent apartments, Tenzin told me. Refugees all saw a doctor for a general checkup and got a government Medicare health account, so health care was basically free. For visits to the hospital or dentist, a government interpreter could accompany them. If needed, a refugee nurse with an interpreter was dispatched to their home.

Tibetan refugees met with a social worker at AMES, Australian Migration Education Services, which had an office in Footscray and other neighborhoods. AMES helped new arrivals enroll in English classes. Tibetans who already spoke proficient English could enroll in vocational training, like Norbu, or start looking for a job.

Considering that rent for a two-bedroom apartment could cost $300 a week, many Tibetans wanted to start earning money as soon as possible. But English was usually the biggest challenge for getting a job, said Tenzin. Although AMES assisted with job placements, it wasn't so easy finding work. Tibetan refugees typically found jobs as chefs, aged care workers, home health aides, airport workers, carpenters, vendors at fruit and vegetable markets, fast food restaurants, and distributing pamphlets on the street. "Finding a job is all about luck and persistence and networks," said Tenzin.

Since the Tibetans granted asylum in Australia had faced political persecution, virtually all had fled their homeland as adults or young adults. Norbu's transition had been relatively smooth due to his studies at the Transit School in Dharamsala, training and support from Gu Chu Sum, and his restaurant job. But many other refugees lacked education, English, and job skills, so it was harder for them to adjust. Some jobs in Australia required drivers' licenses and other skills. Vocational training took months or years. Many refugees had not been in a formal classroom for years—if ever in their lives. It was easy for Tibetan refugees to feel adrift, observed Tenzin.

Under its special program for Tibetans, the Australian government usually granted fifty visas each year to refugees who had faced political persecution. The majority of them arrived from India. In 2014 and 2015, Australia granted as many as 250 visas to Tibetans because there had been a lull in previous years due to Australia's tighter immigration policies under a conservative government. By 2015, there was a small flood of refugees arriving in Australia, and services were stretched.

All this work kept Tenzin very busy. Why did he volunteer? Later he told me it was important to help his community "because my Tibetan people have suffered a lot under brutal Chinese communist regime and now they live in this privileged country. However, due to lack of English, they still suffer and struggle every day." Tenzin continued, "Being a Buddhist, I believe in karma. My service for the underprivileged members is like a light in a dark place to the happier pathway."

. . .

For the fortunate, Australia was a "privileged country" as Tenzin Khangsar had described. The supermarkets had a dazzling bounty of fruits and vegetables and aisles filled with endless varieties of food. Walking on intact sidewalks and breathing clean air was a joy. From my friends' house in Melbourne, I often jogged down a path lined with fragrant eucalyptus trees, their trunks encased in gnarled, sculpted bark. I could walk to the beach and Port Melbourne where I often watched a giant ship called the *Spirit of Tasmania* set off southward as its horn bellowed departure.

From my idyllic base in Melbourne, I went back to Footscray several times. One afternoon I visited the AMES center in a large, bright building with classrooms, offices, and common spaces. Cheerful posters hung on hallway bulletin boards. They announced, "We've learnt 87 languages to help you learn one" and "Working with Refugees to Build New Lives in Australia." Next to fliers for free computer workshops, the Victoria Immigrant and Refugee Women's Coalition, and the Women's Friendship Café a poster read, "AMES has already helped more than 500,000 people to read, write, speak and understand the English language better."

Some thirty-one languages were spoken at that center among students who hailed from Sudan, Indonesia, Croatia, Albania, China, Serbia, Tibet, Russia, Greece, and other far-flung countries. Classrooms were decorated with posters of animals such as kangaroos and of food groups: lettuce, celery, raspberries, toast. Another poster explained what public signs meant: Pedestrian Crossing, Airport, Toilets.

At the center I met with Sahar Ageed, case manager, and Sheree Peterson, communications officer. All clients attend an orientation where they learn about cultural expectations and social etiquette in Australia. For example, they learn that jaywalking and putting one's feet up on train seats is illegal or frowned upon. Sessions with about sixteen students per class teach basic health and "meaningful engagement," such as knitting and crocheting. Attendees might hail from Iran, Iraq, Ethiopia, or Burma.

In addition to teaching English, AMES's employment unit helped people with job interviews, cover letters, and résumés.

But it wasn't easy for many refugees to adapt, especially older ones who couldn't easily learn English. Ageed told me about a Tibetan father and daughter who arrived in Australia in 2014 and lived in Footscray. The daughter was in her twenties. The father, in his sixties and previously a security guard at a temple in Delhi, had physical and mental trauma from being tortured in Tibet. Ageed did not tell me the circumstances of the man's journey, but after twenty years, he still had trouble sleeping. He had problems with his hips and had trouble walking so was in a special tutor program rather than English class.

The congenial atmosphere at AMES was different from the Asylum Seekers Resource Center a few blocks away. The nonprofit ASRC worked with people in limbo, migrants who came without visas to Australia to seek asylum. Kon Karapanagiotidis, founder and CEO of ASRC, called Australia one of the worst countries for settling asylum seekers. Since 1996, conservative politics in Australia had made asylum a contentious issue and even conflated asylum seekers with terrorists. In 2013, Australia spent $8 billion to "lock up asylum seekers" on islands off its coast, according to Kon. Those who came illegally by boat "faced the most brutal situations in the world," he said.

Asylum seekers came from Afghanistan, Iraq, Iran, Pakistan, Sri Lanka, Zimbabwe, Ethiopia, China, and elsewhere. Some 1,500 Chinese asylum seekers were persecuted because they were members of Christian churches or the Falun Gong, according to Kon. In 1993 there were 15,500 asylum seekers in detention. By January 2015, 28,000 were in limbo with 11,000 of them in offshore detention camps. In the previous 14 months, 100 boats had arrived in Australian waters carrying undocumented immigrants.

Others who managed to arrive to Australia's mainland were granted temporary protected visas but had no right to work or access health care. "The majority live on no income," said Kon. They lived in "ghettos" and formed an underclass without a safety net that could turn into another "lost generation"—a reference to brutally oppressed Aboriginal peoples. Kon was adamant that Australia must stop politicizing the situation and take its fair share of refugees. If the government took 1 percent of what it spent on offshore detentions and designated the funds for social programs that supported them, that would be far more productive than locking people up and detaining children indefinitely, Kon said.

I thought of Norbu. His experience as a political refugee was vastly different than that of asylum seekers who waited in limbo in Australia's detention centers. It was an uneasy dichotomy dictated by politics, policies, immigration papers, and luck.

·   ·   ·

For the more fortunate, I saw how immigrant cultures could flourish. Weeks later, in February 2015, Losar celebrations within Tibet itself were still subdued. China again tightened security ahead of the Tibetan New Year to suppress any potential unrest. But an ocean away in Melbourne, the Tibetan community celebrated with great fanfare. It was near the end of February and still warm during the Australian summer when Tenzin Khangsar invited me to the Losar celebration in Collingwood, a Melbourne neighborhood. The air was hot and dry as I walked from the tram station along empty streets. I wasn't sure I was heading in the right direction. But then I spotted welcoming Tibetan prayer flags hanging above the doorway of a large building.

I stepped inside Collingwood Town Hall and was transported to a Tibetan party. Tibetan pop music blasted from speakers and Tibetan and Australian flags hung over the stage. There were women in *chupas* and striped *pangden*, men in traditional shirts and big hats batting balloons around, as well as a few red-robed monks. Children chased each other across the room and little girls turned cartwheels. A man with a thin mustache and brown hat set at a rakish angle smiled broadly and danced in a circle. He wore a white tunic with long, floppy sleeves that fell over his hands as he held out his arms wide. In one hand he held a can of Carlton draught beer. Ladies in *chupas* crooned alongside him. In one corner, some young Tibetans laughed and cheered as they played cards. An older man smiled as he pushed a baby stroller across the floor. People ate fried snacks and candies from straw baskets. It was a microcosm of other diverse and colorful Tibetan gatherings I had seen in Dharamsala, in Sarnath at the Dalai Lama's teachings, and recently at the Australia Day parade in Melbourne. It was sobering to think that in Tibet itself there were no such grand, joyous, and public celebrations.

In the industrial kitchen, people busily rolled tubes of dough to make *momos*. They pulled off plugs then flattened them into floury circles on large wooden boards. I could smell the mounds of pink ground meat filling in large bowls. A production line that included women in aprons and a teenaged boy with spiky bleached hair busily stuffed circles of dough.

Meanwhile, back in the main room a few people got onstage to sing Tibetan songs. One young man rapped in Tibetan to a whooping crowd. The rest of the evening, people ate, drank, and danced. The music got even louder as the deejay played Tibetan tunes and thumping Punjabi bhangra. Bob Marley's "Buffalo Soldier" came on and women started swaying in a circle. Couples, and middle-aged and older ladies, waltzed. The deejay danced with a white balloon and waggled his hips, then yelled into his mic, "It's time to disco!" The crowd cheered as "Gangnam Style" blasted from the speakers. Men, women, and children started the trendy dance from South Korea and mimicked riding a horse and swinging a lasso in the air like the singer Psy.

Some of them had probably done that on a real horse while galloping across the Tibetan plateau.

Even though I had spent Losar in Dharamsala, the home of the Dalai Lama, the Tibetan exile government and thousands of Tibetans, I had never experienced the holiday in its full glory since celebrations were canceled in 2009. But here in a hall in Melbourne, I saw Tibetans truly celebrating the day as they were meant to do. It was a joy to behold.

In the middle of the dance floor, an older Tibetan man in a big hat happily swayed to the music. He tapped his boot heel on the floor and waved to me in invitation to join the party.

[17]

The Only Thing That Counts
Without Culture and Tradition
Then There's No More Tibet

SYDNEY, FEBRUARY 2015

. . .

The town of Dee Why is about twelve miles north of Sydney on a stretch of coast called the Northern Beaches. When I told Australian friends that I would spend most of my Sydney visit in Dee Why, they were puzzled. It took more than an hour to commute there on the L90 city bus; Dee Why was a nondescript suburban beach town of about 20,000 people and not a typical destination. In fact, the Northern Beaches were nicknamed "the insular peninsula."

But Dee Why has a different significance to Tibetans, and a stroll around the town reveals why. In a fast-food restaurant called Aces Charcoal Chicken, friendly Tibetans in uniforms greeted me from behind the counter. Near Coles, the ubiquitous Australian supermarket, was a Gloria Jean's chain coffee shop. The place was full of Tibetan men, some wearing traditional shirts, leisurely sipping coffee as though in a Dharamsala café. And in my first few days wandering around Dee Why, I was flabbergasted to see a familiar face transplanted from the Himalayan foothills to the Pacific Ocean coast.

Dee Why was home to about 700 Tibetans, the largest community in Australia. Gloria Jean's had become a de facto meeting spot for Tibetans due to its central location, not its menu of mudslide mocha espresso and crème brûlée coffee. Pleasant suburban streets had names like Pacific Parade and Oaks Avenue. Shops sold beachwear and sunglasses in a main commercial area called Village Plaza. It was the kind of place where cars honked at you if you crossed the street outside of a crosswalk. Yet there were cross-cultural influences too. I passed a church where people were singing beautiful hymns. I peeked inside and saw a service full of Pacific Islanders— including spiffy men wearing sarongs and suit jackets. They beckoned me to enter so I sat on a pew and listened to a sermon that was perhaps in Samoan or Tongan.

Dee Why's tree-lined streets led to the seafront. The beach was more idyllic than the town's somewhat down-at-the-heels, "daggy" reputation. Maybe by Australian's high standards, Dee Why beach was fairly unremarkable. But by normal standards, it was a lovely crescent of sand that opened to a spectacular turquoise ocean. At one end of the beach sat "rock pools"—large swimming pools fed by seawater. The pools were crowded with people trying to swim laps as children splashed in the bright blue water. At the other end of the beach, in the far distance, colorful houses sat on a hillside overlooking the ocean. The hues—lemon and periwinkle blue with terracotta roofs—reminded me of the bright buildings carved into the steep hills of Dharamsala.

Above the beach, people sat on a grassy lawn to chat, picnic, and enjoy the sea view. Frothy waves carried surfers aloft. On the grass, two older men played Guns N' Roses tunes on electric guitars. A little blonde girl chased squawking seagulls and threw tufts of grass at them. Wetsuit-clad surfers carried boards to and from the ocean in a quintessential Australian beach scene. In addition to these Australian beachgoers, a monk in red robes held a plastic Coles bag around his wrist. Four Tibetan women wearing *chupas* sat on the grass. Two men who looked Tibetan or Nepali sat chatting on a park bench.

Walking around a beach town that was home to Australia's largest population of Tibetans was a bit surreal, and I was glad to see it in person. I hadn't even planned on going to Sydney, but having a base in Melbourne with my new friends gave me the flexibility to extend my Australia trip and do more interviews. And when I emailed Chin Jin, the Chinese democracy activist I met in Dharamsala, to tell him I was in Melbourne, he eagerly invited me to Sydney, his adopted hometown. He would be speaking on a panel, and he invited me to attend. Tencho Gyatso, the Dalai Lama's niece and a director with the International Campaign for Tibet, was coming to Sydney from Washington, DC. She would speak at the event with Lhakpa Tshoko, the Dalai Lama's representative to Australia, a Chinese Australian professor, and Chin Jin about Tibet-China relations.

At first, because of my tight budget, I wasn't sure if I should go to Sydney. But with characteristic enthusiasm, Chin Jin persuaded me to make the trip. He even offered to put me up with his friend so I wouldn't have to worry about accommodations.

It was hard to pass up the invitation. I flew from Melbourne and Chin Jin's nephew, Yang, picked me up at the Sydney airport. I was amazed that a twenty-something would spend his Saturday night fetching a total stranger. We drove to a Sydney suburb called Campsie and had dinner at a local Chinese restaurant. Then Yang dropped me off at a modest but comfortable home owned by Chin Jin's friend Jack and his wife, an older couple who had immigrated from China. Jack was also active with the Chinese democracy movement. "Jack and his wife are very friendly!" Chin Jin had told me over email. The couple were unfazed that a total stranger would be staying with them for several days. Chin Jin had vouched for me, and that was enough for me to take up residence in their spare room.

I was out of the house in Campsie most of the time, but some days I worked on articles for the *Economist* at the small desk in the bedroom that used to belong to the couple's grown daughter. One day Jack's granddaughter arrived at the house with a green lollipop in hand and proceeded to jump on my bed. "She likes to talk to herself everywhere—tram, bus," her grandmother observed. Sometimes I ate breakfast with my generous hosts but I spent most of my days in Dee Why.

Campsie was nearly seven miles west of Sydney and connected to the city by commuter train. The suburb's main street was lined with Asian restaurants, bakeries, and grocery stores. It reminded me of a smaller, calmer version of other Asian immigrant communities like Flushing in Queens, New York. One morning I jogged in the neighborhood and came across a park where older Asians practiced tai chi. Another group of ladies did vigorous arm circles. Some South Asian women in *salwar kameez* joined the tai chi. Along the main road, Chinese bakeries sold egg tarts and sticky rice dough coated with shredded coconut, like in so many Chinatowns around the world.

The day after I arrived in Sydney, Chin Jin picked me up from Jack's house to drive to the city center. He still bristled with energy and looked much the same as when I had last seen him in Dharamsala, though it was a bit strange to see him doing something as mundane as driving along city streets instead of walking through McLeod Ganj accompanied by street dogs.

The panel at the University of Technology in Sydney was well attended, with Chinese and Tibetans in the audience. Tencho Gyatso, the Dalai Lama's niece, worked on Tibetan and Chinese engagement programs at the International Campaign for Tibet. Articulate and calm, she looked professorial. I later learned that she had played the Dalai Lama's mother in *Kundun*, Martin Scorsese's 1997 film.

After the talk, I spoke with Tencho for a few minutes in the lobby and tried to find a quiet place to record her for a Voice of America radio story. I asked what she thought about the Tibetan community in Australia. Tencho acknowledged the challenges of "balancing raising children and living lives as Tibetans, but now also Australia-Tibetans—and learning to weave their lives into this new country."

Then she expressed admiration. "I think they're doing an excellent job. They hold weekend schools. They help each other. They built a network and organize in helping them get into the system."

A few days later I got a chance to see the children's language and culture classes in Dee Why at a local community center. There, about ninety Tibetan children attended Tibetan language and culture classes taught by a dozen teachers. I watched as they rehearsed traditional songs and dance for Losar celebrations.

The classes had started in 2002 and grew as the Tibetan community expanded. The biggest challenge was finding venues large enough for all the students. The current community center was too small, said Phurbu Khonnyi Tsang, president of the Tibetan community association for the state of New South Wales. In his late twenties or thirties, Phurbu had shaggy hair and wore heavy-framed black glasses. His Australian accent was tinged with a Tibetan one too.

"Compared to other nationalities or communities, Tibetans have a different responsibility," Phurbu told me. "We have a big responsibility to keep our language and culture alive within the young generation. As the Dalai Lama says, 'We must keep our language alive.' But many children whose parents are working full time, so they don't get much time to spend with their kids."

That day, I also met Dorjee Dadul, a Tibetan in his sixties who emigrated to Australia from India in 1980. He worked closely with the Tibetan community in Sydney and helped start the Tibetan language classes in Dee Why. Culture "is the very identity of Tibetanness. Without culture and tradition then there's no more Tibet. We can be anyone—Joe Blow, citizen of Australia," Dorjee told me ardently.

Gray-haired Dorjee was outgoing and talkative when I met him in Dee Why at Gloria Jean's. We decided to move to a quieter café nearby. As we walked, a teary, middle-aged Tibetan woman approached Dorjee. They spoke in Tibetan for a while; I could tell he was trying to console her. After she left, he told me she had lost her wallet and asked him for help. As one of the first Tibetans to immigrate to Australia decades before, he was well known in the Tibetan community—and had a colorful history.

Dorjee was just three or four years old when his family fled Tibet for India. Like many Tibetan refugees, his mother worked doing road construction. She was carrying rocks on her back while building roads in the hills of Siliguri to Sikkim in northeast India. Two of her toes were crushed and they had to bring her to a hospital in the town of Kalimpong. When Dorjee was about nine years old, his family settled in Darjeeling, a hill town known for its eponymous tea. His father started working with a group supporting Tibetan guerillas being trained by the CIA for covert operations in Tibet during the Cold War. In 1963, when he was an adolescent, Dorjee started working as a courier for Tibetans helping the CIA. "They found out I was useful because I could interpret," said Dorjee. The resourceful boy carried letters and bought supplies in local markets for the clandestine forces.

In 1966 Dorjee took a typing course in Delhi with the Tibetan exile administration. At the end of 1967 he started working for a new magazine called the *Tibetan Review*. He was the only staff member besides the publisher and did everything and anything needed for seventy-five rupees a month. "I didn't have money to buy a toothbrush!" Dorjee recalled.

In 1972 he got a visa to Canada and worked in a yarn factory with other Tibetans. He also started doing volunteer work for the Tibetan exile administration's office in New York and lived between the United States and Canada for the next eight years. When the Dalai Lama came to the United States for his first visit in 1979, Dorjee worked with the entourage that traveled with him. By 1980, Dorjee contemplated volunteering in Tibet to teach English, since China was starting to open up to the outside world after decades of insularity. But when an opportunity came to go to Australia in 1980, Dorjee found himself working at a Tibetan Buddhist center in Sydney as a temporary interpreter for a teacher whose translator couldn't get a visa from India. "I'll give it a try until your interpreter comes," Dorjee told the center. The translator never arrived. Dorjee originally planned to stay in Australia six months. Three decades later, he is still there.

Dorjee's children were born in Australia, but he tried to instill Tibetan culture in them. He even sent them to a camp at the Tibetan Children's Village in Dharamsala for Tibetan children living abroad. At the school they had to hand-wash their clothes in cold water and, like other Tibetan children in India, live without many creature comforts. Unsurprisingly, his Australian-born kids hated it; they called TCV "Tibetan Crap Village." After growing up with the amenities and everyday luxuries of life in Australia, it was hard to do without them.

But India and Tibet were still vital for Dorjee. Several years after we had met, when he was in his seventies, he told me he hoped to spend time in Dharamsala and go on pilgrimage in India and maybe Tibet. "Hope is always there. I'd like to die in Tibet," said Dorjee.

. . .

Although Dee Why was unremarkable to Australians I spoke with, even Tibetans in Tibet had heard about Dee Why, Dorjee told me. Among Tibetans in India, it was common for them to request relocation to Dee Why, not simply Sydney, when applying for asylum.

Like many communities that sprout up in unlikely places, the diaspora started with one émigré. In 1975 a Tibetan named Namgyal Tsering immigrated to Australia and lived near Dee Why. The same year he founded the Australian-Tibet Society as its president. His brother-in-law was Sogyal Rinpoche, the Tibetan Buddhist teacher who founded the Rigpa centers and wrote *The Tibetan Book of Living and Dying*.

As more Tibetans settled in Australia, they told their friends and relatives about Dee Why and word spread. Teachers and others working in Dee Why know that Tibetans are part of the town's fabric. I saw that when Dorjee and I stopped by the town's public library; it had the warm, familial atmosphere of many public libraries around the world. Tucked in among shelves of Australian newspapers and magazines were copies of Tibetan publications such as the *Tibet Express* and *Tibetan Review*. Dorjee also showed me children's books in Tibetan published through Australia Tibet House. One book featured bright drawings of Australian animals like kangaroos, koalas, and emus. It also included Tibetan animals: yaks, snow leopards, and the black-necked crane. There were no snow leopards in Australia, but a child who picked up the book would know they existed in a storied place where the family of their Tibetan classmates hailed from.

. . .

Tibetans tried to preserve their culture in their new home, but they also had to adapt to life in Australia. One way to do this was learning to swim. The beach and ocean are integral parts of culture for many Australians and most learn to swim at a young age. The beach was Dee Why's front yard and the centerpiece for recreation. Yet most Tibetan refugees had never seen the ocean before arriving in Australia and didn't know how to swim. They were now far from the mountains of their homeland and unaware of the potential dangers of the ocean, from sharks to rip tides.

A swim teacher in Dee Why named Tanya Carmont noticed Tibetans in classes she taught at community pools in the area. They were excited to be at the swimming center—too excited. Even though they didn't know how to swim, some of the Tibetans jumped straight into the pool. "That gave me the biggest scare of my life," Carmont told me. "Tibetans in general are not afraid of the water. They love being near the ocean. They love going in the water—but they really don't know how to swim and they get themselves into trouble down there."

In 2012, having learned that there was a sizable community of Tibetans in Dee Why, Carmont developed a water safety and swimming lesson program for Tibetans with the Manly Community Center. The Tibetan program included a ten-week swim and water safety course that cost just fifteen dollars because it was subsidized by local grants. An illustrated booklet on water safety has been translated into Tibetan.

By 2015, about 300 Tibetans had enrolled in the course. They included Pasang Tsering, a forty-year-old Tibetan who emigrated from India to Australia in 2008. Tsering had also become a certified swim instructor in Carmont's program.

One afternoon, I sat with Tsering on concrete bleachers that overlooked Dee Why's seawater swimming pools with a commanding view of the ocean. There were no lifeguards at this public pool. Tsering and I watched a kid do a dangerous-looking backflip into the pool from a railing. Like most Tibetans in Dee Why, Tsering had never seen the ocean before emigrating to Australia. "Most Tibetans don't know swimming so I hope [to] teach more Tibetan kids and adult," he said in a soft voice. "We live near the ocean. So dangerous for life, so we should learn."

Phurbu, president of Sydney's Tibetan association, approved of the swim program. "Tibet is dry land, snowy mountains. There's no beach and ocean. We have only rivers and lakes. So when you come to Australia all the boundaries are beaches. It is very important to learn swimming and basic important things: swimming, their language, their culture."

While hundreds of Tibetans had learned to swim, many others had no time for recreation. They were preoccupied with finding work and becoming employable. Living in Dee Why was cheaper than living in Sydney but still expensive. Average rent for a one-bedroom apartment in Dee Why was

$350 per week, said Phurbu. Many Tibetans lived together to reduce costs, but finding a job was still imperative. Most people couldn't afford to live on government assistance alone. In the Northern Beaches, there was big demand for cleaners and workers in aged care—roles popular among Tibetans. But these positions still required training and certifications from government vocational schools called Technical and Further Education, or TAFE.

On another afternoon, Dorjee Dadul and I visited TAFE Northern Beaches, which sat on a spacious campus a couple of miles off the main highway. We walked past modern buildings sprawled across verdant grounds full of tropical trees and bushes. Cicadas buzzed and birds whistled as we strolled along manicured paths. Near the cafeteria sat a pool table and ping pong table. Prince crooned on a radio in the distance. Dorjee explained that Tibetan TAFE students sometimes held picnics on the campus even when classes were not in session during holidays because it was a "safe place" for them. It wasn't hard to see why the bucolic campus was a haven.

TAFE was established by the government in the 1970s. TAFE Northern Beaches offered classes ranging from carpentry and accounting to hospitality and information technology and much more. It took two years to earn a certificate in aged care, while a course on house cleaning took one hundred hours. A class to earn a certificate in spoken and written English was popular among Tibetans.

That afternoon ten students including older and younger Tibetans sat in a bright classroom as ceiling fans twirled overhead. A blonde teacher was going over pictures and words in English.

"*K* is for kangaroo," she intoned. She covered pictures and words for possum, kiwi fruit, pineapple, and *yabby*, an Australian word for crayfish. During lunch break, Tibetan students milled around in the lobby holding Tupperware boxes and metal thermoses.

Some Tibetans adapted well to life in Australia, especially if they already knew English from India. Other Tibetans with less English and formal education had a harder time. "Tibetans are generally very adaptable," observed Dorje. "At the same time, they have a lot of issues because of the language."

Learning English wasn't as simple as attending a class, though. A Tibetan who was previously a nomad might not adjust to a nine-to-five city job. Tibetans experiencing post-traumatic stress disorder or other anxiety such as family separation faced special challenges, as I had been told in Melbourne at AMES. One Tibetan woman couldn't concentrate in her English class because she was worried about her children in Tibet, said Philippa Belle-more, a former social worker at TAFE. While there were lots of free services for refugees from the government and other organizations, they could be hard to find and access, especially without English, said Maria Chidzey, a multicultural community worker at the Manly Community Center.

To help fill some of the gaps, in 2007 Philippa and Dorjee set up a Tibetan Mentoring Program. As of 2015, 120 Tibetans had been paired with about 100 Australians. Volunteer mentors might help Tibetans prepare for citizenship tests, make doctor appointments, or translate letters from Australian social services, among other things. The mentors themselves went through thirty hours of training and had to pass an interview to qualify for their roles. However, by 2021 the program was no longer running due to lack of resources.

Other problems that came up for Tibetans were restaurants not paying minimum wage; cleaning jobs that exploited workers, especially school janitors; and landlords who raised rents beyond legal limits. And there were everyday pitfalls. One Tibetan didn't realize how far away a cleaning job was and ended up paying fifty dollars for a taxi ride to outer Sydney. Another Tibetan donated money to a door-to-door solicitor and did not realize his donation recurred every month. Another Tibetan got a customer satisfaction survey from the bank and thought it was an exam he needed to take at the bank. Everyday tasks and seemingly simple interactions could be daunting or demoralizing.

. . .

In addition to aged care, housekeeping, restaurants, and other service industries, Tibetans were entrepreneurial. That was embodied in an unlikely character. One day as I walked past Gloria Jean's café in Dee Why, I saw a familiar face. The last time I had seen Sonam was in Dharamsala in 2008, when he joined a candlelight vigil for a Tibetan man killed in Tibet. I had also interviewed him in the Khanna Nirvana café following a talk he gave about fleeing Tibet after China's March 2008 crackdown.

Sonam stood out in Dharamsala because, with his wide-brimmed hat and goatee, he looked like a rugged cowboy from the steppes of Tibet. And that's what he still looked like as we strolled past each other outside Gloria Jean's. I recognized his square features immediately. My mouth fell open as we stared at each other in surprise. Sonam wore a blue chambray button-down shirt, flip flops, and a bush hat. He remembered me too. We greeted each other excitedly then sat on a bench outside Dee Why's Christian Science Reading Room to catch up.

Sonam had been in Australia for less than a year. He had been jailed in Tibet so was eligible for political asylum in Australia. In fact, he had been jailed several times for involvement in protests. He was at risk again after the 2008 protests in Tibet. He came from a nomadic family and his brother was killed by authorities. But he wasn't scared of Chinese people. He matter-of-factly told me he "had a lot of Chinese friends in jail." He had also first learned smatterings of English while in prison.

In Dharamsala, I had lost touch with Sonam. In Australia he was selling Akubra hats—like the brown one he wore—to Tibetans overseas. Turns out the hat that Crocodile Dundee wore was also very popular among Tibetans. I didn't fully understand his businesses, but apparently the bush hats sold like hotcakes, even at ninety Australian dollars a pop. We spoke in Mandarin because Sonam was from a Tibetan part of China's Sichuan Province, and his Mandarin was much better than his English.

"Did you remember I'm American?" I asked him.

"Yes, because your Chinese isn't that good," he replied.

I laughed. Perhaps my rusty Mandarin was also a good indicator that I was not a Chinese spy. Sonam told me that his wife was born in India, so her Tibetan was not very good.

That afternoon, Tibetans in Dee Why were preparing for a field trip to hear a Tibetan Rinpoche speak in Sydney. On the spot, Sonam invited me and I accepted. I spontaneously boarded an old school bus filled with Tibetans from all walks of life and we sat on one of the vinyl bench seats. In front of us sat a middle-aged woman reading a book of Tibetan scripture. Near me an adolescent boy in shorts listened to music through Sony headphones. A teenaged girl with long, fake eyelashes chewed gum. A Tibetan man in a cream-colored traditional shirt and fedora hat held a plastic bag full of katha scarves for offerings.

The bus lumbered along, and as we entered Sydney we sped over the Harbour Bridge. Below us, the water and the white petal-like shards of the Opera House sparkled in the sun—a surreal view to take in next to Sonam, whom I had last seen on the streets of gritty, landlocked Dharamsala.

When we arrived at our destination in Sydney, the busload of people disembarked and entered the Rigpa Center in the Newtown neighborhood. Colorful photos of the Dalai Lama lined the walls in an entryway where people removed their shoes and piled them together. The place smelled of incense. Upstairs, everyone sat in a prayer hall decorated with colorful *thangkas* and a golden Buddha statue as the centerpiece. Sonam sat in the third row to listen to an esteemed Rinpoche give a talk about Buddhism in Tibetan. I wanted to be inconspicuous, so I sat in the back. I couldn't understand anything except snippets of English that were peppered into his talk, such as "Buddhism is about transforming the mind" and "We are good, but sometimes action is wrong."

The back of the hall, it turns out, was where parents deposited their restless children. A boy in a silk brocade shirt and camouflage shorts stacked purple cushions like a fort. A mother handed out juice boxes. Outside the prayer hall was a table covered with platters of cookies: Arnott's biscuits, Scotch fingers, custard cream. Before long, many of the children, including a girl in a red brocade dress, had fallen asleep on stacks of cushions. I craned my head and saw that Sonam was still listening attentively at the front of the room. An old man near me in a wool fedora fingered prayer beads. In English the Rinpoche said something I understood: "The only thing that counts is how you lived your life."

. . .

A few days after my chance meeting with Sonam in Dee Why, he invited me to his home for lunch and to meet his wife. Saturday seemed like the best time, but I didn't anticipate that Sydney's already cumbersome public transportation system would slow to a crawl over the weekend. In the city center, I waited at the bus depot for an inordinately long time. I wanted to bring Sonam a gift, but there were no bakeries or wine shops nearby and my only option was a 7-Eleven convenience store. I had ample time to browse the aisles but there wasn't anything appropriate. Finally, I had to settle for a box of Krispy Kreme donuts dotted with pink sprinkles because it was nearly Valentine's Day. Donuts from an American company sold at an American chain convenience store in Australia as a gift for a refugee from Tibet I met in India. In this world of overlapping, melded cultures, why not?

I took a bus to Sonam's house: a one-story brick home with terracotta roof tiles in a more suburban part of Dee Why. By the time I arrived I was more than an hour late. When Sonam opened the door, I apologized profusely as he ushered me inside. His wife Yeshi was thirty-six years old and had a round face that was even rounder because she was, I learned, seven months pregnant. I felt even worse about keeping a pregnant woman waiting to eat. I penitently offered the box of Krispy Kreme donuts and Yeshi perked up.

Sonam and Yeshi shared the house with another Tibetan couple who was not home. The living room was spacious, with two sofas facing each other. A TV sat above shelves stocked with jugs of oil, cans of coffee, and jars of peanut butter. One wall was decorated with a small Indian flag next to an Australian one. A glass door looked out onto a large grassy backyard where laundry hung from a clothesline.

We sat down in the living room around a glass coffee table covered with a huge platter of *momos*—bowls of green vegetables, cooked eggplant, and red peppers. Chopsticks rested on the table. Yeshi and Sonam seemed eager to eat, so we wasted no time digging in.

"You can use your hand. I feel most comfortable with spoon," she told me. Blunt and droll, Yeshi spoke English fluently because she was from Mundgod, a large Tibetan settlement in southern India, seven hours northwest of Bangalore. Her family had moved to Pune, a city a few hours from Mumbai, so she spoke Marathi, the language of Maharashtra State, in addition to English and Hindi. As a polyglot, Yeshi was surprised when she met Tibetans from Tibet who couldn't speak Mandarin. "What have they been doing this whole time?" she wondered.

Yeshi was taking a management course near Dee Why and looked forward to working so she could "start earning." It wasn't clear how she and Sonam had met. Yeshi told me she had moved to Australia because a Tibetan astrologist said that Sydney would be good for her future.

Sonam went into the backyard to take a phone call in Tibetan. Yeshi observed that her husband woke up at 6 a.m. every day and was always on the phone doing business. "He likes talking. He's very active! In this business, he made a lot of money."

Yeshi had lived in Delhi for some time, and we reminisced about India. "Food is so cheap! Three bunches of spinach for five rupees!" She waxed nostalgic about *jalebi*, the Indian dessert of fried batter drenched in sugar syrup, and paratha sold near Delhi's Red Fort. Her mother used to make chapatis, as well as dal and *pakoras*. Unlike me, Yeshi was skeptical about Australian produce. "These apples are so perfect. It's not natural," she criticized. "Watermelon is so huge! In Mundgod, the watermelon is so small."

I mentioned I had observed weekend classes in Dee Why for Tibetan children and had been interviewing Tibetans about life in Australia. "Will you send your child to Tibetan school?" I asked.

Yeshi didn't hesitate. "Yes!" she replied.

As she watched me scribbling notes, she asked, "What's your longest interview?"

"Hours," I replied.

"Don't you feel bored writing? I read two pages and I want to fall asleep," Yeshi said with what I was learning was her characteristic frankness.

I burst out laughing. She looked at me mystified; she didn't see what was so funny. I explained that writing didn't bore me. It was interesting, though quite tiring. Yeshi seemed unconvinced. I continued to write everything down, and at the end of our Tibetan meal, my host eagerly bit into dessert: a Krispy Kreme Valentine's donut with pink sprinkles.

Documents and Ability
For the First Time I Have Hope

DECKYI: LEUVEN, BELGIUM, APRIL 2016

. . .

My train from Brussels pulled into Leuven, a town famous for its fifteenth-century university and Stella Artois beer. Hundreds of people streamed out of the station and up the ramp into the late afternoon sun. I was a world away from the beaches of Australia; it had been more than a year since I visited Norbu in Melbourne, and I had just landed in Europe after four busy months in Rwanda, Kenya, and South Africa to write articles. I would soon return to Africa for another fourteen months of journalism. But on my way back from Johannesburg to the United States for a brief visit, I managed to squeeze in a few days' layover in Brussels. The quick trip was an interlude to pick up the thread on Tibetan refugees. It had thinned, but I grabbed it again when I realized there was a chance to see Deckyi in Belgium.

In spite of the crowd, I almost immediately saw her waiting for me on the edge of Leuven Station's wide, cobblestone plaza. She was instantly recognizable, even though it had been more than four years since I last saw her in India in 2012. Her long hair was tied in a bun. On the crisp spring day, she wore khaki capri pants, a white jacket with decorative ties, and pointy cream-colored shoes made with woven leather strips. Deckyi had the same serious, slightly anxious expression, but her face lit up when she saw me.

She greeted me in English in her soft voice and seemed happy if a little shy. I marveled at seeing her again after so long. For some reason, it did not seem so strange to meet her in a historic European university town rather than in a crowded Himalayan hill station or a courthouse in Delhi. We walked to the other side of the terminal where rumbling buses pulled up to numbered stands. Deckyi and Dhondup lived in an apartment about a mile and a half away. People were on their way home after work, so Deckyi and I crowded close together as people jostled around us.

"How is it here? Do you like it?" I asked eagerly.

Deckyi smiled tentatively and replied in English, "It is good. For the first time I have hope." She gave a small laugh. As the bus pulled into the station, she handed me a couple of euro coins to pay my fare.

The bus sailed down a narrow street lined with gray stone row houses and we overtook cyclists in the adjacent bike lane. After a small roundabout, it stopped and we got off. Deckyi and I walked a short distance until we reached a row house with a blue wooden door. A row of bells and name tags lined the side of the entrance. Among a list of Flemish names were those of Deckyi and Dhondup written in black ink.

Their apartment was up a flight of wooden stairs on the second floor, marked by a Tibetan decorative door hanging. Inside, Dhondup greeted me shyly. He wore a T-shirt and sweatpants and his hair was rumpled. Like Deckyi's, his face looked slightly plumper, but he also looked much the same. Afternoon sunlight spilled into the one-room living room and kitchen, whose windows looked out onto a tranquil garden. A sofa faced a flat screen television and a wall decorated with Tibetan *thangkas* and posters of a smiling Dalai Lama. The mantle showcased a decorative plate, a stuffed Winnie the Pooh, plastic toy motorcycle, pencil case, small bottle of Chanel No. 5 perfume, and a softly lit wedding picture of Deckyi and Dhondup. I didn't recall seeing that photo in their room in Dharamsala.

When Deckyi and I sat next to each other on the sofa. I noticed her ears were double pierced with metal studs. She wore a plastic flower ring on her fourth finger—a change from the gold ring she wore in Dharamsala. The last time I'd seen her in 2012, she had talked about applying for asylum in Belgium. More Tibetans were going there, she said. I didn't understand how she would do it, but I knew she was getting documents ready. At that time I was living in Delhi again, and on my next trip to Dharamsala, I found Deckyi suddenly gone. Dhondup remained, and I met him in the small room they used to share together. He told me Deckyi had made it to Belgium and was working on getting documents so he could come too. Then, months later, the next time I went to Dharamsala, Dhondup also was gone. Vinayak, the lawyer who worked with Tibetans, said Belgium was currently the popular destination for refugees. I didn't know how Deckyi and Dhondup had gotten to Belgium or what they were doing there.

Now there I was, sitting in their living room in Leuven. Deckyi and I spoke in a mixture of Mandarin and English, which she spoke with her gentle, melodious voice. Her English had improved, and she made an effort to speak it to me.

I was eager to hear her story. How did you get here? I asked. In India she got a passport and visa to Poland. Was it fake? Yes, replied Deckyi without hesitation. Through word of mouth among Tibetans in Dharamsala, she paid a middleman 700,000 rupees (about $14,000) to get the passport and arrange a visa and flight. It was a small fortune, and she used the rest of her savings and borrowed money from other Tibetans. When Deckyi handed over the money, she wasn't sure what would happen. Would the fixer disappear? If he did, there wasn't any recourse. But ultimately, the fixer got her an Indian passport arranged for her to travel to Europe in the summer of 2012.

On the evening of Deckyi's flight from Delhi airport, she nervously went through airline check-in and then immigration. She didn't speak English, so the fixer shepherded her through. "I don't know what he said," Deckyi told me.

She and five other Tibetans flew from Delhi to Warsaw. They spent three days in Poland before they took a car to Belgium. They left before dawn and drove sixteen hours until they arrived in Leuven, where Deckyi stayed with a Tibetan friend for one night. The next day they went to a refugee reception center in Liège, in eastern Belgium. At the government refugee center there, Deckyi applied for asylum.

More than 100 refugees lived in the center while their applications were reviewed and processed. They hailed from various places: Syria, East Turkistan (Xinjiang, China), Iraq, Iran, Bangladesh, Afghanistan, and the Democratic Republic of the Congo. Life in this new place was challenging at first.

"When started, not good. Didn't know people," recalled Deckyi. "I worried about documents, life." But there were eight or nine Tibetans there so she wasn't lonely. The refugees slept in dorm rooms with six to eight people. The center also had a kitchen, gym, TV room, and ping pong table. The refugees couldn't freely leave, but every ten days they got a pass to go out, as well as train tickets within Belgium. Deckyi visited Tibetan friends or sometimes went to the countryside or the sea with the other Tibetans. During Deckyi's ten months at the center she took French classes once or twice a week. French was very difficult, she admitted, and she still couldn't speak it. Deckyi and Dhondup agreed that Dutch was easier to learn.

At the center in Liège, Deckyi's biggest complaint was the food. She wasn't used to so much bread and potatoes but "Mei you qita de banfa," she said in Mandarin. *There's no other way.* Eventually she got used to life there, "Then ok."

Refugees tended to stick with their compatriots because of language and culture. The Tibetans didn't interact much with others, but there was one universal language. Refugees from all different countries gathered to watch soccer games on TV. Otherwise, there was another thing that brought them together. "The center only had one news," said Deckyi. "Who got documents. Who got second document."

Although the application process was long, it was usually smooth. "Ninety-five percent of people—no problem," she said. Deckyi eventually had two interviews with immigration officials and was granted asylum in Belgium as a political refugee.

Deckyi started planning her journey to Belgium back in 2011. That same year, Europe received 34,795 applications for asylum. When she arrived in 2012, that number swelled to more than 335,000, according to the European Parliament. In early 2011, Arab Spring uprisings roiled Arab and Middle Eastern countries. Refugees fled in droves from instability in Libya, Tunisia, and Egypt, leading to an escalation of asylum seekers in Europe.

Civil war erupted in Syria in 2011 and sparked a wave of forced migration. From 2013, Syrian refugees dominated asylum applications to Europe. By 2016, Europe faced its worst refugee crisis since the Second World War, with more than 1 million people applying for asylum in 2015 and 2016, according to the Migration Policy Institute. Refugees from Syria, Afghanistan, and Iraq were the largest groups of asylum seekers. By 2016, Europe began closing its doors to the influx of migrants. Compared to its neighbors, Belgium received a small number of asylum applications. For example, in 2015, it received more than 27,000 applications, whereas Germany received more than 343,000 from January to October that year—by far the most of any European country. In 2016, the number of applications to Belgium fell to 18,710. Many people in Belgium, a country of 11 million, were uncomfortable with large numbers of migrants, though others were welcoming.

But in February 2016, Carl Decaluwé, governor of West Flanders, discouraged Belgians from feeding refugees, saying "otherwise more will come." The language was reminiscent of park signs that warned people not to feed pigeons. Before that, the mayor of a Belgian town near Zeebrugge recommended building a "camp like Guantanamo" to house refugees. In neighboring France, the government took down makeshift camps housing 4,000 migrants in Calais. Hungary tightened its borders with barbed wire fences on the borders of Serbia and Croatia after nearly 400,000 migrants passed through the country in the summer of 2015. An infamous video showed a Hungarian television camerawoman trying to kick a Syrian refugee carrying his young son as people ran across a field near the Hungary-Serbia border.

By 2016, few if any Tibetans were coming to Belgium anymore, said Deckyi. It was too difficult to make the journey and applications were being denied by the government. She and Dhondup made it through a small window of opportunity just before it closed.

To make matters worse, in March 2016 terrorists from the so-called Islamic State set off bombs in the Brussels airport and at a metro station near the European Union headquarters. The attack killed 32 and injured at least 300 people. It came after another Islamic State terrorist attack in Paris killed 130 in November 2015. In Brussels, when I walked by Maelbeek metro station near where I was staying, flowers, photos, and placards still lined the street outside. Two months before, a twenty-seven-year-old had detonated a bomb on the subway during morning rush hour.

Xenophobia and anti-immigration sentiments were on the rise across Europe, but Deckyi and Dhondup had not felt any ill-will directed at them. After Deckyi was granted asylum and left the refugee center in Liège, she lived in Midi, a neighborhood near the train station in Brussels where other Tibetan refugees resided. It didn't feel very safe to her. Midi was considered a "seedy area where you don't want to hang around if you can help it," opined an article in *The Guardian*.

There, Deckyi used her monthly government allowance of 800 euros to pay her 380-euro rent for a room and a kitchen shared with two other people. She recalled, "Summer is too much hot. Too much zhanglang." *Cockroaches.* "Nighttime when you close the light then you wait five minutes, you open the light, you see, 'Oh, it's group!'" She took Dutch-language classes at a nearby government social services center, tried to find work in restaurants, and met with Tibetan monk friends from India who had also found their way to Belgium. "I would like to live in Leuven or another city but this time it's hard to get room. Where you can find room, first you live here," she explained.

When Deckyi got asylum, she applied for documents so Dhondup could join her. In Delhi, a Tibetan interpreter hired by the Belgian embassy helped her husband navigate complicated paperwork and get a required health checkup. Almost two years later, in April 2014, Dhondup left India for Belgium. He wasn't nervous or afraid.

"When he come, don't worry about anything. All document is real, original," Deckyi declared. Dhondup flew from Delhi directly to Brussels and Deckyi met him at the airport. By then Deckyi had started vocational training through the government's social welfare centers. Not long after Dhondup arrived in Belgium, the couple moved to Leuven. They knew from other Tibetans that this was a good town—safe and livable, with many students. As a couple, they had a monthly government allowance of 1,057 euros to pay rent and living expenses.

It was a far cry from Lhasa, but in picturesque Leuven, Deckyi and Dhondup walked the cobblestone roads past the spire of Saint Peter's Church, the Gothic facade of the fifteenth-century town hall, the stone archways of Leuven University founded in 1425, through the "grand square" of Grote Markt built circa 1450 and then Oude Markt dating back to the twelfth century. Forty outdoor cafés lined the old market and earned it the title of the world's "longest bar."

On a narrow road lined with restaurants and busy with tourists and students, Deckyi found temporary work washing dishes in a Japanese restaurant. Deckyi then went online to check websites for Chinese people in Belgium and found ads from other restaurants looking for workers. She and Dhondup landed regular jobs at a restaurant a twenty-minute bus ride from Leuven Station. The place was modern and spacious, with muted gray walls and red banquettes. The owners were a couple from China's Zhejiang Province. The proprietress was thirty-two years old and briskly efficient.

She is "hen hao," *very good*, said Deckyi, "like friends." Does she care that Deckyi is Tibetan? I asked. "Don't care," she shrugged. "We're not talking about religion."

Seven other people worked there, all Chinese except Deckyi and Dhondup. They spent Saturday nights at the restaurant in staff rooms because they finished work too late to catch the bus back to Leuven.

I visited Deckyi one Saturday evening at the restaurant. The booths and tables were full of families and middle-aged Belgians eating dinner and drinking bottles of wine. The restaurant could seat about ninety people, but that night it was half full. Deckyi wore a uniform of white shirt, black slacks, and a red scarf tied around her neck. She washed and dried glasses at the bar, brought drinks to guests, scooped ice cream, and brought plates of food to tables. She introduced me to the friendly young owner, her boss, with a hint of pride. In the kitchen Dhondup helped the chefs prepare food. After dinner I took a city bus back to Leuven then slept on the sofa at Deckyi and

Dhondup's empty apartment while they finished their shift and stayed overnight at the restaurant.

In addition to restaurant work, Deckyi had started training at a government center in the fall of 2015 to work as a cleaner, and began working in January. When I met them in May 2016, Deckyi was cleaning houses part time for ten families.

"Also you know, when you come here you get 800 euro is coming from another people's tax," she told me in English. "Then you must quickly go work to back to others. I have to say I must go work." Deckyi wanted to study in the afternoons but hadn't started. At 9 euros an hour, Deckyi made about 750 euros a month. Three of her clients were older, in their sixties and seventies. One was eighty-seven. Deckyi felt like she could help these lonely older people, similar to how Norbu in Melbourne felt about his work in the nursing home.

"I like to help them," said Deckyi. She also felt proud of assisting households with three or four children who were very busy with work and family. "Then when you come to other house to cleaning, when they're coming from work they will to see, 'Ah, my house is clean!' Feeling good, I think this is good."

In 2015 Dhondup started six months of training to be a cleaner. He learned to use a vacuum cleaner, washing machine, different soaps and detergents, how to clean glass, how to clean the floor, and iron. It wasn't hard for him to learn, considering he had had a good job as a company manager in Lhasa. In their training, Deckyi and Dhondup also learned how to look up clients' addresses on the Internet and navigate directions, "How to chat with people," explained Deckyi. "When you get the problem with job—how to do. When you're sick, how do you do." She added, "Work is no problem, but talking to people a little *kunnan*," she said in Mandarin. *Difficult*. In Dutch class the teacher spoke slowly and used simple words, but in the real world, people spoke quickly.

In Belgium, the government and people are good, observed Deckyi. In China and Tibet, you need connections (*guanxi*) and money. But in Belgium, you just need documents and *nengli*—ability.

"You don't need *guanxi*," said Dhondup in Mandarin. "*Hen gongping.*" Life was "very fair" in Belgium.

Deckyi guessed there were about 1,000 Tibetans in Belgium and approximately 300 in Leuven. The trendy port city of Antwerp, known for fashion and design, was home to the country's biggest Tibetan community. Near its Chinatown were some Tibetan restaurants that had opened over the last decade, she said.

In Liège, there was a small temple where Tibetans could pray. On Belgian holidays, some Tibetans gathered to have barbecues or they took the train to the seaside town of Ostender. The previous winter, Deckyi and Dhondup went to Denmark for a visit. And the previous year in 2015, the couple went to Frankfurt, where hundreds of Tibetans attended a teaching by the Dalai Lama on one of his regular trips to Europe.

Deckyi was already thinking about the future. "We have no children, we must to think about when I'm old. If we each other can go work, maybe loan little bit money from bank. Maybe buy one apartment. Next time you come, we will have our house," she told me. When they got older and were unable to work, "then maybe go to India, go to a cheap country." One advantage of India was that they could easily pray at Tibetan temples. Deckyi also raised one downside: "I don't know. India is too hot."

Deckyi was forty years old—too old to have children, she reckoned. "We two take money from Belgium government. When we have children, also take money from Belgian government," she said. "So we're waiting to work. Now we are all old. Forty years is difficult. So I think no."

At the end of our conversation, Deckyi asked me in Mandarin what I wanted to eat for dinner. "Wanfan chi shenme?"

We moved to the kitchen area, where Dhondup had started to prepare dinner on a small table crowded with a rice cooker, hot water thermos, and bottles of condiments like soy sauce. As a special treat, they made dumplings filled with cabbage and tofu; Deckyi remembered I was vegetarian. Soon the cutting board was covered with dumplings that Dhondup dropped into a pot of boiling water then fished out with a ladle. The three of us ate the steaming dumplings in hungry, satisfied silence, dipping them into soy sauce and stuffing them into our mouths.

The glass kitchen door opened onto a small balcony lined with colorful potted flowers. A slight smell of incense wafted in from some other apartment. Across the garden I could see through the back windows of stone houses where people were going about their day. A bare-chested guy was putting on a shirt. The sound of voices drifted over red tile rooftops. It was nearly 7 p.m., but it was still light outside as summer approached and days got longer. Birds chirped and trilled before roosting for the night. We were a long way from their noisy, cramped rooms in Dharamsala and their roomy house in Lhasa, their homeland where their tumultuous and unpredictable journey had started. But it felt perfectly natural to have dinner with Deckyi and Dhondop in Leuven, the place they now called home and where Deckyi finally felt hope.

[19]

An Ex-monk Still Loves Basketball
Ohh, America Is Like This

NEW YORK, JULY 2021

. . .

In the spring of 2021, in the middle of the COVID-19 pandemic, I suddenly had to track down Topden. I had finally and unexpectedly found a book publisher after years of rejections. I eagerly picked up the thread on Tibetan refugees that had fallen aside for a long stretch while working in Africa and during graduate studies at Harvard Kennedy School back in Boston.

The last time I was in touch with Topden was in 2015 on my last trip to Dharamsala; I wondered how I would find him. When I lived in India, Topden and I communicated mainly by text message. But I doubted he had the same phone number in 2021. I had no idea how he was doing, especially during India's devastating wave of COVID-19 cases. So one early spring evening, I emailed Topden at an address I had last used in 2009, a dozen years earlier. His email from July 4, 2009, read,

> hi Tashi delek
>   here is every thing well and i am at feridaband near delhi for para-vet training for a month so studying hard and every day checking dictionary and little bit tired. but i will do it well. thanks for thinking of me see you soon Topden.

I sent an email to him though doubted I'd hear back. But in less than an hour, I was surprised to get a reply, and even more surprised by what it said.

> Hi Amy
>   Off cause I remember u. Nice to hear about u, yes m here in USA, working in Main, ME, n going to New York day after tomorrow by Boston, How u doing?

Topden wasn't in Dharamsala or southern India, but in all places, Maine. What on earth was he doing there? It was surreal to think of him in the "vacation state," known for beaches, quaint New England towns, and lobster.

On top of that surprise, Topden told me he was coming through Boston by bus the very next day on his way to New York. What an incredible co-incidence, I exclaimed. "Yes, it is very good karma," Topden remarked. We arranged to meet during his short layover in Boston when he would change buses for New York. He messaged: "Yes love to meet Amy, please come to meet me if u have time. I will reach south station at around 9 am but I will msg u when about to reach, excited to meet you after long time, wow."

By the spring of 2021, the United States was starting to emerge from COVID-19 lockdown. The next day, for the first time that year, I took the subway downtown to South Station. I'm from Boston and had been there countless times over the decades to catch Greyhound and Peter Pan buses to New York and other destinations. But I never imagined it would be the site of a reunion with a Tibetan monk friend I met in the Himalayas.

As I walked through the bus terminal, a voice called out to me. There was Topden standing by a bench next to his two large rolling suitcases. He looked a little older, but his friendly face was much the same. It wasn't too strange to see Topden with a head of thick, wavy hair, unlike his shaved monk's head when I first met him in 2008. I could tell he was smiling although we both wore face masks. Topden held two cups of coffee from McDonald's and of-fered me one. He wore a gray sweatshirt, trim workout pants, and new sneak-ers. Topden looked like just another traveler catching a bus in South Station.

My email of the previous night just happened to find Topden on the last day of his nine-month stint in Maine working in a Chinese restaurant. Topden was no longer a monk. In fact, he was married. In 2017 he married a Tibetan woman living in New York City and then immigrated to the United States the following year. Topden normally lived in Queens in a diverse neighbor-hood with a lot of Tibetans, as well as immigrants from Ecuador, Peru, India, and many more countries. They lived not far from Jackson Heights, where I had lived in my late twenties before moving to India. Topden was now a New Yorker and could have been my neighbor or someone I walked past on the street. That was a bit mind-bending, especially because he seemed like himself, only transported from northern India to a bus station in Boston. He was jovial as usual. His English had been quite good in Dharamsala and was even better now. Topden told me he had a great time working for nice Chinese restaurant owners in Maine, about an hour north of Portland. He worked a lot as a waiter but made good money. Working in America was fruitful, "But if you don't work you are homeless!" he exclaimed, his eyes widening for emphasis.

The previous year, Topden spent the height of the pandemic lockdown in New York. He and his wife, who worked as a cleaner, didn't work during that time. Topden had a bit of savings, and his wife got some unemployment benefits. "Three months, never go outside my door," he said incredulously. "Three months like jail person. It was so scary." The couple bought food online until eventually his wife ventured outside to go shopping.

I thought of Topden walking around New York and taking the subway. During the pandemic, racist harassment and unprovoked attacks on Asian people had surged across the United States, from New York to San Francisco. They were irrationally blamed and scapegoated for a virus that had originated in China and killed thousands of Chinese there. Anyone Asian could be targeted. Even people who were mistaken as Asian, including Latinos, Native Americans, and Caucasians, had been attacked or harassed.

Some of the violent assaults were captured by surveillance cameras. In March 2021, on a highly trafficked street in midtown Manhattan, a sixty-five-year-old Filipina woman on her way to church was kicked in the stomach in broad daylight. As she sprawled on the sidewalk, her attacker stomped on her head several times. It was a miracle the petite woman survived. In April 2021, Yao Pan Ma, a sixty-one-year-old recent immigrant from China, was collecting cans on busy 125th Street in Harlem. Ma was attacked and fatally head stomped as cars whizzed by. Across the country, elderly Asians in particular had been punched on their doorsteps in San Francisco, stabbed on the street after doing their morning shopping, and murdered during muggings in Oakland.

Topden had seen some of the viral videos too. "Be careful, especially on the subway," I warned. Ironically, despite my travels in low-income, developing countries, I was usually more concerned about violent crime in the United States, so I worried about him. He nodded but did not seem as bothered as me. Topden had already been in New York during the pandemic, while I just read alarming news about the city. He had a much better sense of what was happening.

Before long, Topden had to board his next bus. We agreed to catch up again; already I started considering when I could visit him in New York. I handed him back a McDonald's cup since I don't drink coffee, and Topden amiably said he would drink both cups on the bus. The four-and-a-half-hour journey on a bus with a bathroom on smooth, flat highways seemed luxurious compared to the twelve-hour overnight bus from Dharamsala to Delhi that we had taken in India.

That evening I messaged Topden when I estimated he had arrived in New York. I imagined him lugging two big suitcases on the subway home. What could he do if anyone attacked him? Even on my way home from South Station I constantly looked over my shoulder. That evening at 11 p.m. he replied: "Yes just arrived. It was good to see u. Good night."

. . .

A few months later, in early summer, I started a new staff journalism job and worked out of the company's New York headquarters. On the morning of July 4, a holiday, Topden arrived at my friend's place in Chelsea where I was staying while she was away. I went downstairs to let him in, and there was Topden standing on the sunny street. He wore a Puma sweatshirt, dark pants, and black loafers with no socks and looked a bit sleepy. The previous night he had gotten home from his new job around midnight. Now he was in Chelsea at 9:30 a.m. Topden's hair was slightly mussed, but he claimed he wasn't tired. He had arrived in Chelsea quite quickly from Brooklyn, where he was staying at his cousin's place. Did he ever get confused by the subway? I asked. Even after living in New York for years, every so often I mistakenly got on an express train that shot me up to 125th Street, seventy blocks north of my destination.

Topden said the subway was no problem. In fact, a couple of days before, he was in a Brooklyn station when some "Americans," as he described them, approached him for directions. They were lost and trying to make sense of the multicolored spaghetti of New York's subway map. "Where am I??" the bewildered guy asked.

Topden gave directions and told them they needed to go upstairs, then to the other side to get the green G train uptown. "Thanks, man!" the guy gushed as he fist-bumped Topden.

Now this Tibetan transplanted to New York via India sat in a pink upholstered chair in Chelsea as he told me the story of how he came to the United States.

. . .

Around 2014, Topden's cousin in Dharamsala started asking him about his plans for the future. The cousin was thinking ahead and warned Topden, "You are getting old."

Even when I was still living in India, many Tibetans in India were immigrating abroad, sometimes as political refugees, like Norbu, Deckyi, and Dhondup, but often for work, a chance to make money and have a better quality of life. Some Tibetans in India criticized people for leaving the exile communities there to chase money in the West. His cousin brought up the idea of Topden's immigrating to the United States, but he wasn't interested and wanted to continue his veterinary work. "Then I say no," Topden recalled. "I want to take care of animals, that's my life. Then we never talking about it."

But a couple of years later, Topden's cousin brought up the prospect again. "I don't want to come to United States. He insist me a lot. Then I say ok. How can I do?" Not long after, the cousin "introduced" him to Dawa, a Tibetan immigrant living in New York City. "He give me her number. We talk a little bit, little bit, little bit. We talked, liked each other." His cousin remarked, "Now you're thinking about your life." As he talked to me, Topden never mentioned the Indian girl he'd had a crush on back in Dharamsala. She seemed to be a distant memory.

Dawa was a few years younger than him and originally from Kham, like Topden. She had married a Tibetan in the United States and had immigrated to New York about a decade before. But she divorced after six years and was looking to remarry. Topden had been a monk since he was a child and a devoted monastic for three decades. For Tibetans, it was an honor to be a monk and no small thing to withdraw from monastic life. But Topden told me he had already been thinking of leaving his monastery to work full time at the vet clinic. Even when I knew him in Dharamsala, Topden seemed to relish his stylish layperson's clothes. Before he met his future wife, he had already decided to "sacrifice monastery" for his veterinary work. Topden finally had to inform the monastery he was leaving. He explained, "I'm helping the animals. I had already plan. Not sudden plan. I have to tell them."

When he described what happened, it did not seem like a very hard decision. Nor did he mention fallout from the monastery. In fact, many monks had become laypeople. Critics in the Tibetan refugee community would say too many monks were going that route. Topden admitted it was challenging to live without the monastery's community he had relied on for most of his life.

"After leave monastery, then have to think about my future. I can't go back to monastery. Always open for me. Whatever happened, you can go, always open. After that, always closed the door for me," said Topden about no longer having its safety net. "Then I talk to my cousin. Before he introduced me to my wife. 'If you want, you can marry with her. You can come to USA.' Then I was really busy with animals. After I leave monastery, he ask, 'What about that girl? Important you guys talk.'" After being introduced to each other, Dawa and Topden started talking on the phone, but she still had to be convinced that he had good intentions. "Her ex-husband has other girlfriend," Topden explained. "She hurt much. She don't believe. Then we meet, talk, then decide."

In 2017, Dawa visited India for a big religious prayer ceremony called the Kalachakra Puja in Bodh Gaya, where the Buddha attained enlightenment. The town in the state of Bihar was a major Buddhist pilgrimage site, like Sarnath. Topden met Dawa for the first time in person in that auspicious town.

Dawa traveled by car from Delhi to Bodh Gaya. The fourteen-hour overnight journey made Dawa irate; and then she couldn't reach Topden when she arrived because of problems with his cell phone connection. "She was so mad. So angry," he remembered. To make matters worse, the ride was uncomfortable in other ways. "She need bathroom—she hold her pee," Topden chuckled.

Things smoothed out after that rocky start. Topden and Dawa spent ten days in Bodh Gaya, then hired a car to Sarnath, the Buddhist holy site that I visited in 2009. After spending some time there, they drove to Delhi and then Dharamsala. In total, they spent about fifteen days together. Topden told me, "Then we know each other, know each other, know each other. Then I propose. She said yes. She has two months. Then we know each other. She's comfortable to me. We had small celebration in my house."

After they got married, Topden started his visa application. "If I do late, they ask, 'Why you not come to United States?'" By May 2018, Topden got his visa and the following month he left India. He didn't feel sad leaving. "I can go back whenever I want. If it's from Tibet, I feel so sad because I couldn't go often to Tibet."

He did miss some things in India. "I miss my dogs. Skinny and Mary." His long flight from Delhi to New York was "completely fine." Topden watched four Bollywood movies and time passed quickly. When he arrived at the airport in New York, no one talked to him. But then the immigration officer who checked his passport greeted him in Tibetan by saying "Tashi delek." Topden was surprised and delighted. "He makes me feel so comfortable. Oh my god, knows tashi delek!" he exclaimed. "He didn't ask me anything. He said, 'Look at camera.' I clasped hands. It's my feelings. We believe karma—my life is good."

His wife and cousin were waiting for him at the airport and they took a taxi to his cousin's apartment in eastern Brooklyn. On the way home, they passed sprawling Highland Park. Even as the scenery flew past, Topden was impressed by the greenery. "Park is so nice! I will come back here," he vowed. The street scenes looked "totally different from India. It's like new in my life. 'Ohh, America is like this,'" he recalled thinking.

Topden spent almost three months settling into New York. He and his wife lived in an apartment in Queens with other Tibetan roommates, and Dawa worked during the week at her cleaning job in New Jersey. In the mornings, Topden would play basketball or go running. At the supermarket, he spoke with people to practice English. When he went to the Indian supermarket in Jackson Heights to buy dal and masala, he spoke Hindi and got a welcome taste of India, his first adopted home. "I love speaking Hindi," enthused Topden.

I asked how he improved his English—did he listen or watch the news? Topden shook his head. He watched a favorite police show on the Internet. That was much more interesting to him than depressing news about the real world. "News always: 'Two people killed.' Accidents. Fire. Every morning it's 'Oh my goodness!'" But with his favorite crime show, at least Topden could learn about the law instead of being depressed by news of the day.

Sometimes he would walk from home in Queens to his cousin's apartment in Brooklyn. It took an hour and a half, but Topden enjoyed exploring, though "sometimes it's smelly." He laughed. "Wow, this smells so bad! Is this really New York? Homeless people pee and poop."

New York wasn't a shock because Dawa had told him about life there during almost daily phone calls when he was still in India. "Wherever you go—if you have job, your life is easy. If you can't job, you have no job, then it's not easy," he explained. If old people approached him for money, he would give a dollar or two. But Topden was puzzled when young, able-bodied people panhandled on the streets instead of working.

A few times a week, Topden went to Manhattan's Chinatown to eat and shop. Sometimes he walked there and crossed into Manhattan over the bridge and the glittering East River. "I like noodle lo mein," he laughed. Chinatown's colorful street vendors and shops made him feel at home. "I was born in Tibet. Sometimes we go to city. They sell vegetables. Makes feel remember when we were young," he said of Chinatown. Topden also went to Flushing, a large Asian neighborhood in Queens. Later in the summer, I met him there one Sunday afternoon. As we walked the crowded streets lined chockablock with Asian shops, he joked, "I'm in China? Everybody is like Chinese people."

A couple of weeks after Topden arrived in New York, he went to an annual picnic for former monks from his monastery in India. About twenty Tibetan men who had immigrated to the United States gathered in Corona Park in Flushing. Topden already knew many of the ex-monks who were now living in New York working various jobs: construction, cooks and sushi chefs, hotel staff, and Uber drivers. He showed me videos of the picnic on his phone. Beneath an azure sky, they ate Tibetan food and barbecue, played basketball and soccer, said prayers and collected money for their monastery, though not necessarily in that order. They reminisced about their monastery near Mysore, south of Bangalore.

"Sometimes miss. We grow in monastery, like second home," explained Topden. After the day of camaraderie among these former monks who "grew up" in India, they returned to their lives as new New Yorkers, cooking, driving, and literally building the city.

After his first few months in New York, Topden looked for a job. His big advantage was knowing English. He had better job opportunities, like being a waiter, and could navigate the city on his own. As a monk, he had been in an environment of learning most of his life and was accustomed to the discipline of study. Some of his ex-monk friends could speak English. Other Tibetans were not as fortunate. Topden's cousin had a Tibetan roommate who spoke no English and worked at a Chinese restaurant. The roommate did speak Chinese, though, which gave him some advantages.

Like many of his Tibetan friends, Topden went to an agency in Manhattan's Chinatown that placed Asian immigrants in jobs, usually Chinese restaurants, across the country. The woman at the agency asked what position he wanted. Topden was candid. "I said, 'I have no experience. I'm new, I'm Tibetan. I can promise you I can work hard.'"

The woman replied, "Ok, no problem, you come. We'll see." She placed him at a Chinese restaurant in a suburb outside Detroit. It was common for immigrants from Tibet and China to migrate to wherever there were jobs and spend time away from family. So Topden was matter-of-fact about the fourteen-hour bus ride from New York to Michigan. It was a big coach bus and much more comfortable than the rickety ones careening around hairpin turns in India.

The restaurant's owner picked Topden up from the bus station. The job came with free housing for workers in a shared apartment. The next day, Topden went to work at the Chinese buffet although he had never worked in a restaurant before. "I was really confused about what to do," he recalled. His first job was carrying ice from the ice machine and cleaning tables.

The Chinese owner had two young teenage sons who were on school vacation and trained Topden. "They helped me very much. Next day I can catch," he said.

The other workers spoke Chinese—or, more precisely, Fujianese dialect from Fujian Province—except the manager and owner, who communicated with Topden in English. No one cared that Topden was Tibetan, and he wasn't treated differently from the Chinese workers. "Owners are nice. If you work, they like you. If you don't work well, then they don't like you. They like me," explained Topden. "New people come, they introduce me. 'He's Topden, he good person.'" The owner's mother worked at the restaurant and took a shine to him. "She feed me whatever she cooks. She give me, said, 'Don't show others okay?'" He chuckled.

Within three months, Topden learned the ropes in the restaurant. "The job is not hard. It's good. All day everything is new. I like this job. If I don't like, I quit," he stated simply. Sometimes there were Indian customers. "When Indian people came to restaurant, feel so good! Punjabi came. We talked in Hindi, it feel so good. Surprised I speak Hindi! Of course, I grow [up] in India, my god!" After a while, a few other Tibetans workers joined the restaurant.

Topden's plan was to work in Michigan for six months and then return home in time for Losar. After his stint in the Midwest, that winter he spent a month in New York with his wife and celebrated Tibetan New Year. Then he looked for another job. This time the Chinatown agency found him a job at a Chinese restaurant in Maine. "I love it," Topden enthused about his time there. "Manager is so good. Owner from Taiwan, manager is from Maine."

The restaurant's workers there also shared an apartment. They all spoke some English so it was a closer-knit group. It was also more diverse: a staffer from Indonesia, three Mexican cooks, two young women from the Philippines, as well as Americans. One Chinese worker came, but he couldn't work properly; he smoked one to two packets of cigarettes daily, Topden recalled.

When the restaurant needed more staff, Topden recommended four Tibetans he had worked with in Michigan. "I call people who are nice. There's network," he said. They had moved on to a restaurant in Alabama, but it was easy to connect through WeChat, the Chinese messaging app. "Wherever they go, WeChat is there. Hi!" he told me. They came to Maine per Topden's recommendation. More Tibetan friends made life in Maine even better. "Maine so nice people! So kind. Not rich, but so nice life, simple life. Not much rush," Topden observed.

There was an Indian restaurant close to his restaurant and the Punjabi owners liked Topden too. They toned down the spiciness of their food for regular customers, but they made authentic cuisine for Topden. "They cook me more masala, more spices, like original Indian food." Life was fairly pleasant, and he had a routine. On Thursdays, his day off, he usually woke up late at 11 a.m., had breakfast, and did laundry and other chores. "Change a lot of socks every day—smells!" he laughed. On his day off, Topden might go shopping at Walmart, Shaw's, JC Penney, or TJ Maxx, which were within walking distance. The restaurant offered staff free food from its buffet, but Topden made dinner on his day off. Then he talked to Dawa on the phone in the evening. During his time in Maine, Topden didn't go to the beach, but he did go to the L.L. Bean and North Face stores in Freeport, a half-hour drive away. "They give you sale. I like L.L. Bean," he said approvingly of the iconic Maine brand.

Topden was no stranger to freezing temperatures. "In Tibet I never feel it's cold, because I was born in there," said Topden. But in Maine winter seemed more intense. "From November to March, you live in snow. Make paths in snow. Almost my apartment covered like snow." He had learned a bit of Spanish from his Mexican coworkers, including the useful phrase, "Mucho frio, amigo."

Topden enjoyed his time in Maine. Even after he returned to New York, the restaurant owners there would text him. "'We are getting busy. Are you coming back?'" they wrote. Topden smiled fondly. "Very nice people. We are like family."

Now that he was back in New York, I thought Topden would work at another Chinese restaurant. But one of his Tibetan friends had referred him to a job at a small hotel in Brooklyn. Topden had never worked in hospitality and during his job interview admitted that to the manager. It wasn't an issue though. "Manager like me. He didn't ask me much. 'You have Social Security number, New York ID. Okay, I'm going to hire you. Sixteen dollars an hour. I'll call you tomorrow,'" Topden told me.

He started working at the small hotel in Park Slope, Brooklyn as a "house man." He carried guests' bags to their rooms and brought them anything they needed: ice, towels, blankets, pillows. One day a week he worked in the laundry room and another day he cleaned rooms. "New job is very easy," he said.

When I talked to Topden on July 4, Dawa was away visiting her relatives in Minnesota, home to a large Tibetan community. He was staying in Brooklyn at his cousin's apartment because it was a shorter commute to the hotel. "I like Brooklyn. Quite quiet, nice. Queens is so rush and then Manhattan is more rush," Topden opined.

Each week he worked morning or midday shifts. When he started at 8 a.m. he left home around 6 a.m. so he could play basketball at a court near the hotel before work. "Some people so good!" said Topden in awe of the other players. If he finished by 4 p.m., he might play basketball again. "Basketball always in my bag. Makes me happy. Love basketball," he said enthusiastically. I remembered our conversations about basketball in Dharamsala; I was glad some things didn't change.

A couple of hours passed as Topden told me about his life in the United States, and then he had to head to work. We had a bit of time, so I suggested we take a walk on the High Line, the Manhattan greenway park built on refurbished train tracks running above Chelsea. Topden hadn't visited yet and was eager to see it.

It was July 4, Independence Day, and droves of people were out enjoying the holiday after being in COVID lockdown for months. There was a queue for the High Line and an attendant asked if we had registered online for our visit. We could register by scanning a QR code, she instructed. I didn't know how to do it, but Topden showed me how to scan the code on his smart phone. He learned to use QR codes because his bank used them. This wasn't the first time a monastic had showed me a new technology; another monk had introduced me to Facebook in Dharamsala.

The High Line was packed with hordes of people, a human river that propelled us along the boardwalk. I pointed out some of the High Line's features: original weathered railroad tracks underfoot; landscaping of wildflowers designed to look rustic and unmanicured. Topden admired the funky architecture along the way and glimpses of the sparkling Hudson River. I told him he could probably see fireworks from Brooklyn later that night over the East River.

Topden had to get to work, so we walked to the subway station at Thirty-Fourth Street. I went downstairs with him and, like an anxious mother, reminded him to take the A train downtown, not uptown. He nodded, then breezed through the turnstile.

. . .

The next day, I met Topden in Brooklyn when he finished work in the late afternoon. His shift at the hotel had been particularly hectic that day but he was in good spirits. The hotel had been booked full for July 4, so the next morning was busy with checkouts and lots of laundry. Topden met me outside the subway station. He wore shorts and a T-shirt, and a basketball bulged from a mesh pocket of his backpack. We had planned to go to the basketball court near the hotel, but it was too crowded.

The hotel was a narrow building with blue reflective glass and a parking lot in front. Photos on its website were more glamorous than the reality, but Topden was proud of the hotel and said it was clean and nice. We went inside and said hello to the receptionist who greeted us warmly from behind a plexiglass partition. She suggested we go upstairs to see the view. We took the elevator upstairs to an empty hall, then walked up a flight of stairs to the roof with a view of Manhattan's skyscrapers in the distance. People weren't allowed up there, but the previous night Topden had slipped out to glimpse the July 4 fireworks that bloomed in the sky over the East River.

In lieu of playing basketball, we decided to have an early dinner. We walked to nearby Fourth Avenue and passed a restaurant with a patio built for pandemic outdoor dining. That appealed to Topden, but the young waiter told us they were only serving inside. Only when he walked inside did he realize it was an Indian restaurant. He smiled. When the waiter came over, Topden excitedly tried to speak in Hindi, but the friendly young man was actually from Bangladesh. Then I told the waiter that I had spent many months there and enjoyed it.

Although the Brooklyn Indian restaurant was run by Bangladeshis, Topden felt comfortable there. India was like home. "1992 to India. I was fourteen years old," he reminisced. That afternoon in Brooklyn, Topden was hungry after a hard day's work at the hotel. He ordered chicken tikka, while I ordered palak—pureed spinach—with Impossible vegetarian meat. I told Topden about vegan meat substitutes. He tasted the Impossible Palak dish and declared it was better than his chicken. As we ate, Topden told me something else about his decision to emigrate. "I came to the United States for my mom.

I sent money to her." When his mother had fallen ill a few years ago, Topden asked his sister not to work and said he would send money for her to care for their mother. His sister used his money to treat his mother at a hospital in Chengdu in Sichuan, but she eventually passed away.

Before 2008, even from India, he couldn't easily contact his family. Topden received a letter about his grandmother's death two years after she died. After he arrived in the United States, Topden had hoped that once he became a citizen he would be able to travel to Tibet to see his mother. "That's my aim," he told me. He wanted to see his family after more than thirty years, but now his mother was gone. "Definitely yes I will go to India," said Topden. Now he was unsure about ever going to Tibet. "My parents are not there. It will be so sad."

· · ·

When we left the restaurant, it was still light outside as we walked toward the subway station. It was a pleasant summer evening in Brooklyn and people filled sidewalk restaurant tables. Topden carried his backpack bulging with the basketball and a bag of leftover chicken tikka and Impossible palak. At the subway station, I wasn't sure which train I should take to get back to Manhattan, but Topden said we could both take the green G line and then switch. I wasn't familiar with that train, but he had taken it so many times between Queens and Brooklyn that he called it "my subway."

A few months later, that winter, I suggested to Topden that we visit the American Museum of Natural History in Manhattan. He hadn't experienced too many tourist sites and I wanted to show him around New York—one of the places in the world that is home to me. In the cavernous halls of the iconic museum, Topden was awed. He was bowled over by towering dinosaur skeletons in their atrium abode and how ancient they were, especially when I double-checked they were indeed as much as 150 million years old. I explained what fossils are and recalled to Topden that during my cross-country Jeep ride across Tibet years ago, children had run up to us to offer heavy, palm-sized fossils of shells pulled from the earth. I later realized they were likely authentic. Once upon a time, those rocky Tibetan steppes were likely covered with a lost ocean before the landscape shifted ages ago, as part of the world's endless transformation.

In the museum, there was a diorama featuring the Potala Palace and displays about Tibet. Topden peered at some artifacts in the glass cases. He clarified that one device was used like flint to spark fires, and that the horn of a Tibetan deer was used to make nose rings for yaks. "My family is half-nomad, half-farmer," Topden mentioned offhand. "We have a lot of yaks."

He was impressed with the diorama of a Kenyan landscape showing trees and low hills. "I want to live there," he said longingly. Is that like Florida or North Carolina or Georgia? he asked. It had been years since he had seen mountains after immigrating to the United States.

"Oh, there are mountains not far from New York!" I told him. Topden was excited when I said we could take a train trip upstate. Then we perused displays showcasing animals in their natural habitats. Topden told me about vultures, wild dogs, and porcupines in Tibet and how their quills were used for medicinal purposes. At the elephant display, he recalled how a pachyderm near his monastery in southern India had killed a man, ripped him in half and thrown the torso in a river. A Tibetan farmer tried to make peace with the angry animal by telling him he had children. "Elephant, he forgive him," Topden said of the peacemaker.

Then suddenly he wondered, Where was the yak display? I assured him the museum must have a yak given how essential they are to rural life in Tibet and other countries. We strode down the darkened hallways in search of the woolly animal and realized with disappointment that this preeminent natural history museum did not have a yak after all.

Topden murmured disapprovingly. "Where is the complaint box?" he joked. I laughed out loud. During our museum visit, I learned new things about Tibet and Topden—and was reminded that he was very funny.

Back on that summer night after dinner in Brooklyn, we both got off "his subway" to change to the gray L train. I followed Topden as he strode through a tunnel bustling with people. At a fork, he instructed me to take the left path to get the train back to Manhattan.

"I go here," he said, indicating the other path to Brooklyn. In the rushing crowd, I hurriedly said goodbye to Topden before we diverged in the stream of people. I glimpsed him confidently striding up the ramp like the other New Yorkers going somewhere else. Then I parted ways with him to head toward home.

[AFTERWORD]

I started working on this book in 2008 and thought the project would take a few years to complete. I finished writing most of the manuscript within that time frame, but I had no idea the journey to publication would take more than fourteen years. Despite that passage of time, the challenges Tibetans face have persisted, and their repression has arguably worsened under an increasingly authoritarian administration in China. Tibetans in exile acknowledge a particular responsibility to preserve culture, religion, language, and identity that are under threat in their homeland. As the Dalai Lama—Tibet's spiritual leader, greatest ambassador, and champion—turns eighty-eight in 2023, preserving Tibetan culture and identity into an uncertain future is more urgent than ever.

As I write this near the end of 2022, issues related to immigration are at the top of geopolitical agendas. Refugees and their plights are in the spotlight as the world grapples with historic levels of migration, much of it forced by conflict or political turmoil. By the end of 2015 more than 65 million people were displaced, the highest number since World War Two, according to the UN High Commissioner for Refugees. Many were from Syria, Iraq, and Afghanistan. They represent the world's highest share of forcibly displaced people since the UNHCR began collecting data on them in 1951.

The movement of peoples from one country to another, particularly related to conflict, continues. In 2021, the US military abruptly withdrew from Afghanistan two decades after the September 11, 2001, terrorist attacks in New York and Washington, DC. That withdrawal created another wave of 120,000 Afghan refugees. About 76,000 arrived in the United States, representing its largest influx of war refugees since the fall of Saigon, Vietnam, in 1975.

Other examples abound. Most recently in 2022, Russia's war in Ukraine led to some 7.7 million becoming refugees in Europe alone. Since 2015, more than 7 million Venezuelans have migrated in what is the world's second-largest external displacement crisis, according to the UNHCR.

Although refugees and migration issues are covered by the media, it is difficult to get deeper insight into how people adjust—or don't—as they forge new lives in their adopted homes. One benefit of working on this book for so long is that it afforded the chance to do a rare longitudinal study told through an even rarer lens of narrative.

. . .

Of course, it was remarkable and memorable that the Dalai Lama spoke to me and hugged me at that press conference in March 2008. But it was the Tibetans in Dharamsala, both refugees and exiles born in India, who compelled me to move to the hill town. They inspired me to return and keep following them around the world even when I was unsure where the journey would lead. "Unsure" would become a nearly comic understatement: I left my prestigious job at the *Financial Times* after nine years with the newspaper and declined the possibility of working for them in London to become a freelance journalist on a shoestring budget. The respect of working for a big global newspaper was gone—not to mention steady income, health insurance, benefits, and institutional support.

But I wanted to write in-depth stories about things that intrigued and moved me—like the ordinary but extraordinary Tibetan refugees and exiles I met. I deliberately focused on them rather than high-profile leaders, elites, or activists. Society usually fixates on celebrity, rather than the fundamental connective tissue of ordinary people, their everyday trials, tribulations, and triumphs, and how they preserve culture and identity.

In retrospect, freelancing and working on this book was a big risk: solo reporting over four continents with no budget, no book advance, and no idea if this project would ever get published. But in spite of the strain, I wrote my best journalistic articles while freelancing. And I had a unique, perhaps once-in-a-lifetime, opportunity to live in Dharamsala, immerse myself there, and begin what would become this book.

In spite of all the uncertainty over the years, one thing remained constant: I never doubted that the stories of Tibetan exiles and refugees are precious and invaluable. They deserve to be told, remembered, preserved, and shared. I never doubted that.

. . .

As I resumed finishing this book in 2021 during the COVID-19 pandemic, I was reminded how remarkable it is that the Tibetans I met around the world did not conflate me—a person of Chinese descent—with the actions of China's government, which oppressed and drove them into exile. To some, it may seem silly to think that a person born, raised, and educated in the United States to parents with zero connection to the Chinese government—and indeed an ingrained apprehension of it—would be associated with the actions of China's authoritarian regime. Imagine if, say, an American of German descent (the largest ethnic group in the United States) were associated with the actions of the Nazi regime during the Holocaust. But many people make the woeful mistake of conflation because of race, ethnicity, nationality, or religion.

From the start of the pandemic in 2020, the horrific and tragic spike in anti-Asian racism, harassment, and violence reminded me of how easy it is to blame individuals for circumstances that have nothing to do with them. More than 2 billion people of East Asian descent around the world were not to blame for the outbreak of the virus. And people in China themselves died and suffered terribly—a fact many people seem to forget. Chinese citizens were the first victims of the virus and any government mishandlings of the pandemic. But too many people had a knee-jerk reaction and conflated East Asian features with the cause of COVID-19. That conflation led to unwarranted and unprovoked harassment and attacks on anyone who looked East Asian—even if they were not even of Asian descent.

More than two years after the start of the pandemic, the crisis of anti-Asian racism persists. In the United States, brutal attacks on Asians and harassment of them still happen regularly. But while finishing this book, I recalled the remarkable, open-minded magnanimity of the Tibetans I met who made me feel welcome wherever I was in the world. I wish others could follow their example. And thanks to the tremendous generosity of spirit of Tibetan people, this book exists.

[ACKNOWLEDGMENTS]

I am enormously grateful to all the Tibetans who told me their stories, translated, shared insights, and welcomed me. Some Tibetans have not been named in the book to protect them and their families in Tibet, but this book would not be possible without them. The Tibetan exile administration was always open and helpful. Special thanks to Chhime Chhoekyapa and Tenzin Taklha, joint-secretaries for His Holiness the Dalai Lama, as well as Tempa Tsering, former representative in Delhi. And of course, I am grateful to the Dalai Lama for writing the foreword for *Far from the Rooftop of the World*.

Many organizations were valuable resources, especially the International Campaign for Tibet. Huge thanks to Kate Saunders, who read this manuscript and gave valuable feedback, as well as critical suggestions along the way. Gabriel Lafitte and others in Australia shared their knowledge and time. My apologies if I have forgotten to acknowledge anyone. There are far too many people to whom I owe thanks. I got invaluable validation from residencies at MacDowell and at the Logan Nonfiction Program, supported by Jonathan Logan. Many editors published my articles about Tibet issues in the *New York Times, Financial Times, Wall Street Journal, Washington Post, Christian Science Monitor, The Nation, Atlantic.com, International Herald Tribune, Roads & Kingdoms, Far Eastern Economic Review.com, Doublex (Slate)*, and *BuddhaDharma*, as well as for National Public Radio and the Voice of America. *Crab Orchard Review* published the chapter "Deckyi's Journey." Years ago Robert Thomson hired me at the *Financial Times*, and I am indebted to him.

The Solutions Journalism Network and Pulitzer Center gave important support for my journalism in general, as did the Economic Hardship Reporting Project for my work about the experience of Asian Americans and Pacific Islanders during the COVID-19 pandemic. My journalism from Bangladesh was assisted by a grant from the McGraw Center at Newmark Graduate School of Journalism at the City University of New York.

I am also extremely grateful to the Harvard Kennedy School, Columbia Journalism School, Columbia Business School, and Knight-Bagehot

Fellowship. Donna Masini of Hunter College's MFA program burnished my love of poetry. Wellesley College gave me the opportunity to live and work in Asia for the first time years ago. After teaching at Ginling College in China through the Wellesley-Yenching fellowship, I traveled in Tibet, which made a deep impression and helped me understand Dharamsala's uniqueness years later.

From kindergarten through high school, I went to stellar public schools in Brookline, Massachusetts, and had wonderful teachers who gave me so much. Thanks especially to my extraordinary high school English teachers, Abby Erdmann and Beth Thomspon, who introduced me to W. E. B. DuBois and his concept of *twoness*, which was foundational for me. Years later, I was surprised when I realized that not all fifteen-year-olds read *The Souls of Black Folk, Invisible Man,* and *The Autobiography of Malcolm X* in high school.

Awards and accolades from the United Nations Correspondents Association, South Asian Journalists Association, Association of Healthcare Journalists, Asian American Journalists Association, Society of Environmental Journalists, Fetisov Journalism Awards, and Chicago Journalists Association were extremely encouraging. *The Best American Essays* anthology recognized my work with four Notable Essays. Asian American Journalists Association has also been supportive over the years.

I am eternally grateful to my wonderful and generous friends. I could not survive without them. Many of them opened their homes to me in Asia, Africa, Australia, and Europe. Without them, my work would not have been possible, especially Lynn Howard and Ian Wood in Melbourne via Michael Wood. Thanks also to Chin Jin, Yang, Jack and family, and Jenny Wiggins (Australia); Andre B. (Belgium); Kazi Inam Ahmed, Beth Hain and Raim Habil, Gerben de Jong, and Dana Ward and Gertrude Kangah (Bangladesh); Celeste Fulgham, Deepika Mehra, and Chamsai Menasveta (India); Joey Fox and Chris Pastorella (Sweden); Suvi Rajamäki and Heli Lehto (Finland); Nenad and Ivan Jukic (Croatia); and friends in Bosnia.

For their hospitality and help in Africa for other journalism, I must thank Emmanuel Dogbevi, Nikki Germany, Leisa Gibson and Jeremy Green, Risha Hess, Sreeratna Kancherla, Melissa Lo, Robin Mardeusz and Kinsy Hood, Luis Rodriguez, Paola San Martini, Kathy Sturm-Ramirez and Leyfou Dabo, Ananthy Thambinayagam and Dharma Sears, Cairn Verhuslt, Peter Vrooman and Johnette Iris, and Tanya W. In Philadelphia, Tally and Raji Malik; in Washington, DC, Steve Herman, Mattito Watson, and Colin and Margaret Warren. In New York, Lincoln Bickford, Alex Dranovsky and Ting

Wang, Pat Duffy and Josh Cohen, Lavanya D. J. and Deepak S. J., Vanessa and David Franklin, Vanita Gowda, Alice Hsu, Anupah Makoond, Eoin O'Sullivan, Sejal Shah, Kejia Tang, and Radhika Tewari. In London, Terri Moyer and Anna Budgen. In San Francisco, Hsin I Liu, Ben and Jacqueline Arnoldy, and Bogomil Balkansky. In Dubai, Caroline and Jeff Wilson.

Dear friends have been lifelines, especially Pat Duffy, Deepu Gowda, and Emily Heaphy. Pat, Colin Warren, and Bruce Ashby read drafts of this book. Sarah Antine and Minal Hajratwala read drafts of other books. Against the odds, my immigrant parents carved out a life in the United States through their hard, unsung work and sheer grit and determination. For years, Zarko has been ever reliable and patient. I am grateful to my unflappable agent, Jessica Papin, for her steadfast optimism and support. Amy Holmes-Tagchungdarpa and Kimberly Meyer gave valuable input. And thanks to the entire team at the University of North Carolina Press: Dino Battista, Ann Bingham, Sonya Bonczek, Valerie Burton, Cate Hodorowicz, Elizabeth Orange Lane, Alex Martin, Brock Schnoke, Lindsay Starr, Susan Koski Zucker, and everyone who worked on this book.

In 2017 *Far from the Rooftop of the World* got a boost as a finalist for the Restless Books Prize for New Immigrant Writing. In 2021, *Far from the Rooftop of the World* won the University of Massachusetts Press's Juniper Prize for Creative Nonfiction. I ultimately declined this wonderful honor, but I am very grateful to the University of Massachusetts Press and judge Shayla Lawson for much-needed validation.

Finally, I'm grateful for public libraries in New York, Chicago, Boston, Brookline, Massachusetts, San Francisco, Washington, DC, and Helsinki, as well as the Newberry Library in Chicago—welcoming havens where I worked on this book and kept it alive.

[WORKS CITED]

PROLOGUE

BBC News. "China Accused of Excessive Force over Tibet Unrest." July 22, 2010.

Central Tibetan Administration. "Glimpses on History of Tibet." 2021. https://tibet
.net/about-tibet/glimpses-on-history-of-tibet/.

Congressional Executive Commission on China. "Officials Report Release of More
than 3,000 of the More than 4,400 Detained Tibetan 'Rioters.'" July 9, 2008.
www.cecc.gov/publications/commission-analysis/officials-report-release-of-more
-than-3000-of-the-more-than-4400.

International Campaign for Tibet. "Tibet at a Turning Point." August 6, 2008.
https://savetibet.org/tibet-at-a-turning-point/.

McCawley, Tom. "Violence in Tibet Strains China's Relations with
India, Nepal." *Christian Science Monitor*, March 20, 2008.

O'Neill, Mark. "45 Million Died in Mao's Great Leap Forward, Hong Kong
Historian Says in New Book." *South China Morning Post*, September 5, 2010.

Phayul. "Over 66,000 Tibetans in Indian Subcontinent: CTA Population Census."
August 10, 2022. www.phayul.com/2022/08/10/47418/.

Phillips, Tom. "The Cultural Revolution: All You Need to Know about China's
Political Convulsion." *Guardian*, May 10, 2016.

Reuters. "TIMELINE: A Year of Unrest in Tibetan Regions." March 14, 2009.

CHAPTER 1. MONKS AND BASKETBALL

International Campaign for Tibet. "A Struggle of Blood and Fire: The Imposition of
Martial Law in 1989 and the Lhasa Uprising in 1959." February 25, 1999.
https://savetibet.org/a-struggle-of-blood-and-fire/.

Jaggi, Maya. "The Long Fight." *Guardian*, June 9, 2006.

CHAPTER 2. HERE TO THIS OTHER COUNTRY

Gu-Chu-Sum Movement Association of Tibet website. Accessed November 1, 2022.
https://en.guchusum1991.org/.

CHAPTER 3. DHARAMSALA MEANS SHELTER

Bilham, Roger, and Susan Hough. "Future Earthquakes on the Indian Subcontinent:
Inevitable Hazard, Preventable Risk." *South Asian Journal* 12, no. 5 (April–June
2006): 1–9.

Chander, Ramesh. "Excavation at Chaitru." Kangra Museum.
    Unpublished manuscript, accessed November 2008. Photocopy.

City Population. "Dharmsala, India." Accessed November 1, 2022. https://citypopulation
    .de/en/india/himachalpradesh/kangra/0240202000__dharmsala/.

"A Culture at Risk: An Initial Assessment of Seismic Vulnerabilities in Upper
    Dharamsala, India." Palo Alto, CA: GeoHazards International, October 31, 2006.

Encyclopaedia Britannica Online. s.v. "Buddhism." Last modified August 23, 2022.
    www.britannica.com/topic/Buddhism.

Himachal Pradesh State Disaster Management Authority. "Earthquake Hazards."
    Last modified January 12, 2018. https://hpsdma.nic.in/Index1.aspx?lid=1180
    &lsid=1184&pid=70&lev=3&langid=1.

"The Indian Empire." *Imperial Gazetteer of India*, v. 1, p. 98, Digital South Asia
    Library, University of Chicago website. Last modified January 28, 2021. http://dsal
    .uchicago.edu/reference/gazetteer/pager.html?objectid=DS405.1.I34_V01_128.gif.

"McLeodganj's Iconic Nowrojee General Store to Shut Shop after 160
    Years." *Hindustan Times* (Chandigarh, India), August 24, 2020.

Ministry of Tourism (India). "St. John in the Wilderness Church." Incredible
    India. Accessed November 1, 2022. www.incredibleindia.org/content/incredible
    -india-v2/en/destinations/dharamsala/st-john-in-the-wilderness-church.html.

O'Brien, Hettie. "The Bells v the Boutique Hotel: The Battle to Save Britain's
    Oldest Factory." *Guardian*, May 11, 2021.

Punjab District Gazetteers, Kangra District, vol. 7, part A, 1924–25, Public Library
    of India. Superintendent Government Press, Lahore, India.

"RGI Releases Census 2011 Data on Population by Religious Communities." Press
    Information Bureau, Government of India, August 25, 2015. https://pib.gov.in
    /newsite/printrelease.aspx?relid=126326.

Roy, Malini. "The Accident That Befell Sir Donald Friell McLeod." *Asian and
    African Studies Blog*, British Library Blogs, August 14, 2014. https://blogs.bl.uk
    /asian-and-african/2014/08/the-accident-that-befell-sir-donald-friell-mcleod.html.

"Shutters Will Soon Down on Heritage Shop Synonymous with Dalai Lama's Abode."
    National Herald (New Delhi), August 28, 2020.

"Thousands of Students Participate in India Earthquake Drill." GeoHazards
    International. Last modified February 9, 2021. www.geohaz.org/post/2012/04/01
    /thousands-of-students-participate-in-india-earthquake-drill.

US Geological Survey. "Today in Earthquake History: October 8th." Earthquake
    Hazards Program. Accessed November 1, 2022. https://earthquake.usgs.gov
    /learn/today/index.php?month=10&day=8&submit=View+Date.

Wikipedia. s.v. "James Bruce, 8th Earl of Elgin." Last modified November 22, 2022, 20:33.
    https://en.wikipedia.org/wiki/James_Bruce,_8th_Earl_of_Elgin.

CHAPTER 4. WINTER AUDIENCE WITH THE DALAI LAMA

Avedon, John F. *In Exile from the Land of Snows: The Definitive Account of the Dalai Lama and Tibet since the Chinese Conquest.* New York: Harper Perennial, 1994.

Bauer, Manuel. "Act of Faith." Noorderlicht, 2007. https://old.noorderlicht.com /en/archive/manuel-bauer/.

Brehm, Denise. "Dalai Lama Enlists Science in Quest for 'a Happy Mind.'" MIT News, September 17, 2003. https://news.mit.edu/2003/dalai-lama-enlists -science-quest-happy-mind.

Dugdale, Joshua, dir. *The Unwinking Gaze: The Inside Story of the Dalai Lama's Struggle for Tibet.* New York: World in Vision, 2008. DVD.

Pema, Jetsun. *Tibet: My Story.* Shaftesbury, UK: Element, 1997.

Tibet Museum. *Tibet's Journey in Exile.* Dharamsala, India, 2008. Exhibition wall notes.

Tibet Post. "The Fate of Tibet's Nomadic Peoples and the Decline of Global Cultural Diversity." Last modified October 22, 2012. www.thetibetpost.com/en/outlook /47-opinions-and-columns/2777-the-fate-of-tibets-nomadic-peoples-and-the -decline-of-global-cultural-diversity.

Yee, Amy. "Tibetan Education Thrives—In Exile." *Christian Science Monitor,* March 6, 2009.

Yee, Amy. "Young Lawyer Aids Exile Tibetans with His Language and Legal Skills." *Christian Science Monitor,* September 6, 2011.

CHAPTER 5. THE LONGEST NIGHT

Foundation for the Preservation of the Mahayana Tradition. "Lama Tsongkhapa Day (Ganden Ngamchoe) Is on December 29." December 21, 2021. https://fpmt .org/edu-news/lama-tsongkhapa-day-ganden-ngamchoe-is-on-december-29/.

Karmapa. "Buddhism in Tibet." Accessed November 1, 2022. https://kagyuoffice .org/buddhism/buddhism-in-tibet/the-gelug-school/.

Pema, Jetsun. *Tibet: My Story.* Shaftesbury, UK: Element, 1997.

CHAPTER 6. A CHANCE TO ENHANCE

Encyclopaedia Britannica Online. s.v. "Sir Alexander Cunningham." Last modified November 24, 2022. www.britannica.com/biography/Alexander-Cunningham.

Balachandran, Sudhakar (Sid) V. "The Satyam Scandal." *Forbes,* January 7, 2009.

Census India. "2001 Census of India." Accessed November 15, 2022. www .censusindia.gov.in/Census_Data_2001/Census_data_finder/C_Series /Population_by_religious_communities.htm.

Central Institute of Higher Tibetan Studies. Accessed December 6, 2022. www.cihts .ac.in/webpage/index.aspx#.

Economic Times. "China Says Arunachal Pradesh Part of It 'since Ancient Times.'"
    Last modified December 31, 2021. https://economictimes.indiatimes
    .com/news/india/china-says-arunachal-pradesh-part-of-it-since-ancient
    -times/articleshow/88618947.cms.

Google and Archaeological Survey of India website. Accessed December 6, 2022.
    https://artsandculture.google.com/story/sarnath-turning-the-wheel
    -of-law-archaeological-survey-of-india/kQWR2ftWElFKKQ?hl=en.

Office of His Holiness the Dalai Lama. "Dalai Lama Stresses on Environment
    Protection." January 14, 2009. www.dalailama.com/news/2009/dalai-lama
    -stresses-on-environment-protection.

Vail, Lise F. "The Origins of Buddhism." Asia Society. Accessed November
    1, 2022. https://asiasociety.org/education/origins-buddhism.

Varanasi: Government of Uttar Pradesh. "Tourism." Accessed December
    6, 2022. www.uptourism.gov.in/en/post/dhamek-stupa.

Wong, Edward. "Dalai Lama to Visit Indian Region Claimed by China."
    New York Times, October 22, 2009.

World Factbook. "Bhutan: Country Summary." Last modified November 16,
    2022. www.cia.gov/the-world-factbook/countries/bhutan/summaries.

CHAPTER 7. NO LOSAR AND MURDER IN THE SNOW

Arsu, Sebnem. "'Bush Shoe' Gives Firm a Footing in the Market." *New York Times*,
    December 20, 2008.

Dalai Lama. *Freedom in Exile: The Autobiography of His Holiness the Dalai Lama
    of Tibet.* London: Abacus, 1992.

Damdul, Dorjee. "Tibetan Youth Dies in Custody." Radio Free Asia, January 30,
    2009. Translated by Joshua Lipes. www.rfa.org/english/news/tibet
    /tibetandeathincustody-01302009131007.html.

Gould, Mark, dir. *Murder in the Snow.* Melbourne: 360 Degree Films, 2008. DVD.

International Campaign for Tibet. "Self-Immolation Fact Sheet." April 2022.
    https://savetibet.org/tibetan-self-immolations/.

International Campaign for Tibet. "Torture and Impunity: 29 Cases of Tibetan
    Political Prisoners." February 26, 2015. https://savetibet.org/torture-and
    -impunity-29-cases-of-tibetan-political-prisoners/.

Karadsheh, Jomana, and Octavia Nasr. "Iraqi Journalist Throws Shoes at Bush in
    Baghdad." CNN, December 14, 2008. www.cnn.com/2008/WORLD/meast
    /12/14/bush.iraq/index.html.

Latulippe, Hugo, and François Prévost, dirs. *What Remains of Us.* Montreal:
    Nomadik Films, 2004. DVD.

Long, Qiao. "China 'Strikes Hard' in Tibet." Radio Free Asia, January 26, 2009.
    Translated by Luisetta Mudie. www.rfa.org/english/news/tibet/lhasa
    -01262009081502.html.

Office of His Holiness the Dalai Lama. "Dalai Lama Visits West Tennessee to Accept Freedom Award." September 24, 2009. www.dalailama.com/news/2009/dalai -lama-visits-west-tennessee-to-accept-freedom-award.

Staples, Darren. "Shoe Thrown at Chinese Premier in Cambridge." MSNBC, February 2, 2009. www.nbcnews.com/id/wbna28978669.

Stolberg, Sheryl Gay. "Shy U.S. Intellectual Created Playbook Used in a Revolution." *New York Times*, February 27, 2011.

Yee, Amy. "From India, a Homespun Brand of Hospitality." *New York Times*, October 14, 2009.

Yee, Amy. "King of India: Gandhi Was a Source of Inspiration for Martin Luther King Jr." *Wall Street Journal*, February 27, 2009.

Yee, Amy. "Murder in the Snow." *Far Eastern Economic Review* (Hong Kong), March 17, 2009. www.feer.com/international-relations/20098/march58 /Murder-in-the-Snow (site discontinued).

Yee, Amy. "Tibetan Exiles: 'We Shall Overcome.'" *The Nation*, February 26, 2009.

CHAPTER 8. FIFTY YEARS

Avedon, John F. *In Exile from the Land of Snows: The Definitive Account of the Dalai Lama and Tibet since the Chinese Conquest.* New York: Harper Perennial, 1994.

Rawcliffe, Rosemary, dir. *Women of Tibet: A Quiet Revolution.* Berkeley, CA: Frame of Mind Films, 2008. DVD.

Yee, Amy. "Tibetans Find Freedom in Exile." *Wall Street Journal*, October 8, 2010.

CHAPTER 9. I STILL HAVE FAITH IN CHINESE PEOPLE

Al Jazeera. "Xinjiang Leak Reveals Extent of Chinese Abuses in Uighur Camps." May 24, 2022. www.aljazeera.com/news/2022/5/24/xinjiang-leak-sheds -new-light-on-chinas-uighur-camps.

Kahn, Joseph. "Rioting in China over Label on College Diplomas." *New York Times*, June 22, 2006.

Maizland, Lindsay. "China's Repression of Uyghurs in Xinjiang." Council on Foreign Relations. Last modified September 22, 2022. www.cfr.org/backgrounder /china-xinjiang-uyghurs-muslims-repression-genocide-human-rights.

O'Neill, Mark. "45 Million Died in Mao's Great Leap Forward, Hong Kong Historian Says in New Book." *South China Morning Post*, September 5, 2010. www.scmp.com/article/723956/revisiting-calamitous-time.

Phillips, Tom. "The Cultural Revolution: All You Need to Know about China's Political Convulsion." *Guardian*, May 10, 2016.

CHAPTER 10. WOMEN OF TIBET

Dharmakara. "Tibet Facts 10: Role of Women in the Protest Movement." 1996. http://tibet.dharmakara.net/TibetFacts10.html.

Kristof, Nicholas D. "Martial Law Ends in Tibet's Capital." *New York Times*, May 1, 1990.

Rawcliffe, Rosemary, dir. *Women of Tibet: A Quiet Revolution*. Berkeley, CA: Frame of Mind Films, 2008. DVD.

Tibetan Nuns Project website. Last modified 2022. https://tnp.org/.

Yee, Amy. "Breaking Through." *Lion's Roar*, February 11, 2012. www.lionsroar.com /breaking-through/.

Yee, Amy. "The Next Dalai Lama Should Be a Woman." *Doublex* (*Slate*), October 8, 2009. www.doublex.com/section/news-politics/next-dalai-lama-should-be -woman?page=0,0 (page discontinued).

CHAPTER 12. DECKYI'S JOURNEY

CNN. "A Timeline of Tibetan Protests." March 14, 2008. www.cnn.com/2008 /WORLD/asiapcf/03/14/tibet.timeline/index.html.

International Campaign for Tibet. "A Struggle of Blood and Fire: The Imposition of Martial Law in 1989 and the Lhasa Uprising in 1959." February 25, 1999. https://savetibet.org/a-struggle-of-blood-and-fire/.

International Campaign for Tibet. "Tibet at a Turning Point." August 6, 2008. https://savetibet.org/tibet-at-a-turning-point/.

Richardson, Sophie. "25 Years after 'Disappearing' Tibetan Panchen Lama, China Is No Nearer to Its Goal." Human Rights Watch, May 15, 2020. www.hrw.org/news /2020/05/15/25-years-after-disappearing-tibetan-panchen-lama-china-no-nearer -its-goal.

Yee, Amy. "Tibetans Find Freedom in Exile." *Wall Street Journal*, October 8, 2010.

CHAPTER 14. FAR FROM THE ROOFTOP OF THE WORLD

Avedon, John F. *In Exile from the Land of Snows: The Definitive Account of the Dalai Lama and Tibet since the Chinese Conquest*. New York: Harper Perennial, 1994.

Central Tibetan Administration. "Tibetans Celebrate Historic 50th Anniversary of Democracy Day." September 2, 2010. https://tibet.net/tibetans-celebrate -historic-50th-anniversary-of-democracy-day/.

Namdroling Monastery. "11th H.H. Drubwang Prada Norbu Thubtan Chosky Drayang." Accessed November 1, 2022. www.namdroling.net/Portal/Page /11th-Drubwang-Padma-Norbu-Thubtan-Choskyi-Drayang.

Namdroling Monastery. "How the Main Temple Was Named the Golden Temple." Accessed November 1, 2022. www.namdroling.net/Portal/Page/How-the-main -temple-was-named-the-Golden-Temple.

Tibetan Children's Village website. "Bylakuppee." Accessed November 1, 2022. https://tcv.org.in/school/tcv-bylakuppee/.

Yee, Amy. "Tibetans Find Freedom in Exile." *Wall Street Journal*, October 8, 2010.

Yee, Amy. "Tibetan Monks and Nuns Turn Their Minds toward Science."
   New York Times, May 30, 2009.

CHAPTER 15. NEW YEAR, NEW LAND
Anzac Day Commemoration Committee. "ANZAC Biscuits." Accessed
   November 1, 2022. https://anzacday.org.au/ww1-ANZAC-biscuits.

CHAPTER 16. AUSTRALIA DAY AND LOSAR
Landy, Samantha. "New Citizens Pledge Allegiance before Australia Day Parade
   through Melbourne." *Herald Sun* (Melbourne), January 26, 2015. www.heraldsun
   .com.au/news/victoria/new-citizens-pledge-allegiance-before-australia-day-parade
   -through-melbourne/news-story/85b2befdc48eef2d6aaac3cdf424190d.
Parliament of New South Wales. "1788 to 1810—Early European Settlement."
   Accessed November 1, 2022. www.parliament.nsw.gov.au/about/Pages/1788-to
   -1810-Early-European-Settlement.aspx.
State Government of Victoria. "Victorian 26ers Club." Last modified November
   17, 2020. www.vic.gov.au/australia-day-26ers-club-victorians-born-26-january.
Worrall, Allison. "Aboriginal Rights Protest Disrupts Australia Day Parade." *The Age*.
   Last modified January 27, 2015. www.theage.com.au/national/victoria/aboriginal
   -rights-protest-disrupts-australia-day-parade-in-melbourne-20150126-12ya7z.html.
Yee, Amy. "Tibetans in Australia Focus on Tradition during New Year Celebrations."
   Voice of America, February 20, 2015. www.voanews.com/a/tibetans-in-australia
   -focus-on-tradition-during-new-year-celebrations/2651510.html.

CHAPTER 17. THE ONLY THING THAT COUNTS
Central Tibetan Administration. "Tibetan Receives Top Australian Honours."
   July 9, 2007. https://tibet.net/tibetan-receives-top-australian-honours/.
NEWS.com.au. "The 'Insular Peninsula': Reason Sydney Cluster May Not Be as
   Worrying as It Might Otherwise Have Been." December 22, 2020. www.news
   .com.au/national/nsw-act/news/the-reason-sydney-cluster-isnt-as-scary-as-it
   -could-be/news-story/abd98369703e9c9f76b4c1fd9a8c902d.
RIGPA. "About Sogyal Rinpoche." Accessed November 1, 2022. www.rigpa.org
   /sogyal-rinpoche.
TAFE NSW. "Our History." Accessed November 1, 2022. www.tafensw.edu
   .au/about/history.
Yee, Amy. "In Australia, New Tibetan Migrants Learn to Swim." Voice of America,
   April 10, 2015. www.voanews.com/a/in-australia-new-tibetan-migrants-learn
   -to-swim/2713806.html.
Yee, Amy. "Tibetans in Australia Focus on Tradition during New Year Celebrations."
   Voice of America, February 20, 2015. www.voanews.com/a/tibetans-in-australia
   -focus-on-tradition-during-new-year-celebrations/2651510.html.

CHAPTER 18. DOCUMENTS AND ABILITY

Associated Press. "Number of Refugees Reaching Europe Plunged in 2016." *Al Jazeera*, January 6, 2017. www.aljazeera.com/news/2017/1/6/number-of-refugees-reaching-europe-plunged-in-2016.

Asylum Information Database. "Country Report: Belgium." Fourth Update, December 2015, and 2016 Update, February 2017. https://asylumineurope.org/reports/country/belgium/.

Asylum Information Database. "Country Report: Germany." Fourth Update, November 2015. https://asylumineurope.org/reports/country/germany/.

BBC News. "Brussels Explosions: What We Know about Airport and Metro Attacks." April 9, 2016. www.bbc.com/news/world-europe-35869985.

BBC News. "Hungarian Camerawoman Who Kicked Refugees Charged." September 8, 2016. www.bbc.com/news/world-europe-37304489.

BBC News. "Migrant Crisis: Germany Sees Massive Drop in Asylum Seekers." January 11, 2017. www.bbc.com/news/world-europe-38584705.

Blyth, Derek. "Gare du Midi: Where to Eat, Drink and Stay near Brussels' Eurostar Terminal." *Guardian*, November 13, 2014.

Dufrasne, Edouard. "Belgium Spooked by Migrant Influx as Europe's Refugees Crisis Spirals." NBC News, March 12, 2016. www.nbcnews.com/storyline/europes-border-crisis/belgium-spooked-migrant-influx-europe-s-refugees-crisis-spirals-n527911.

European Parliament. "Asylum and Migration in the EU: 2012." Accessed November 1, 2022. www.europarl.europa.eu/infographic/asylum-migration/index_en.html#filter=2012.

Hume, Tim, Tiffany Ap, and Ray Sanchez. "Here's What We Know about the Brussels Terror Attacks." CNN, March 25, 2016. www.cnn.com/2016/03/23/europe/brussels-belgium-attacks-what-we-know.

Katsiaficas, Caitlin. "Asylum Seeker and Migrant Flows in the Mediterranean Adapt Rapidly to Changing Conditions." Migration Policy Institute, June 22, 2016. www.migrationpolicy.org/article/asylum-seeker-and-migrant-flows-mediterranean-adapt-rapidly-changing-conditions.

Migration Policy Institute. "Moving Europe beyond Crisis." Accessed November 1, 2022. www.migrationpolicy.org/programs/moving-europe-beyond-crisis?gclid=CP-Q3NDWvNECFeEpowodYMABuQ.

Reuters. "Camerawoman Who 'Tripped Refugees' in Hungary Faces Charges." *Guardian*, September 7, 2016.

Vlaanderen (Government of Flanders). "Dienstverlening van de Openbare Centra voor Maatschappelijk Welzijn (OCMW)." Accessed November 1, 2022. www.vlaanderen.be/dienstverlening-van-de-openbare-centra-voor-maatschappelijk-welzijn-ocmw.

CHAPTER 19. AN EX-MONK STILL LOVES BASKETBALL

Associated Press. "Man pleads guilty to hate crime in Chinese immigrant's death."
   January 12, 2023.

Closson, Troy. "Asian Immigrant Attacked in Hate Crime Last Year Dies."
   New York Times, August 12, 2022.

Fieldstadt, Elisha and Wong, Wilson. "Doormen Who Appeared to Watch Attack on
   Asian Woman in N.Y.C. Fired." NBC News.com. April 6, 2021. www.nbcnews
   .com/news/asian-america/doormen-who-appeared-watch-attack-asian-woman
   -n-y-c-n1263168.

Hu, Xiumian, Anlin Ma, Weiwei Xue, Eduardo Garzanti, Yong Cao,
   Shi-Min Li, Gaoyuan Sun, and Wen Lai. "Exploring a Lost Ocean
   in the Tibetan Plateau: Birth, Growth, and Demise of the Bangong-
   Nujiang Ocean" *Earth-Science Reviews* 29 (June 2022): 104031.

AFTERWORD

The Economist. "The Silent Majority: America's Largest Ethnic Group Has
   Assimilated So Well That People Barely Notice It." February 5, 2015.

Inter-agency Coordination Platform for Refugees and Migrants from Venezuela.
   "Refugees and Migrants from Venezuela." Last modified November 5,
   2022. www.r4v.info/en/refugeeandmigrants.

Jordan, Miriam. "We Can't Claim Mission Accomplished." *New York Times*,
   August 12, 2022.

McKirdy, Euan. "UNHCR Report: More Displaced Now than after WWII." CNN.
   Last modified June 20, 2016. www.cnn.com/2016/06/20/world/unhcr-displaced
   -peoples-report/index.html.

UN High Commissioner for Refugees. "Ukraine Situation." October 2022.
   https://data.unhcr.org/en/situations/ukraine.

UN High Commissioner for Refugees. "Venezuela Situation." Accessed November 1,
   2022. www.unhcr.org/en-us/venezuela-emergency.